education
be smarter.

New PSAT 10/11/NMSQT
Strategy Guide
Intensive Prep

Developed in conjunction with Test Prep Genius

New PSAT 10/11/NMSQT Strategy Guide Intensive Prep

C2 Education is a registered trademark of C2 Educational Center, Inc.

2015 Edition

This product was developed by Test Prep Genius, a premiere education support services company that delivers a comprehensive package for education institutions and services.

C2 Education: http://www.c2educate.com/
Test Prep Genius: http://www.tpgenius.com/

Development support was provided by C2 Education and Edward Kim, the Director of Curriculum. Please report any errors or feedback to the nearest C2 center and support@tpgenius.com.

Table of Contents

Section 1
The New PSAT

Introduction: The Redesign
College Board's Announcement

The Announcement

On March 5, 2014, in Austin, Texas, College Board President David Coleman presented a renewed mission by the organization to provide a redesigned SAT and PSAT. Still in the midst of implementing vast changes to their AP Courses, College Board announced that in spring of 2016, high school students would begin taking a radically changed, redesigned standardized test.

President Coleman and a number of College Board's team members had been integral in guiding and executing the mission to develop the Common Core State Standards (CCSS). To align with the CCSS, College Board and President Coleman continued their work with the SAT and PSAT by re-assessing test questions and the structure of the existing exam.

In order to provide high school students with a stronger predictive assessment for college success, College Board redesigned the PSAT in drastic ways. The new PSAT is very different in both test structure and test questions; the new exam will strive to answer one very important question: Is the average high school student prepared for first-year college work?

The PSAT 10/11 will be designed for sophomores and juniors to take during the school year in October; the PSAT 8/9, which is covered in another book, will be designed for 8th graders and freshmen to take during the school year in October.

Our Mission – YOU

Test Prep Genius has one mission: to provide you with curriculum and support that maximizes your progress without wasting time. Instructional content should be short and effective; practice material should be plentiful.

Test Prep Genius is excited to offer you the C2 Education PSAT 10/11/NMSQT Strategy Guide. This guide will show you short, effective strategies for every major concept the new PSAT incorporates.

We wish you the best of luck in your work, progress, and results on the new PSAT!

Test Structure Changes
Overall Changes to the New PSAT

There are major structural changes to the new PSAT 10/11 that you should keep in mind. These changes were made to better meet the needs of the average high school student and to provide you with an optimized exam.

Timing and Question Counts

Reading:	60 minutes for 47 Questions
Writing and Language:	35 minutes for 44 Questions
Math:	70 minutes for 48 Questions

Total Time = 2 hours and 45 minutes

Raw Scores

Raw Scores are calculated based on the total number of questions you answered correctly. You will not be penalized an extra -0.25 points for answering questions incorrectly since the College Board wants to encourage educated guessing without penalty on the new exam.

Score Reporting

Your final new PSAT 10/11 score is composed of two pieces – 1 Math Score, 1 Reading and Writing Score.

Both Math and Reading and Writing Scores are scaled from 160 to 760 for a total PSAT 10/11 score ranging from 320 to 1520. Why the weird scale? The College Board wants to be able to take your PSAT scores and New SAT scores to compare them to each other on one composite scale. The PSAT 8/9, PSAT 10/11, and New SAT score will be compared to gauge the progress each student has made on the tests.

Although the old PSAT only provided a general report with the overall section scores and a student error report by question, the new PSAT 10/11 offers a detailed breakdown of scores. Parents, students, college admission officers, and counselors will gain greater insight into your abilities by using these scores.

1 Total Score
The Total Score is your composite score ranging from 320 to 1420.

2 Section Scores
The 2 Section Scores are your respective scores in Math and in Reading and Writing ranging from 160 to 760.
3 Test Scores
The 3 Test Scores are your individual scores for Math, Reading, and Writing. The Math, Reading, and Writing Scores are scaled from 8-38.

2 Cross-Test Scores

The Cross-Test Scores are two scores that look at specific topics that are covered on the new PSAT: History/Social Studies and Science. These scores are scaled from 8 to 38 and provide insight into your mastery over the aforementioned topics across all sections, not just one.

7 Subscores

There are also 7 Subscores for Math, Reading, and Writing that provide insight into each major content dimension within the subjects. Content Dimensions are general categories of concepts and question types that make up each section on the exam. Two of the subscores are common in both Reading and Writing. All subscores are scaled from 1 to 15.

Math Subscores
Heart of Algebra
Problem Solving & Data Analysis
Passport to Advanced Math

Reading Subscores
* Words in Context
* Command of Evidence

Writing Subscores
Expression of Ideas
Standard English Conventions
* Words in Context
* Command of Evidence

Indicates common subscores across different sections

Subject-specific Changes
Changes to each subject: Evidence-based Reading & Writing, Math, Essay

There are detailed changes to each subject on the new PSAT:

Evidence-based Reading

The new Reading section is no longer broken into three sections; it is one long 60-minute section with 47 questions.

There will be 4 single passages and 1 paired passage, and all passages will stay within a 500-750 word count; the paired passage will have 1000-1500 words. There are also specific topics for the passages to be used – 1 U.S. and World Literature passage, 2 History/Social Studies passages, and 2 Science passages.

1 of the History/Social passages and 1 of the Science passages will also contain graphics, which will be incorporated in some way, shape, or form on a number of questions. The graphics will be somewhat challenging, utilizing high data density, several variables, and complex interactions. Your goal will be to understand the core information the graphic intends to show and how it ties into the passage as a whole or in part.

Reading passages will range in text complexity from grades 9 – 11. However, they will focus on topics and content relevant to today's students instead of focusing on outdated literature and facts like the old PSAT's passages.

Each passage will definitely contain 1 Words in Context question and 1 Command of Evidence question.

> The Words in Context questions are similar to passage vocabulary questions in the old PSAT Reading – the old PSAT presented questions like "In Line 87, the word ____ most nearly means". The new PSAT provides similarly phrased questions but focuses on vocabulary that has different connotations depending on the context of the passage; the vocabulary is also noticeably easier so students do not need to rote memorize words. Students should focus on utilizing vocabulary in different ways. For example, the word "synthesis", as presented by the College Board, has different meanings in science and business.

> The Command of Evidence question is a new question type. For certain questions, you will rely on definitive proof within the passage to answer them. Sometimes, a Command of Evidence question will follow directly after, to ask you to select the specific lines used for reference when answer the previous question.

Despite the changes to the Reading section of the new PSAT, keep in mind that Reading Comprehension is still just Reading Comprehension. You must read each passage carefully, take notes, and answer questions that test your understanding of what you read.

Evidence-based Writing

The new Writing section is no longer broken into two sections; it is one short 35-minute section with 44 questions.

There will be 4 single passages with 400-450 words each. Like Reading passages, Writing passages will have set topics, but also specific styles of writing. There will be 1 passage each based on Careers, History/Social Studies, Humanities, and Science; each passage will have exactly 11 questions. Passages will incorporate various writing styles: 1 Nonfiction Narrative, 1-2 Argumentative, and 1-2 Informative/Explanatory. While the writing styles may not impact your understanding of each passage, the topics may if you favor certain topics over others.

Like Reading passages, Writing passages will also incorporate 1 or more graphics in 1 of the passages. These graphics will serve a similar purpose for the passage – to present data that correlates to the bulk of the passage but your focus will be incorporating grammar, graphic information, and language to answer questions.

Writing passage will range in text complexity from grades 9 – 11. The passage topics mentioned before will be relevant to today's student.

Each passage also contains 1 Words in Context question and 1 Command of Evidence question. The focus of the majority of questions will be on the key grammar rules and English conventions we use in the proper English language.

Math

The new PSAT Math has been changed from a 3-section component to a 2-section component. One section will allow you to use a calculator, but the other section will not! This is a major change College Board has focused on because it is important the students can solve math problems with and without tools like calculators.

The Calculator section will have 31 questions for you to complete in 45 minutes. 27 of these questions will be multiple-choice questions and 4 questions will be grid-in.

The No-Calculator section will have 17 questions for you to complete in 25 minutes. 13 of these questions will be multiple-choice questions and 4 questions will be grid-in.

To contribute to the Cross-Test scores for Science and History/Social Studies, 16 questions (8 questions for each Cross-Test score) will be focused on topics in Science and History/Social Studies.

Math will be broken down into a number of major content dimensions:

> **Heart of Algebra** will focus on your mastery of Pre-Algebra and Algebra I. You will solve equations, manipulate expressions and inequalities, and interpret formulas.

> **Problem Solving & Data Analysis** will focus on your ability to analyze relationships using ratios, proportions, percentages, and units, and summarize qualitative and quantitative data. This dimension essentially assesses your ability to apply concepts from the Heart of Algebra and other mathematical concepts to word problems and complex situations.

> **Passport to Advanced Math** will contain higher-level math concepts such as re-writing expressions using structure or analyzing and solving quadratic equations and higher-order equations. Polynomials will also appear.

> **Additional Topics in Math** covers miscellaneous topics found in Geometry and basic Trigonometry. You will utilize area and volume formulas, investigate various shapes and their properties, and work with trigonometric functions. This dimension will contribute to the total Math Test Score but will not be displayed as a subscore on your score report.

The Calculator section will contain problems from all four content dimensions listed above but the No-Calculator section will not have Problem Solving & Data Analysis questions. This means that the Calculator section will contain all the problems for Problem Solving & Data Analysis!

How to Use This Book
Maximizing your experience with this book

The C2 Education PSAT 10/11/NMSQT Strategy Guides are designed to provide you with strategies, concept lessons, and deeper understanding into solving the problems you will see on the new PSAT. While you will need to spend sufficient time studying the materials in this book, we have simplified the best approach to every concept on the new PSAT.

Whether or not you have also obtained the TPGenius 2016 Redesigned Strategy & Practice Guide, there are dozens of practice workbooks available from many other education services with hundreds of practice problems. Regardless of the practice workbooks you have at your disposal, you should take the lessons and strategies you learn from this guide and apply them to the practice questions you tackle.

This guide splits "lessons" by specific concept or question type. Take lessons one or a few at a time – the most important thing is for you to carefully absorb all the knowledge you need to master and conquer the new PSAT.

There are two workbooks in this series for the PSAT 10/11/NMSQT:

The **New PSAT 10/11/NSMQT Strategy/Practice Guide** has a huge volume of practice problems for you to tackle and one full-length practice test at the end of the book for you to try. This edition is designed to provide a more comprehensive look at the test for students who need more practice problems covering a wider variety of approaches and methods.

The **New PSAT 10/11/NMSQT Strategy Guide Intensive Prep** is designed to be more compact and condensed – while there are about the half the number of practice problems compared to the Practice Edition, there are two new, full-length practice tests for you to try. This edition is geared towards students who prefer a direct, get-in-get-out method for tackling the PSAT and for students who have little time to prepare.

We wish you the best of luck in your work, progress, and results on the new PSAT!

About the National Merit Scholarship

The National Merit® Scholarship Program recognizes students with excellent academic performance. High school students enter the National Merit® Program by taking the PSAT® during October of their school year. Many high schools offer the PSAT on a set day each year for students free of charge.

Entry Requirements

Students must adhere to the following requirements in order to enter the National Merit® Program via the PSAT:

1. Students must take the PSAT/NMSQT® no later than their third year in grades 9 through 12, regardless of grade classification or educational pattern.
2. Students must be enrolled as a high school student, progressing normally toward graduation/completion of high school, and planning to enroll full-time in college no later than the fall following completion of high school.
3. Students must be citizens of the United States or be a U.S. lawful permanent resident or have applied for permanent residence in the U.S.

All students may take the PSAT/NMSQT®, but must adhere to the above requirements in order to be entered into the National Merit® Program.

National Merit® Program Recognition

Based on PSAT/NMSQT® score performance, students are recognized and notified by their high school administrators of said recognition. There are multiple levels of recognition:

- **Commended Students**: In September, approximately two-thirds of approximately 50,000 top test scorers receive Letters of Commendation in recognition of their academic potential. Commended Students achieve high scores but score just below the level required for participants to be recognized as Semifinalists. Commended Students do not continue in the competition for National Merit® Scholarships, but may become candidates for Special Scholarships, which are sponsored by corporations and businesses.
- **Semifinalist**: In September, approximately one-third of approximately 50,000 top test scorers receive notifications that they have qualified as Semifinalists. Semifinalists are the highest scorers in each state; these Semifinalists will receive scholarship application materials from their respective high schools. Semifinalists may advance to Finalist standing by meeting high academic standards and all other requirements explained in the information provided to Semifinalists.
- **Finalists**: In February, approximately 15,000 Semifinalists are notified by mail at their home addresses that they have become Finalists in the program. High school principals are also notified and sent certificates to present to each Finalist.
- **Winners**: Winners of the National Merit Scholarship® are chosen from the Finalists based on abilities, skills, and accomplishments without regard to gender, race, ethnic origin, or religious preference. NMS committees select winners based on Finalists' academic records, information about school curricula and grading systems, two sets of test scores, the high school official's written recommendation, student activities and leadership roles, and the Finalist's personal essay.

Types of National Merit Scholarship® Awards

From March to mid-June, approximately 7,600 Finalists are awarded a Merit Scholarship® award. There are three types of awards:

1. **National Merit® $2500 Scholarships**: All Finalists compete for these scholarships, which are awarded based on state representation. Winners are given these single payment scholarships for college tuition or other use.
2. **Corporate-sponsored Merit Scholarships**: Corporate sponsors can designate these scholarships to children of their employees, associated communities, or Finalists with career plans the sponsor wants to encourage. These scholarships can be renewable for four years of undergraduate study or as single payment one-time awards.
3. **College-sponsored Merit Scholarships**: A number of sponsor colleges select winners based on which Finalists have been accepted for admission to respective schools. These awards are renewable up to four years of undergraduate study.

Special Scholarships

Every year, approximately 1,300 National Merit® Program participants, who are outstanding but not Finalists, are awarded Special Sponsorships by corporations and business organizations. Students must meet each sponsor's criteria and submit an entry form to the sponsor organization. These scholarships are renewable up to four years of undergraduate study or as one-time awards.

For more information, check out the National Merit® website:
http://www.nationalmerit.org/

Section 2
Evidence-based Reading

Implicit and Explicit Information
Citing Evidence
Words in Context
Central Ideas and Themes
Analyzing Purpose
Quantitative Information
Multiple Texts
Evaluating Arguments
Relationships
Point of View

Implicit and Explicit Information

Concept Introduction

Among the most commonly asked questions on the PSAT are those dealing with **implicit** and **explicit** information. Implicit information is information that is suggested or implied rather than directly stated; explicit information is information that is clearly stated. For example:

Implicit Information:

I sighed with resignation as I looked from the seemingly nonchalant cat to the broken glass on the floor.

Explicit Information:

The cat had made a habit of knocking glasses onto the floor.

Even without the information in the second sentence, we can infer from the first sentence that the cat had broken the glass and, given the speaker's feeling of resignation, that this was likely a regular occurrence. This is implicit information. The implication that the cat routinely breaks glasses is clearly stated in the second sentence; the second sentence gives us explicit information.

Spotting Implicit and Explicit Information Questions

Most implicit and explicit information questions will feature certain phrases. Questions that look for implicit information will usually feature phrases like:

- "It can be inferred..."
- "The passage suggests..."
- "The author implies..."

Words such as *infer*, *suggest*, or *imply* all suggest that the question is asking you to draw a conclusion based on implicit information.

Explicit information questions will often include phrases such as:

- "According to the passage..."
- "The author states..."

When a question references specific information in the passage, it is often an explicit information question.

Answering Explicit Information Questions

Explicit information questions are essentially reading comprehension questions. These are the most straightforward of all PSAT reading questions because they simply ask you for information that is given in the passage.

As with many PSAT reading questions, explicit information questions can often be best answered through the process of elimination. If you are not able to spot the correct answer immediately, then begin eliminating answers you know are incorrect. There are several types of incorrect answer choices that are common to explicit information questions:

- **Not Supported:** If there is no clear evidence to support an answer choice, that answer cannot be correct. Eliminate any answers that are not directly supported by the text.
- **Too Specific:** Answer choices that contain details that are not referenced in the passage are overly specific and can be eliminated.
- **Too General:** Answer choices that make broad generalizations or that include extreme language like "all," "none," "always," or "never" can almost always be eliminated.

- **Proven Incorrect:** Answer choices that are disproved by evidence in the passage can be eliminated. This seems obvious, but the test makers will sometimes include answer choices that are tempting because they are phrased similarly to lines in the passage; even though the answer itself may be proven incorrect in the passage, the language of the answer sounds so familiar that it seems correct.
- **Correct Answer, Wrong Piece of Information:** Some answer choices will be technically correct but will be supported by either outside information (*never* use outside knowledge to answer a question!) or by information that is given in a different part of the passage than the part referenced by the question.

Once you have eliminated these incorrect answers, you will often find yourself left with just one choice remaining. If there is more than one option remaining, choose the answer that you believe is most strongly supported by the passage. Remember that there is no penalty for an incorrect guess!

Answering Implicit Information Questions

Implicit information questions require a slightly larger leap in logic, but they will still be supported by information in the passage. Whereas you may be able to identify a very specific sentence or set of lines that clearly supports the answer to an explicit information question, the answer to an implicit information question may be supported by more than one piece of information. To answer implicit information questions, you may need to take multiple pieces of information and put them together to draw a logical conclusion.

As with explicit information questions, if you cannot determine the correct answer quickly, you should use the process of elimination to narrow down your choices. You should eliminate the following types of answer choices:

- **Side-step the Question:** Answer choices that fail to actually answer the question being asked can be eliminated. These answer choices will often tangentially reference the question, but fail to adequately answer the question.
- **Leap of Logic:** Answer choices that are only vaguely supported by the passage or that require you to make big assumptions can be eliminated.
- **Proven Incorrect:** Much like explicit information questions, implicit information questions may also feature answer choices that reflect wording similar to that in the passage but that are actually disproven by information in the passage. These answers can be eliminated.

Once you have eliminated answers that you know to be incorrect, select the answer choice that is most strongly supported by information in the passage. Although there will likely not be a specific piece of information that clearly states the correct answer, the correct answer will still be supported by evidence!

Example Questions:

1   A recent news story focused on the success of two security
      researchers in remotely hacking a Jeep. The researchers took
      over the car's accelerator while still in motion, rendering the driver
      helpless. This event prompted a class-action lawsuit, a Senate bill
5   to require automakers to take steps to protect vehicles from such
      attacks, and the recall of 1.4 million vehicles. Although many cars
      have long been susceptible to hacks such as keyless theft, not a
      single incident of malicious hacking similar to that undertaken by
      the security researchers has occurred. But as computer
10   processors become increasingly involved with the running of
      various components of cars, vehicles become more vulnerable to
      hacking.

1. It can be inferred from the passage that the cars that are LEAST likely to be hacked would
    A) be recalled by the manufacturer.
    B) not have remote entry.
    C) limit the number of components run by computers.
    D) be protected from attacks by law.

2. According to the passage, which of the following is true of car hacking?
    A) Malicious hacking similar to that conducted by researchers has become commonplace.
    B) All modern cars are susceptible to malicious hacking.
    C) Many drivers have dismissed concerns about car hacking.
    D) Computerized components make cars more likely to be hacked.

The first question uses the word "inferred," so we know it is likely an implicit information question. Let's assume that we cannot spot the correct answer immediately -- we need to eliminate some answer choices. Although the passage does reference recalled vehicles, nothing suggests that these vehicles are unlikely to be hacked (and, in fact, that would be illogical -- after all, recalled vehicles usually have something wrong with them). Although the passage does reference keyless theft, it would require outside knowledge to know that keyless theft is related to remote entry, and we can't use outside knowledge. Although it might seem to make sense that those cars protected from attacks by law would be less likely to be hacked, there is no specific information in the passage to support this statement. Instead, choice C is the best supported answer. The final sentence of the passage tells us that more computerized components makes a car more vulnerable to hacking, therefore it is logical that cars with fewer computerized components would be less vulnerable to hacking.

The second question uses the phrase "According to the passage," which suggests that it is an explicit information question. Choice A is disproved by the passage because the passage states that "not a single incident of malicious hacking similar to that undertaken by the security researchers has occurred." Choice B can be eliminated because of the extreme "all" -- surely not *all* modern cars are susceptible to hacking. Choice C is not supported by any information in the passage, so we can eliminate that option as well. Choice D, however, is clearly supported by the final sentence of the passage.

Citing Evidence

Concept Introduction

All passages on the PSAT reading section will include citing evidence questions. These questions require that you locate the evidence in the passage that supports the answer to another question.

Spotting Citing Evidence Questions

Citing evidence questions are easy to spot. They will always ask you which answer choice best supports or provides the best evidence for the answer to the previous question. The answer choices will always be sets of lines.

These questions are paired with another analysis question, such as an implicit information question. The first question of the pair is an analysis question and the second is the citing evidence question.

Answering Citing Evidence Questions

Although citing evidence questions are easy to spot, they are not always easy to answer. They can often be time consuming because they require that you locate, read, and evaluate several sets of lines from the passage; on a timed test, that's a challenge in and of itself. At the same time, these questions can sometimes help us to answer the analysis question.

Answering these questions will depend on whether you were able to easily answer the analysis question. If you can easily answer the analysis question, follow these steps to answer the citing evidence question:

1. Look for key words, phrases, or ideas from the answer to the analysis question in each of the sets of lines provided. Eliminate any answer choices that don't contain these key ideas.
2. Of the remaining answer choices, choose the one that most clearly supports the ideas in the answer to the analysis question.

If you cannot easily answer the analysis question, you can use the citing evidence question to help. In this case, the process is as follows:

1. Eliminate answer choices that you know are wrong.
2. Since the answer to the analysis question has to be supported by one of the sets of lines given in the citing evidence question, you can eliminate any answer choices in the analysis question that cannot be supported by any of the given sets of lines. Similarly, any answer choices in the citing evidence question that do not support one of the answer choices in the analysis question can also be eliminated. This dual process of elimination can help you narrow down your options for both questions.
3. Of the remaining answer choices, select the answers that have the clearest relationship to one another.

Example Questions:

1   On Wednesday, NASA scientists announced the very first findings captured by the agency's New Horizons probe. The spacecraft completed a gravitational dance with the tiny world and its moon, Charon, on Tuesday morning, but it was so

5   occupied with observing the two orbs that it only began beaming back the very first and most compressed images hours later.
      NASA released two historic new images. The first is the highest-resolution photo of Charon ever, capturing the full disk of the moon. The second is a close-up on Pluto's surface. Both

10   were full of surprises: It was the kind of press conference where giddy scientists chuckle and repeat, "I don't know" over and over again.

1. Which of the following can be inferred from the passage?
    A) Gravity is strong on Pluto and Charon.
    B) There have been no previous pictures of Charon that show the moon clearly.
    C) The scientists studying Pluto are ill-informed about their subject of study.
    D) It takes hours for the New Horizons probe to send pictures back to Earth.

2. Which of the following best supports the answer to the previous question?
    A) Lines 2-3 ("The spacecraft… moon,")
    B) Lines 4-6 ("but… later.")
    C) Lines 7-8 ("The first… moon.")
    D) Lines 9-11 ("It was… again.")

The first question uses the word "inferred," so we know it is likely an implicit information question. Let's assume that we cannot spot the correct answer immediately -- we need to eliminate some answer choices. We can do this with the help of the answer choices of the second question.

Lines 2-3 say "the spacecraft completed a gravitational dance with the tiny world and its moon" – while this line does mention gravity, it doesn't support the conclusion that Pluto and Charon's gravity is strong. Thus, choice A can be eliminated.

Lines 4-6 mention that "it [the spacecraft] was so occupied with observing the two orbs that it only began beaming back the… images hours later." That would imply that the spacecraft was too busy to send the images back to Earth – not that the process of sending them back takes hours.   We can get rid of choice D.

Lines 8-9 say "The first is the highest-resolution photo of Charon ever, capturing the full disk of the moon." This would relate to answer choice B – there have been no CLEAR pictures of Charon before.

Lines 10-12 mention that "It was the kind of press conference where giddy scientists chuckle and repeat "I don't know" over and over again." Extrapolating that these scientists don't know what they're talking about (choice C) is not a logical conclusion; the sentence communicates more of their excitement than their ignorance.

Using elimination, we can eliminate choices A, C, and D from question 1, leaving us with B. Since answer choice C from the second question gives us the evidence for that answer, we can use that as our answer for question 2.

Words in Context

Concept Introduction

All passages on the PSAT reading section will include words in context questions. Rather than testing obscure vocabulary words through sentence completion exercises, the updated PSAT tests your understanding of vocabulary in the context of a passage. The words tested will be terms that appear in normal conversation or academic writing, and most of the words tested will have multiple possible meanings. Your job will be to determine the meaning of the word within the context of the passage.

Spotting Words in Context Questions

These questions are easy to spot. The answer choices will generally be just one or two words long, and the question itself will give you a word and the line number where the word can be found.

Answering Words in Context Questions

The answer choices for words in context questions will usually fall into one of two categories: They will either be alternative definitions for the same word (for instance, "contract" can mean either an agreement or the act of catching a disease, depending on context) or they will have a similar definition but a different connotation.

Because it's common for answer choices to have different connotations, it is important to recognize the difference between **denotation** and **connotation** of words. A word's denotation is the literal meaning of the word. A word's connotation is the feeling or emotion commonly associated with a word. For example:

> **Sample Sentence:** After years in management, she had learned that it was important to be **assertive** in order to gain the respect of new employees.

Let's take a look at the word "assertive." If we were asked what this word means within the context of the sentence, we could probably eliminate answer choices like "aggressive" or "pushy." Although the actual denotation of these words is similar to assertive, both of these words suggest a more negative connotation than the sentence calls for. After all, people are less likely to respect a manager who is pushy or aggressive.

The best way to answer words in context questions is to pay more attention to the passage than to the answer choices. After all, the answer choices will often include several correct definitions of the given word; it is the passage that will tell you which one to choose. Use this strategy to answer words in context questions:

1. Locate the word in the passage. Cover the word up and come up with a replacement word that suits the context of the sentence.
2. Compare your chosen replacement word to the answer choices. Eliminate any answer choices that clearly don't match the word you've chosen.
3. Plug the remaining answer choices into the sentence in the passage. Eliminate those choices that have a connotation that does not suit the sentence. This includes words that are too extreme, overly specific, or too vague.
4. Of the remaining answer choices, choose the one that most closely suits the context of the sentence.

Example Question:

1   Other scientists are more skeptical, stating that it would be
     difficult, if not impossible, to differentiate the dark matter signal
     from the background noise of pulsars and black holes. Many
     physicists go as far as stating that they will not be mollified that
5   dark matter exists or has been found until there is proof from
     particle accelerators and underground experiments that seek to
     detect the particles directly.

1. As it is used in line 4, "mollified" most nearly means
    A) soothed.
    B) lessened.
    C) appeased.
    D) moderated.

We can recognize this type of question by its wording, 'as it is used in this line,' and 'most nearly means.' As it gives us a line reference number, we can go to that line and find "mollified." If we remove the word from that sentence, we'll have this:

"Many physicists go as far as stating that they will not be _____ that dark matter exists or has been found until there is proof…"

What concept is the author trying to communicate with this sentence? That the scientists will not believe that dark matter exists without proof. What word could we put in that sentence that would make the sentence communicate that same idea?

"….they will not be *convinced* that dark matter exists…"

"…they will not be *persuaded* that dark matter exists…"

With these potential guesses in mind, we can now look at the answer choices. Which of these choices do not match?

Soothed means "calmed down."

Lessened means "made less, made fewer".

Appeased means "satisfied".

Moderated means "made less extreme."

While the dictionary definition of "mollified" often means 'soothed' or 'calmed', it makes little sense to say that scientists will be calmed by the fact that dark matter exists. *Lessened* also makes little sense in the context of the sentence – how can a person's opinion be *lessened* by evidence? Both choices A and B can be eliminated.

By plugging the remaining answer choices in the sentence, we can see which one works the best.

"…they will not be *appeased (satisfied)* that dark matter exists…"

"…they will not be *moderated (made less extreme)* that dark matter exists…"

Which of these would best communicate the idea that they will be convinced? If you are convinced of something, you would be *satisfied* that it is correct. Our answer is C, "appeased."

Central Ideas and Themes

Concept Introduction

The PSAT reading section encourages you to not only look at individual pieces of a given passage, but also to look at overarching ideas and themes within the passage. One way to help you catch all of the main ideas of the passage and to spot overall themes of the passage is to take notes as you read. By noting the main idea or argument of each paragraph, the thesis or central claim of the passage as a whole, and any other particularly important arguments, events, or ideas, you can provide yourself with a sort of "cheat sheet" for answering questions. This strategy can be particularly helpful with central ideas and themes questions.

Spotting Central Ideas and Themes Questions

These questions will usually ask you about main ideas or arguments seen in the passage. Look for phrases like:

- "The main idea of the second paragraph..."
- "The central claim of the passage..."
- "Overall, the author argues that..."
- "Which of the following best summarizes the main claim..."

Words like "main," "central," "overall," and "summarize" likely indicate a question that will ask for a central idea. Sometimes that central idea will be drawn from one paragraph or section of the passage while other questions will focus on the passage as a whole. Either way, noting main ideas will be useful to you in answering these questions.

Answering Central Ideas and Themes Questions

The first step to answering central ideas and themes questions -- and several other types of questions! -- is to take notes while you read. In the margins, write down a very brief summary of the main idea of each passage. Consider noting the location of the passage's thesis or main idea, places where evidence is used, or paragraphs that primarily serve as transitions from one main idea to another. By doing this, you can create a guide that will help you to connect information in order to identify central ideas and themes.

After reading the passage (and taking notes!), follow these steps to answer central ideas and themes questions:

1. Summarize the passage as a whole in just one sentence. Keep this sentence in mind as you answer the question.
2. Eliminate any answer choices that have little connection to your summarized main idea.
3. Eliminate any answer choices that reference things that are barely referenced in the passage. Remember that a central claim or idea will appear throughout the passage!
4. Eliminate any answer choices that are overly generalized. For instance, if the passage discusses a specific battle of the Civil War and the answer choice discusses the Civil War in general, it is overly broad.
5. Eliminate any answer choices that are too specific. For instance, if the question asks for the central idea of the passage but the answer choice offers the main idea of a single paragraph, the answer is likely too specific.
6. Of the remaining choices, choose the one that best reflects your idea of the central idea of the passage.

Example Questions:

1   The thought of Hawaii usually brings to mind surfers, shaved ice, and sleek beach resorts. One thing you may not know about the 50th state is that it has one of the highest rates of homelessness in America. High rents, displacement from development, and

5   income inequality have resulted in approximately 7,000 people in Hawaii without a roof over their heads.

Now, architects at the Honolulu-based firm Group 70 International have developed an innovative solution to the homelessness problem: turn a fleet of retired city buses into temporary mobile shelters.

1.   The main idea of the passage is that
   A) most people's impression of Hawaii is incorrect.
   B) city buses can be used for innovative purposes.
   C) Hawaii has a surprisingly large homeless population.
   D) One solution to Hawaii's homelessness problem may come from the use of city buses.

First, we should summarize the ideas of the passage in one quick, simple sentence. Make sure that this statement addresses all aspects of the passage, not focusing on any one particular idea. Perhaps we could say "while Hawaii has a large homeless population, solutions are being found through the use of retired city buses."

Can we eliminate any answer choices that have little to do with our idea or that have little to do with the passage? Choice A, "most people's impression of Hawaii is incorrect," is mentioned in the first line, but does not have much to do with the general idea that these paragraphs are trying to get across. It can be eliminated.

Are there any answer choices that are overly generalized? Choice B, "city buses can be used for innovative purposes," while relevant to the passage's idea as a whole, does not focus on the Hawaiian problem and leaves itself open to several other interpretations – city buses could be used for many things beyond homeless shelters. Choice B can be eliminated.

Are there any answer choices that are overly specific? Choice C focuses only on one detail of the passage – that Hawaii has a homeless problem – and doesn't address the general idea of trying to *fix* the problem. It can be eliminated.

This leaves us with only answer choice D, which references both the problem – Hawaii's homelessness problem – and the solution – the use of city buses.

Analyzing Purpose

Concept Introduction
Until now, most of the question types we've discussed have dealt with the actual content of a passage, but the PSAT reading section also wants to see how well you can examine why an author does the things he does. This includes the author's word choice and the structure of the passage.

Spotting Analyzing Purpose Questions
Since analyzing purpose questions could be asking about word choice or structure, they can be slightly more difficult to identify than some other question types. Look for phrases like these to give you a clue:

- "The author's purpose..."
- "The paragraph serves to..."
- "The most likely reason for..."
- "The rhetorical purpose of..."
- "Effect of the word choice..."

Look for key words that indicate that a question is asking you to identify the author's intention, the purpose of an element of the passage, or the effect of certain words, phrases, or sentences.

Answering Analyzing Purpose Questions
Regardless of whether the question focuses on word choice or passage structure, you should pay close attention to the main ideas of the passage in order to determine the author's intent. After all, you'll be answering questions about why the author did things a certain way, so it's important to know what the author's overall intention was. As we noted in the last lesson, the best way to spot main ideas is to take brief notes in the margin while you read.

If a question asks about the purpose of a specific part of the passage, follow these steps:

1. Look at your notes to determine what the main idea of the paragraph in question is. Consider this main idea within the context of the passage as a whole. How does this particular paragraph contribute to the development of the author's ideas? Some options might include (but are definitely not limited to) acting as a transition between two larger themes, presenting a new supporting argument or a counterargument, offering supporting evidence for an argument, or appealing to the reader's senses or emotions.
2. Eliminate any answer choices that do not seem to match the purpose that you came up with in step one.
3. Examine the remaining answer choices. Choose the one that best reflects your understanding of the passage's structure.

The process is somewhat different when a question asks about the author's word choice. For these questions, follow these steps:

1. Underline the specific words, phrases, or sentences referenced by the question.
2. Reference your notes to remind yourself of the author's purpose in both the passage as a whole and the paragraph being referenced by the paragraph.
3. Consider the connotations -- the emotions or feelings associated with a word -- of the words or phrases in question. Using your knowledge of the author's purpose, consider why the author would have chosen that particular word and that particular connotation.
4. Choose the answer that best matches your understanding of the author's purpose and the connotations of the words in question.

Note that the strategies for both of these specific question types require that you examine your notes. Notes can make a big difference in your ability to answer reading questions quickly and accurately.

Example Questions:

1   The requirements of the homeless vary. Though a small portion of the homeless are habitually adrift, most are individuals facing tough transitions – losing a house to foreclosure, escaping domestic violence, being dislocated by natural disaster.

5   Progressively, designers and architects are attempting to satisfy these needs through innovative design-based solutions.

But transitory shelters are still unable to resolve the conundrum of chronic homelessness. It's gradually thought that merely giving homeless people homes – a philosophy called Housing First – is

10   more successful than trying to solve the underlying reasons for homelessness as they're still living in shelters. Housing First is also budget-friendly, since people with homes end up requiring less public support and are less prone to end up in prisons or emergency rooms.

15   Nevertheless, the fact remains that with homelessness on the upsurge in America, we'll surely be in need of more innovative solutions.

1. The second paragraph serves to
   A) emphasize the importance of transitory shelters.
   B) underscore the benefits of the Housing First philosophy.
   C) denigrate those who argue that homelessness can't be solved.
   D) describe the changing attitudes towards giving housing to the homeless.

2. The author's word choice in the third paragraph is most likely intended to
   A) stress the importance of innovation in approaching homelessness.
   B) bemoan the lack of innovative solutions.
   C) warn of the rise of homelessness in America.
   D) argue for the improvement of homes for the homeless.

Seeing the phrase "this paragraph serves to" in the first question should indicate that this is an Authorial Purpose question. First, we need a straightforward summary of the second paragraph. What is its main idea? Perhaps it could best be phrased as, "Chronic homelessness is still a problem, and one of the potential solutions is giving the homeless places to stay in." Thus, which of our answer choices would best show what the second paragraph is trying to do? Choice A, "emphasize the importance of transitory shelters," can be eliminated – the first sentence of the paragraph contradicts that intention. Choice B stresses the benefits of this movement, which – given the facts provided in the second half of the paragraph – could be a potentially correct answer. The intention of the paragraph certainly does not attempt to insult anyone, so choice C could be eliminated. Finally, choice D does mention something mentioned in the paragraph – that the idea of giving homeless people homes is 'gradually thought', which would show a change in attitude. But in the end, the primary purpose is not to show how people are changing their minds – a relatively minor aspect of the paragraph as a whole - but rather to emphasize how this movement may be useful. B is the best answer.

The second question mentions the author's *word choice*. Let's take a look at the words used in that sentence that makes up the third paragraph. The author uses the words *upsurge, surely,* and *innovation.* The connotation of those words suggests a certain urgency in the author's intention. The content suggests a need for action. In choice B, there's no call for action and no sense for urgency. Choice C may suggest a sense of urgency, but doesn't make a call for action, whereas choice D calls for action without a sense of urgency. Only choice A suggests a sense of urgency *and* a call for action; thus, it would be our best answer.

Quantitative Information

Concept Introduction

At least one of the reading passages on each PSAT will include some sort of graphic, be it a graph, table, or chart. At least one of the questions for this passage will reference that graphic. These questions require that you analyze the quantitative information presented in the graphic and consider that information in light of the passage.

Spotting Quantitative Information Questions

These questions are easy to find because they will reference a graphic. Typically, these questions will include a phrase like "Based on information in the passage and the graph..." or "According to the chart..."

Answering Analyzing Purpose Questions

These questions can vary widely in difficulty. Some simply expect you to interpret the data in the graphic while others require that you synthesize the data in the graphic and the information in the passage. Questions that require synthesis mean that you must combine information from both sources to draw a conclusion.

Regardless of whether a question requires synthesis or is based primarily on information in the graphic, we know that the correct answer will have to reflect accurate data from the graphic. This can help to narrow down answer choices. To answer quantitative information questions, follow these steps:

1. Carefully examine the graphic. Be sure you understand what the graphic is saying.
2. Eliminate any answer choices that disagree with information in the graphic. Look out for misinterpretations of the graphic; this includes answer choices that misinterpret the axis labels or that make general statements that aren't fully supported by the graphic.
3. If the question requires use of information from the passage, eliminate any answer choices that disagree with the passage. As with implicit and explicit information questions, look out for answer choices that are worded similarly to the passage but that don't really reflect the claims of the passage.
4. Of the remaining answer choices, choose the one that best reflects the information from the graphic and the passage.

Example Questions:

1   Sociologists and economists have long warned of socioeconomic inequality and a lack of social mobility in American society, which is perhaps most clearly illustrated by the link between parental income and the economic potential of their

5   children. A new Pew report suggests that the effects of parental income are even higher than previously estimated.

      This new study tells us that the amount of money one makes can be roughly predicted by how much money one's parents made, a trend that grows stronger as one moves upward along

10   the income spectrum. The numbers can be jarring: Both male and female children born to 90th percentile earners are on track to earn more than three times as much as children of 10th percentile earners, simply by dint of being born into the right family.

      Such statistics may well indicate the death of the American

15   Dream. We like to believe that those who work hard will succeed, no matter their background, but it seems that it is your parents' income rather than your work ethic that matters most.

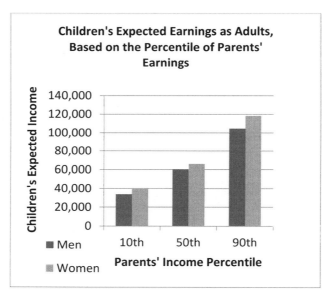

1. Information from the passage and the graph suggests that
   A) only men are impacted by parental income.
   B) women may receive even greater benefit from high parental income than men do.
   C) only women are impacted by parental income.
   D) men may receive even greater benefit from high parental income than men do.

2. Which of the following lines from the passage most clearly reflects information from the graph?
   A) Lines 1-4 ("Sociologists...children")
   B) Lines 4-6 ("A new...estimated")
   C) Lines 9-13 ("The numbers...family")
   D) Lines 14-17 ("We like...most")

Before we begin work on the questions, it is important to understand what the graph is telling us. This graph shows how much children are likely to earn based on the income percentile of their parents. There is a clear upward trend, indicating that the higher one's parents' income is, the higher one's potential earnings are.

Now we can look at the first question. This question asks us to use information from the passage and the graph, so we know the answer is likely to be found in both places. In the graph, we can see that the incomes of men from low-income households seem to be more limited than the incomes of their female counterparts, which could possibly support choice A - that only men feel the impact of parental income. However, the phrase "Both male and female children," found in line 10, directly negates this answer choice, so choice A can be eliminated. This same line negates answer choice C, that only women are impacted by parental income, so we can also eliminate choice C. We must now determine whether the best answer is choice B or D. Though we know that children of both genders are affected by parental income, these two answer choices ask whether men or women see greater benefit from high parental incomes. If we look at the chart, we can see that women from high income households earn more money than men from high income households, thus supporting choice B over choice D.

The second question asks us to find a set of lines from the passage that is directly linked to the data in the chart. Although the chart might be used to support the assertions made in the lines in choices A, B, and D, none of these options is a direct reflection of the data; these lines *interpret* the data. Only choice C offers a clear reflection of the data in the chart - that children born to parents in the 90th percentile of income earn roughly three times as much as those born to parents in the 10th percentile.

Multiple Texts

Concept Introduction

On every PSAT reading section, there will be a paired passage. Most of the questions accompanying the paired passages will only reference one of the two passages, but at least one or two questions will require that you consider both passages. These questions are known as multiple texts questions.

Spotting Multiple Texts Questions

Multiple texts questions are generally easy to spot because they will reference both passages or both authors. Questions might include the following phrases:

- "Based on information in both passages..."
- "Both authors..."
- "The author of the first passage would likely respond to the argument in the second passage..."

Any question that references both passages or authors will require that you consider both passages to arrive at the correct answer.

Answering Multiple Texts Questions

Much as with other question types, multiple texts questions will be much easier to answer if you take notes while you read. This will allow you to more easily spot similarities and differences between the two passages. When dealing with dual passages, look for:

- The authors' respective positions on the issue at hand
- The authors' tones
- Arguments in each passage that are similar or that directly contradict one another

As with quantitative information questions or citing evidence questions, the additional information can help us to eliminate incorrect answer choices. After all, we know that the correct answer will need to accurately reflect *both* passages. To answer multiple texts questions, follow these steps:

1. If the question references the overall ideas or positions of both passages, look at your notes. Use your notes to come up with a summary of the main claim of each passage.
2. If the question refers to specific parts of the passages, carefully reread these specific parts. Consider the similarities and differences in the ideas of these parts of the passages.
3. Eliminate any answer choices that fail to accurately reflect information from *both* passages. Incorrect answer choices will often accurately reflect the ideas of one passage but not the other.
4. Eliminate any answer choices that mix up the perspectives or ideas of the passages. It is not uncommon for incorrect answer choices to flip the ideas of the passages in an attempt to catch you unawares.
5. Of the remaining choices, choose the one that best reflects the ideas and perspectives of both passages.

Example Questions:

Passage 1

1   Even as the mental health community sees an uptick in complaints about screen addition, whether or not screen addition is a diagnosable disorder remains a point of debate. Part of the confusion stems from the fact that we have pushed to incorporate
5   technology in our schools, blurring the lines between entertainment and education and making moderation an even harder goal to attain. As a result, our children are becoming increasingly isolated and detached as technology pervades their lives from waking to sleeping.
10   Among young children, screen time in any amount has been shown to impair social communication and the development of relationships. As children grow older, the negative impacts of screen time are less severe, but excessive screen time can eliminate many of the important growing experiences that
15   contribute to a child's development. After all, if our teens are glued to screens, how can they be expected to socialize with friends, get involved with school activities, work a first job, and test the boundaries of their independence?

Passage 2

20   Some children wanted to play baseball all day, but I wanted to play videogames. Fearing that videogames would rot my brain, my parents imposed strict limitations on screen time, which resulted in covert binging. I look back on those years and wonder why my parents thought that videogames were so very harmful. After all, it
25   is because of videogames that I learned to tell stories, create worlds, and even how to save and spend money. Videogames were my first introduction to programming, and they helped me realize my career in technology.
    Today, technology is so prevalent that it is almost impossible to
30   keep children away from it. To be honest, I don't think we should even try. Restricting our children's access to technology even as they watch us check our smartphones at regular intervals merely teaches them not to respect rules when they have a chance to get around them. On the other hand, allowing children to learn to
35   regulate their behavior like adults gives them room to naturally modify their own habits.
    Technology is not going anywhere. Rather than trying to keep our children away from it, we should teach them to live with it. Let
40   them explore new worlds, exercise their imaginations, and embrace the ever-changing world of technology so that they will be prepared to engage in a creative technological marketplace.

1. Both authors would likely agree that
   A) screen time contributes little to a child's education.
   B) it is impossible to limit children's screen time.
   C) very young children should not be allowed screen time.
   D) modern life is surrounded by technology.

2. How would the author of Passage 2 most likely respond to the argument made in lines 10-17?
   A) Children can learn many important life skills through technology.
   B) Today's teens don't need to participate in the same activities that were expected of teens in prior generations.
   C) It isn't worth trying to limit screen time because children will just find a way to break the rules.
   D) Technology is used in schools.

Before we look at the questions, it's important to review the passages to establish the main claims in each. Both passages discuss limiting screen time for children and teens. Passage one argues that it is important to moderate screen time so that children can meaningfully develop in the real world. Passage two argues that technology teaches many valuable life lessons and plays an important role in modern life, so we should allow children to regulate their own technology use.

The first question asks us for a point of agreement between these two passages. Neither passage supports choice A; passage one points out that technology plays a role in school, while passage two points out that technology teaches valuable skills. We can eliminate choice A. Passage two seemingly supports choice B (although the use of the extreme word "impossible" may be overstating things a bit) by arguing that children whose screen time is strictly limited will simply find a way around the rules. Passage one, however, directly negates choice B by suggesting that parents should limit screen time, which means that the author of passage one must believe that it is possible to limit screen time. We can eliminate choice B. Only passage one supports choice C; passage two says nothing about young children and states that children in general should be allowed to regulate their own technology use. This leaves us with choice D, which is supported both by lines 4-9 in passage one and by the entirety of passage two.

The second question is slightly more complex in that it requires that we anticipate how one author might respond to another author. At the same time, the question helpfully narrows our focus on passage one to a specific set of lines. We should begin by examining those lines. In the cited paragraph, the author of passage one argues that excessive screen time negatively impacts the development of important life skills. We must figure out how the author of passage two would respond to this.

Choice A seems probable as the author of passage two argues that technology teaches important skills; he does this in lines 22-25 and again in lines 34-37. Let's check the other answer choices to be sure that choice A is correct. Nothing in the second passage suggests that the author believes that activities like school activities or first jobs are unimportant, so choice B is not supported. Although the author of passage two does argue that children with strict screen limitations will likely break the rules, this argument does not seem to be a very logical response to the argument that screen time negatively impacts the development of life skills, so choice C is weak. Although passage two does note the possible educational impacts of technology, it does not reference the use of technology in schools; only passage one does that. Choice D confuses the arguments in the passage. Of the given answer choices, choice A is by far the best supported.

Evaluating Arguments

Concept Introduction
Many PSAT reading passages are persuasive in nature. In these passages, the author will make a variety of arguments. Questions accompanying persuasive passages will ask you to evaluate the author's claims, reasoning, and evidence. Let's quickly review some important terms:

- Claim: An author's argument. For example: "Improving school quality requires addressing issues caused by student poverty."
- Counterclaim: A possible counterargument that the author will refute in order to strengthen his claim. For example: "Some argue that all students should be held to the same academic standards regardless of socioeconomic background. This position ignores the reality of poverty, which impacts academic performance more than almost any other factor of a student's life."
- Evidence: Used to support an author's argument. Can come in the form of statistics, survey results, study results, polls, expert testimony, personal experience, or anecdotes. "National surveys of public school teachers overwhelmingly show that students from low-income households lack the level of academic support enjoyed by students from higher-income households."
- Reasoning: Used to support an author's argument. Often links the use of evidence to the claim. For example: "After all, students from low-income households often don't have access to a variety of reading material; their parents are less likely to be able to attend parent-teacher conferences or otherwise engage with their educational experiences; and they are less likely to have adult oversight to ensure that homework gets done in a timely manner. These add up to an academic experience that is less effective than that enjoyed by higher-income students, even when these students are in the same classrooms."

Spotting Evaluating Arguments Questions
These questions will usually include at least one of the terms listed above. You might be asked to summarize a claim or counterclaim, identify which claims are included in the passage, identify the type of evidence used in the passage, summarize the author's reasoning, or evaluate whether an argument or reasoning is effective.

Answering Evaluating Arguments Questions
If you are taking notes while you read, you should have identified the claims and counterclaims made in the passage. It's also a good idea to mark an author's use of evidence so that it's easier to spot while you're answering questions. To answer evaluating arguments questions, follow these steps:

1. Use your notes to identify the argument referenced by the question.
2. Eliminate any answer choices that do not reflect the information in this part of the passage. This includes answer choices that misstate the claim or counterclaim, misidentify the evidence, or misstate the author's reasoning.
3. Of the remaining answer choices, choose the one that best reflects the information in the passage and your understanding of the author's arguments.

Example Questions:

1   If an individual has an ailing kidney, a donor's spare organ can
be transplanted into the injured individual so both individuals can
survive. What if it were possible to do something comparable for
someone with a deteriorating brain?

5   In recent lab research, Miguel Nicolelis and his colleagues
connected the brains of multiple monkeys to operate as shared
networks capable of working together to manipulate a cybernetic
arm and make deliberations and decisions. Nicolelis is hopeful
that linking human brains in this manner may make possible a

10   collection of new neurological instruments that could assist people
with conditions from Parkinson's disease to paralysis.

His team implanted electrodes in the brains of three monkeys to
monitor and document neural activity, which would subsequently
be linked by a computer. The monkeys were placed in separate

15   rooms, each of which included a digital display that allowed the
monkey to control its brain-machine interface to operate a
cybernetic arm to get a reward. None of the animals were aware
that they were working together to maneuver the arm, yet they not
only completed the task, but they also improved with repetition.

20   In another similar experiment described in *Scientific Reports,*
four rats were physically connected with a microwire to discover
how their brains collaborated as a linked unit when undertaking
various puzzles. The rats were supplied with information via
electrical pulse and rewarded when their brains synchronized. The

25   rats were able to store, retrieve, and communicate data on
temperature and barometric pressure, allowing their combined
brain network to make analyses that were superior to those of a
single rat.

After the success of the of such studies, Nicolelis and his team

30   are attempting to translate the findings to noninvasive clinical trials
to test whether such brain networks could effectively assist
paralyzed humans with rehabilitation. He believes that such
technology could provide millions of people around the world with
a second chance they probably thought they would never get.

1. Which of the following best summarizes Nicolelis's primary claim?
    A) Human brains could work together to accomplish a task, but only if the people were in the same room.
    B) Monkey brains and human brains are remarkably similar in the ways in which they function.
    C) Human brain transplants will soon be possible, just as kidney transplants are possible today.
    D) Technology that links people's brains could one day be used to help people with neurological conditions such as paralysis.

2. Nicolelis's claim is supported by which of the following types of evidence?
    A) The results of two similar animal studies
    B) An analogy that compares kidney transplants to brain transplants
    C) The results of a noninvasive clinical trial regarding paralysis
    D) A study on rats that was published in *Scientific Reports*

3. Nicolelis reasons that
   A) if kidneys can be transplanted, so can brains.
   B) if groups of monkeys can make decisions together, so can humans.
   C) if the brains of multiple animals can be linked to achieve a goal, so can the brains of humans.
   D) if paralyzed humans can receive cybernetic limbs, then their brains can control those limbs.

The first question references Nicolelis's main claim. This can be found in lines 8-11 and is repeated in the final paragraph. Nicolelis believes that his brain experiments will lead to technology that will link people's brains in order to help treat neurological conditions. Right away, we can see that choice D is most likely correct. Let's quickly examine the remaining answer choices. Choice A is not supported by the passage; the only reference to subjects being in the same room is in reference to the monkeys in Nicolelis's experiment, who were able to collaborate without being in the same room, thus directly negating choice A. Choice B is tempting because the passage suggests that Nicolelis's belief that his idea will work is based on his success with monkeys; however, when compared to choice D, which is very clearly supported by the passage, this choice represents a weak inference rather than a primary claim. Choice C might be tempting if we failed to read beyond the first paragraph; however, a further analysis of the passage shows that there is no discussion of brain transplants. Choice D is the best choice.

If we look for evidence in the passage, we see an analogy between the kidney and the brain, a study on monkeys, and a study on rats. A noninvasive clinical trial is referenced, but a closer reading reveals that this clinical study is planned for the future and has not yet occurred, so it cannot be considered evidence. We can thus eliminate choice C. Within context, the analogy between the kidney and the brain serves to introduce the general concept of linking brains to treat brain disorders; a brain transplant is never mentioned, and this analogy is not used to support Nicolelis's beliefs. We can eliminate choice B. This leaves us with choices A and D. Although the study on rats is specifically mentioned, it is not the only evidence used to support Nicolelis's belief; this study is paired with Nicolelis's monkey study. As a result, choice A is a stronger answer than choice D.

Finally, we are asked to examine Nicolelis's reasoning. We've already noticed that the analogy between the kidney and the brain is not intended to suggest that we will soon be able to do brain transplants, so we can eliminate choice A. Choice B is tempting because Nicolelis hopes to translate his success with linking monkey brains to linking human brains. We will keep this answer choice. The same can be said for choice C. Nothing in the passage supports choice D, so we can eliminate choice D. We must now choose between choice B and choice C. Although choice B is tempting, it is much more generalized than choice C is. After all, Nicolelis is not really focused on group decision making so much as he is on linking brains to achieve a goal. Thus choice C is the better answer.

Relationships

Concept Introduction

The PSAT will test your ability to identify relationships within passages. This includes relationships between people, events, or ideas as well as analogical relationships. Roughly one question per test will ask about analogous scenarios; questions about other types of relationships are more common.

Spotting Relationships Questions

Most relationships questions can be identified by key words indicating a relationship, including:

- Similar/similarities
- Compare/comparison
- Contrast/contrasting
- Different/differences
- Related to/relationship
- Caused by

Such questions will usually ask us to look at more than one element of the passage, which also provides clues to help identify relationships questions.

Questions that look for analogical reasoning will often include the words "analogous" or "similar." These questions usually ask you to identify a situation that is similar to a situation discussed in the passage. For instance, if the passage discusses the restoration of a historical building, an analogous situation might be reconstructive surgery following an accident -- both situations return something to its original state.

Answering Relationships Questions

First, let's focus on the more common relationships questions. To answer questions that ask about the relationship between two things in the passage, follow these steps:

1. Locate the items (people, events, ideas, etc.) that are referenced by the question.
2. In your own words, summarize the relationship between these items. Some possible relationships include:
   a. Contradiction or counterexample
   b. Agreement or support
   c. Adding details
   d. Comparison/contrast
   e. Cause/effect
3. Eliminate any answer choices that do not reflect your analysis of the relationship between the items.
4. Examine the remaining answer choices. Choose the one that is most strongly supported by evidence in the passage.

To answer analogical reasoning questions, follow these steps:

1. Reread the part of the passage referenced by the question. Try to summarize the information in simple, general terms. For instance, in our prior example, we noted that restoring a historical building is returning the building to its original state.
2. Analyze each situation offered by the answer choices. For each situation, rephrase it in simple, general terms.
3. Compare the situation in the passage to the ones in the answer choices. Choose the one that seems to best reflect your general summary of the situation in the passage.

Example Questions:

1   Amidst a nationwide discussion about gender-based income inequality, it may seem shallow to raise the issue of the so-called "makeup tax," but it is a very real concern for many women. After all, women spend a lot of time and money on makeup because it

5   affects not merely their personal relationships, but also their paychecks. In comparison, though both men and women invest in things like haircuts and shaving cream, men are generally unconcerned about the cost of makeup.

      Studies show that the average woman will spend about $15,000

10   on makeup in her lifetime. This counts only the monetary cost; women also spend a great deal of time -- an average of 10 minutes to an hour per day -- simply to appear acceptable in the workplace.

      Some respond to concerns over the "makeup tax" by saying,

15   "Just don't wear makeup." And while many women do choose to go without makeup for a variety of reasons, polls show that approximately 50 to 80 percent of women use makeup at least occasionally. A survey conducted in 2012 in New Hampshire showed that at least half of women wear makeup to work,

20   interviews, and other professional settings. It turns out that there is good reason for this practice: In a 2014 study, male and female participants agreed that women seem more competent, likable, and attractive with makeup.

      All of this correlates to years of research that concludes that

25   attractive people get paid higher wages. Thus, the makeup tax: Good-looking men and women both excel, but men don't need makeup to be considered good-looking. This isn't mere conjecture. One study found that women who wore makeup were promoted over women who did not wear makeup; another found

30   that waitresses who wear makeup earn higher tips.

      Compound this with the fact that women still earn less than men -- even when data is adjusted for education and even in female-dominated occupations. In other words, women earn less than men but are expected to spend thousands of dollars more than

35   men in order to look "professional." That is the makeup tax at work.

1. Based on the passage, which of the following is a similarity between male and female workers?
   A) Both spend up to an hour per day to improve their appearance in the workplace.
   B) Both are concerned about income inequality between men and women.
   C) Both are rewarded professionally for an attractive physical appearance.
   D) They spend comparable amounts of money to appear professional.

2. Which of the following situations is most analogous to the makeup tax?
   A) A student from one background is required to earn a higher test score than a student from another background in order to earn admission at the same college.
   B) A slow reader must spend the same amount of time to read a short book as a fast reader spends to read a much longer book.
   C) A person who chooses to buy a very expensive car must pay higher taxes than a person who owns a much less expensive car.
   D) A doctor who has more patients must spend more time at work than a doctor who has fewer patients.

Thanks to the word "similarity," we know we are dealing with a relationships question. Although both man and women are discussed in various parts of the passage, we can narrow down our search by looking for specific parts of the passage that discuss men since they are less of a main focus than women and thus appear in the passage less frequently. Since the passage focuses primarily on differences between men and women, we can further narrow our search by looking for keywords like "both" or "similar." This narrows our focus to line 6, lines 18-20, and lines 25-27. Although line 6 tells us that both men and women spend money on certain appearance-related products, nothing suggests that men and women spend similar amounts of money; quite the opposite, in fact. We can eliminate choice D. Lines 18-20 don't support any of the given answer choices, so we know our answer won't be found there. Lines 25-27 tell us that both men and women are rewarded in the workplace for being good-looking. This supports choice C. Nothing anywhere in the passage supports choice B, and lines 10-12 specify that it is women, not men, who spend up to an hour per day on their appearance, so we can eliminate choice A. Choice C is the strongest answer.

In the second question, we're looking for an analogous situation. First, let's try to rephrase the concept of the makeup tax in general terms. The makeup tax requires that women put in more time and money on their appearance than men to succeed in the workplace. Put even more generally, through no fault of its own, one group spends more than another to achieve the same goal. We can eliminate choice B because the two people spend the same amount of time to achieve a different goal. We can eliminate choice C because the person spending more does so due to his own choice. We can eliminate choice D because one doctor spends more time to achieve a different goal (the care of a greater number of patients). Choice A is most similar to the makeup tax because one student must put in greater effort to achieve the same goal as another student due to circumstances beyond their control.

Point of View

Concept Introduction

Just as the PSAT tests your ability to understand the author's intention, it will also ask you about the author's point of view. To determine point of view, pay close attention to the author's position on an issue, writing style, and tone.

Spotting Point of View Questions

Point of view questions may be presented in several different ways. In general, look for phrases such as:

- "Perspective"
- "Point of view"
- "Author is most likely a..."

Any question that asks about where the author is coming from will usually be a point of view question.

Answering Relationships Questions

While reading the passage, pay close attention to the author's attitude toward the subject matter. Is the passage persuasive? Informative? Why do you think the author wrote this passage? What do you think the author does for a living and would this affect his/her perspective? Who is the intended audience and how might this influence the author's point of view?

Follow these steps to answer point of view questions:

1. Identify the author/speaker and audience. What is the author/speaker's relationship to the audience? Eliminate any answer choices that disagree with this relationship.
2. In one sentence, summarize the purpose of the passage. Eliminate any answer choices that disagree with the passage's primary purpose.
3. Consider the author's style and tone. For example, a formal style and dry tone would likely indicate a more academic point of view, whereas a less formal style and an emotional tone would suggest a more passionate point of view. Eliminate any answer choices that fail to reflect the passage's style and tone.
4. Examine the remaining answer choices. Choose the one that is most strongly supported by evidence from the passage.

Example Questions:

1　　Richard Nixon played an implausibly large role in American
　　politics over the course of a public career that spanned almost 50
　　years after his election to Congress in 1946. He returned over and
　　over again to prominence even after losses and a scandal that
5　　would have sent other politicians into permanent exile. At the time
　　of his death, he had fought hard to overcome the Watergate
　　scandal that had forced him out of the White House in 1974,
　　managing to attain a relatively respected position as elder
　　statement and political analyst. In fact, but the time he died, Nixon
10　　had become such a familiar figure in American politics that many
　　felt it unfathomable that the nation would no "have Nixon to kick
　　around anymore."
　　　　That infamous statement, aimed at the press with which he so
　　frequently battled, was the departure line in a self-proclaimed "last
15　　press conference" after his loss in the race for governor of
　　California in 1962. That loss came only two years after Nixon had
　　lost to John F. Kennedy in one of the closest Presidential elections
　　of the modern era. Nonetheless, despite those devastating upsets,
　　he was elected as the 37th President of the United States in 1968,
20　　marking what seemed to be the beginning of an upward trajectory
　　in his political career. Just six years later, he resigned amid the
　　most famous political scandal in our history.
　　　　To those born after Nixon's election, he is likely known primarily
　　as the first President forced to resign the nation's highest office.
25　　His distinctive -- even comical -- features and mannerisms, such
　　as his jowly face with the ski-jump nose and the widow's peak,
　　and the arms extended displaying the peace sign, made him a
　　prime subject for caricatures. That depiction is true and perhaps
　　fair enough, but it ignores so much about the only American other
30　　than Franklin D. Roosevelt to have been nominated on five
　　national tickets, to run for President or Vice President.

1. Which of the following best describes the author's point of view regarding Richard Nixon?
   A) The author feels the public view of Nixon unfairly ignores certain aspects of Nixon's life.
   B) The author views Nixon as a long-running political joke.
   C) The author believes that Nixon has been unfairly maligned.
   D) The author hopes to redeem Nixon by emphasizing only his positive accomplishments.

2. Based on evidence from the passage, the author is most likely a
   A) personal friend of Nixon's who is reminiscing about Nixon's life.
   B) journalist reporting the event of Richard Nixon's death.
   C) biographer hoping to explain the nuances of a generally misunderstood figure.
   D) former adversary of Nixon's who hopes to remind the public of Nixon's misdeeds.

We begin by identifying the author and the audience, but there is little in the passage to provide a clear answer to this question. Instead, we may have greater luck identifying the purpose of the passage. Although there are a few somewhat persuasive lines in the passage, for the most part the passage seems intended to inform an audience about the life of a famous figure. Since the passage discusses both positive and negative aspects of Nixon's life, it is relatively unbiased. Based on this information, we can eliminate choices B and D, which would suggest a much more persuasive intention. Choice C has some merit since the passage ends with a positive note about Nixon, but the author willingly admits that the negative depictions of Nixon are "true and perhaps fair enough." Choice A best reflects the author's viewpoint on Nixon given that the author both admits the truth of the public view of Nixon and notes that this view ignores quite a bit about Nixon.

The second question asks us to identify the author's likely identity based on information in the passage, something that we felt was unclear when we first addressed question one. These answer choices can help us narrow things down because they all include a possible purpose for the passage. We've already determined that the passage, which is mostly unbiased, is primarily intended to inform rather than to persuade. Based on this, we can eliminate choice D, which would suggest a more negative piece. Nothing in the author's style or tone suggests a relationship with Nixon, so we can eliminate choice A. Although the piece is rather journalistic in style, it does not focus on Nixon's death, nor does it actually report any information about his death, so we can eliminate choice B. Only choice B matches both the purpose and the style of the passage.

Questions 1-10 are based on the following passage.

The following passage is adapted from an article titled "Kepler 452b: What It Would Be Like to Live on Earth's Cousin," written by Mike Wall and published in *Scientific American*.

Kepler-452b may be Earth's close cousin, but living on the newfound world would still be an alien experience.

If a group of pioneers were to be magically
5　teleported to the surface of Kepler-452b, the closest planet to an "Earth twin" discovered, they would immediately recognize they were not on their home planet anymore. (Magic, or some sort of warp drive, must be used for such a journey, since Kepler-452b is
10　located over 1,400 light-years away.)

Sixty percent wider than Earth and approximately five times more massive, Kepler-452b's gravitational force is significantly stronger than the gravitational pull of Earth. Hypothetical explorers would feel
15　around twice as heavy on the cousin planet as they do on Earth.

"It might be quite challenging at first," Jon Jenkins, of NASA's Ames Research Center in Moffett Field, California, said during a news conference. Jenkins is
20　data analysis lead for the space agency's Kepler spacecraft, which discovered Kepler-452b.

But the foreign visitors to the planet would most likely be able to meet that challenge, said John Grunsfeld, a former astronaut and associate
25　administrator of NASA's Science Mission Directorate. He said that firefighters and backpackers routinely carry heavy loads that mimic the effect of increased gravity.

"If we were there, we'd get stronger," Grunsfeld
30　said. "Our bones would actually get stronger. It would be like a workout every day."

If people were to settle on Kepler-452b for long periods of time, there would probably be significant changes to their bodies, he and Jenkins said.
35　"I suspect that, over time, we would adapt to the conditions, and perhaps become stockier over a long period of many generations," Jenkins said.

Other aspects of life on Kepler-452b would be more similar to Earth. For instance, the exoplanet orbits a
40　solar star at about the same distance at which Earth circles the sun.

"It would feel a lot like home, from the standpoint of the sunshine that you would experience," Jenkins said. Earth plants "would photosynthesize, just

45　perfectly fine," he added.

Envisioning other circumstances of life on Kepler-452b is much more speculative because the exoplanet is too far away to examine closely. Researchers believe that the planet is rocky, like Earth, but are
50　unsure. Kepler-452b has been hypothesized to most likely have a thick atmosphere, liquid water, and active volcanoes.

Models suggest that Kepler-452b may soon experience a runaway greenhouse effect, comparable
55　to the one that hindered Venus from being a potentially habitable world billions of years ago to the scorching hothouse it is today.

The star that Kepler-452b orbits is apparently older than the sun – six billion years old compared to four
60　and a half billion years. Therefore, it is in a more energetic phase of its life cycle than the sun; the star is about ten percent larger and twenty percent brighter than Earth's sun. This makes the sunlight on Kepler-452b slightly different than the light familiar to those
65　on Earth.

The high energy level outputs of Kepler-452b's sun might cause the exoplanet to heat up and lose its oceans – if the planet does have oceans in the first place – by evaporation, causing breakup by ultraviolet
70　light and atmospheric escape.

This hypothetical scenario most likely will not occur on Kepler-452b for another 500 million years or so, on the assumption that the estimates and calculations of the planet's size and star's age are
75　accurate, Jenkins said. Larger planets have stronger gravity which allows them to retain their surface water for longer periods of time than smaller planets can.

"But, you know, we don't know exactly," Jenkins added.
80　Jenkins and his discovery team helped create an artist's rendition of that depicts how Kepler-452b would look if a runaway greenhouse effect began to unfold.

The imagery shows "not oceans, but residual bodies
85　of water that are highly concentrated in minerals after the oceans are largely gone, and you have lakes and pools and rivers left," Jenkins said.

"It's a fascinating thing to think about, and I think it gives us an opportunity to take a pause and reflect on
90　our own environment that we find ourselves in," he added. "We've been lucky and fortunate to live in a habitable zone for the last several billion years, and we'd like that to continue on."

As it is used in line 2, "alien" most nearly means

A) extraneous.
B) immigrant.
C) remote.
D) foreign.

In the second paragraph, the author refers to "magic" (lines 4 and 8) most likely in order to

A) emphasize the impossibility of travelling to Kepler-452b.
B) illustrate the fantastic qualities of Kepler-452b.
C) suggest that Kepler-452b would make an interesting setting for an imaginary novel.
D) cast doubt on the existence of a planet like Kepler-452b.

3

The passage suggests that Jenkins believes that humans would grow "stockier" (line 36) after several generations on Kepler-452b primarily because

A) people would need to carry large backpacks filled with supplies, which would stunt growth.
B) there would not be enough nutritious food to allow people to grow taller.
C) life on Kepler-452b would likely be much harder than life of Earth.
D) the stronger pull of gravity would likely force people to grown more muscular to offset the pull.

4

According to the passage, which of the following is something that people would need to adjust to in order to live on Kepler-452b?

A) The overly thin atmosphere, which would likely make plant photosynthesis difficult
B) The lack of a reliable day/night cycle due to the differences in Kelper-452b's solar star
C) Cope with greater weight as a result of the stronger gravitational pull
D) The lack of plant-life

Which of the following best supports the answer to the previous question?

A) Lines 14-16 ("Hypothetical...Earth")
B) Lines 39-41 ("For...sun")
C) Lines 44-45 ("Earth...added")
D) Lines 50-52 ("Kepler...volcanoes")

Which of the following is NOT mentioned in the passage as a similarity between Kepler-452b and Earth?

A) Distance to a solar star
B) Age of solar star
C) Terrain
D) Water availability

According to the passage, how are Venus and Kepler-452b similar?

A) Kepler-452b underwent a similar greenhouse effect as the one Venus underwent, although Kepler-452b remains inhabitable.
B) Kepler-452b seems likely to undergo a greenhouse effect similar to the one Venus experienced long ago.
C) Kepler-452b is already undergoing a greenhouse effect identical to that experienced by Venus.
D) The sunlight on Kepler-452b is very similar to the sunlight on Venus.

Which of the following provides the best support for the answer to the previous question?

A) Lines 50-52 ("Kepler...volcanoes")
B) Lines 53-57 ("Models...today")
C) Lines 60-65 ("Therefore...Earth")
D) Lines 84-87 ("The imagery...said")

9

As it is used in line 76, "retain" most nearly means

A) detain.
B) employ.
C) enjoy.
D) maintain.

10

The passage concludes by suggesting that

A) Earth will likely follow the same path as that predicted by Jenkins for Kepler-452b.
B) when Earth inevitably becomes uninhabitable, the human population will be able to relocate to Kepler-452b.
C) we can learn how to cope with climate change by studying the potential greenhouse effects on Kepler-452b.
D) in several billion years, we will be able to travel to Kepler-452b.

The following passage is adapted from a *Smithsonian Magazine* article titled "What Was on the Menu at the First Thanksgiving?" by Megan Gambino.

What are the traditional Thanksgiving dishes of today? Turkey, stuffing, mashed potatoes, cranberry sauce, and pumpkin pie come to mind. However, if you wanted to host a historically accurate feast,
5 comprised of only those foods that historians are positive were eaten at the alleged "first Thanksgiving," you would be faced with slimmer pickings.

Two chief sources—the only remaining texts that
10 mention the meal—recount some of the staples served at the harvest celebration shared by the Pilgrims and Wampanoag at Plymouth Colony in 1621. An English leader in attendance, Edward Winslow, wrote home to a friend:

15 "Our harvest being gotten in, our governor sent four men on fowling, that so we might after a special manner rejoice together after we had gathered the fruit of our labors. They four in one day killed as much fowl as, with a little help beside, served the
20 company almost a week. At which time, amongst other recreations, we exercised our arms, many of the Indians coming amongst us, and among the rest their greatest king Massasoit, with some ninety men, whom for three days we entertained and feasted, and
25 they went out and killed five deer, which they brought to the plantation and bestowed on our governor, and upon the captain and others."

William Bradford, the governor Winslow references, also described the fall of 1621, adding,
30 "And besides waterfowl there was great store of wild turkeys, of which they took many, besides venison, etc. Besides, they had about a peck a meal a week to a person, or now since harvest, Indian corn to that proportion."

35 Nevertheless, determining any other fare that might have been present at the feast of the colonists and Wampanoag is more difficult. To formulate educated guesses, Kathleen Wall, a culinarian at a living history museum in Plymouth, Massachusetts,
40 analyzed cookbooks and garden records from the period.

Let's begin with the bird. While the colonists and American Indians could have prepared wild turkey, Wall believes that goose or duck was the wildfowl of
45 choice. In her investigation, she has concluded that swan and passenger pigeons would have also been options.

What methods were used to cook the birds? Smaller birds were spit-roasted, while larger birds
50 were boiled and then roasted. The birds may have been stuffed, though probably not with bread. The Pilgrims typically stuffed birds with chunks of onion and herbs. "There is a wonderful stuffing for goose in the 17th-century that is just shelled chestnuts," says
55 Wall. Seeing as the first Thanksgiving was a three-day celebration, she continues, "I have no doubt whatsoever that birds that are roasted one day, the remains of them are all thrown in a pot and boiled up to make broth the next day. That broth thickened with
60 grain to make a pottage."

What else might have been available? In addition to wildfowl, the colonists and Wampanoag likely enjoyed deer, eels, and shellfish, such as lobster, clams and mussels. Like most eastern woodlands
65 people, the Wampanoag were extremely familiar with the forest. This means that they probably brought nuts, such as chestnuts, walnuts and beechnuts, in addition to the food they farmed. "Flint corn was their staple. They grew beans, which they used from
70 when they were small and green until when they were mature," says Wall. "They also had different sorts of pumpkins or squashes."

But, at some point, reproducing the 1621 feast is simply a process of elimination. "You look at what an
75 English celebration in England is at this time. What are the things on the table? You see lots of pies in the first course and in the second course, meat and fish pies. To cook a turkey in a pie was not terribly uncommon," says Wall. "But it is like, no, the pastry
80 isn't there." There was no butter or wheat flour to make crusts for pies and tarts.

Meat with potatoes? No. White potatoes, from South America, and sweet potatoes, from the Caribbean, were not yet available in North America.
85 Cranberry sauce? No. It would be an additional 50 years before there were any records of combining cranberries and sugar into a "Sauce to eat with. . . .Meat."

Now you might be wondering how the
90 Thanksgiving menu developed into what it is today.

The Thanksgiving holiday of today began in the mid-19th century. When Edward Winslow's letter and Governor Bradford's manuscript were recovered and recirculated, the colonial nostalgia of the times
95 meant that by the 1850s, most states and territories

had begun celebrating was had been arbitrarily coined "Thanksgiving."

Sarah Josepha Hale, editor of a popular women's magazine, became a vocal advocate for instituting
100 Thanksgiving as an annual event. Beginning in 1827, Hale lobbied 13 presidents, the last being Abraham Lincoln. She delivered her idea to as a means of uniting the country in the midst of the Civil War, and, in 1863, President Lincoln made Thanksgiving a
105 national holiday. A few cookbooks and hundreds of recipes later, Sarah's vision of the traditional Thanksgiving meal started on the path to the celebration we know and love today.

11

As it is used in line 9, "chief" most nearly means

A) main.
B) champion.
C) commanding.
D) head.

12

Within the context of the passage as a whole, the paragraphs in lines 15 to 34 primarily serve to

A) offer first-person descriptions from those present at the First Thanksgiving.
B) prove the author's assertion that there are only two remaining texts that mention the First Thanksgiving.
C) show that the Native Americans played a much smaller role in the First Thanksgiving than previously thought.
D) continue on a path of violence regardless of whether his request is fulfilled.

13

As it is used in line 35, "fare" most nearly means

A) prosper.
B) expense.
C) food.
D) menu.

14

According to the passage, nuts typically came from

A) gardens of the period.
B) England.
C) Native American farms.
D) the forest.

15

Which of the following provides the best support for the answer to the previous question?

A) Lines 37-41 ("To formulate...period")
B) Lines 64-67 ("Like...beechnuts")
C) Lines 68-71 ("Flint...mature")
D) Lines 74-76 ("You...table")

16

Which of the following best summarizes the central claim of the passage?

A) The Wampanoag actually provided most of the food for the First Thanksgiving feast.
B) Historians have long been curious about the foods served at the First Thanksgiving.
C) Thanksgiving ought to be a longer celebration since the First Thanksgiving lasted for three days.
D) Modern Thanksgiving celebrations bear little resemblance to the First Thanksgiving.

17

Which is NOT a source of evidence mentioned in the passage?

A) Historical cookbooks
B) Native American artwork depicting the feast
C) Garden records from the 1600s
D) Writings of people who attended the feast

18

The author's style and tone can best be described as

A) Persuasive and formal, but still accessible
B) Informative and highly academic
C) Informative and formal, but still accessible
D) Persuasive and highly academic

19

Thanksgiving was made a national holiday in large part to

A) celebrate colonial nostalgia
B) Abraham Lincoln wanted to be more popular.
C) unite the country during the Civil War.
D) create a new market for cookbooks.

20

Which of the following provides the best support for the answer to the previous question?

A) Lines 92-97 ("When...Thanksgiving")
B) Lines 100-102 ("Beginning...Lincoln")
C) Lines 102-105 ("She...holiday")
D) Lines 105-108 ("A few...today")

Questions 21-30 are based on the following passage.

The following passage is excerpted from Theodore Roosevelt's speech "Duties of American Citizenship," delivered on January 26, 1883.

Of course, in one sense, the first essential for a man's being a good citizen is his possession of the home virtues of which we think when we call a man by the emphatic adjective of manly. No man can be a
5 good citizen who is not a good husband and a good father, who is not honest in his dealings with other men and women, faithful to his friends and fearless in the presence of his foes, who has not got a sound heart, a sound mind, and a sound body; exactly as no
10 amount of attention to civil duties will save a nation if the domestic life is undermined, or there is lack of the rude military virtues which alone can assure a country's position in the world. In a free republic the ideal citizen must be one willing and able to take arms
15 for the defense of the flag, exactly as the ideal citizen must be the father of many healthy children. A race must be strong and vigorous; it must be a race of good fighters and good breeders, else its wisdom will come to naught and its virtue be ineffective; and no
20 sweetness and delicacy, no love for and appreciation of beauty in art or literature, no capacity for building up material prosperity can possibly atone for the lack of the great virile virtues.
     But this is aside from my subject, for what I wish
25 to talk of is the attitude of the American citizen in civic life. It ought to be axiomatic in this country that every man must devote a reasonable share of his time to doing his duty in the Political life of the community. No man has a right to shirk his political
30 duties under whatever plea of pleasure or business; and while such shirking may be pardoned in those of small means it is entirely unpardonable in those among whom it is most common—in the people whose circumstances give them freedom in the struggle for
35 life. In so far as the community grows to think rightly, it will likewise grow to regard the young man of means who shirks his duty to the State in time of peace as being only one degree worse than the man who thus shirks it in time of war. A great many of our
40 men in business, or of our young men who are bent on enjoying life (as they have a perfect right to do if only they do not sacrifice other things to enjoyment), rather plume themselves upon being good citizens if they even vote; yet voting is the very least of their duties.
45   Nothing worth gaining is ever gained without

effort. You can no more have freedom without striving and suffering for it than you can win success as a banker or a lawyer without labor and effort, without self-denial in youth and the display of a ready and
50 alert intelligence in middle age. The people who say that they have not time to attend to politics are simply saying that they are unfit to live in a free community....If freedom is worth having, if the right of self-government is a valuable right, then the one
55 and the other must be retained exactly as our forefathers acquired them, by labor, and especially by labor in organization, that is in combination with our fellows who have the same interests and the same principles. We should not accept the excuse of the
60 business man who attributed his failure to the fact that his social duties were so pleasant and engrossing that he had no time left for work in his office; nor would we pay much heed to his further statement that he did not like business anyhow because he thought the
65 morals of the business community by no means what they should be, and saw that the great successes were most often won by men of the Jay Gould stamp. It is just the same way with politics. It makes one feel half angry and half amused, and wholly contemptuous, to
70 find men of high business or social standing in the community saying that they really have not got time to go toward meetings, to organize political clubs, and to take a personal share in all the important details of practical politics; men who further urge against their
75 going note the fact that they think the condition of political morality low, and are afraid that they may be required to do what is not right if they go into politics.

21

According to the author, which of the following are the most important non-civic responsibilities of citizenship?

A) To defend his country and to reproduce
B) To be manly
C)To appreciate beauty and build prosperity
D) To be a good husband and father

22

Which of the following provides the best support for the answer to the previous question?

A) Lines 1-4 ("Of course...manly")
B) Lines 4-6 ("No man...father")
C) Lines 13-16 ("In a...children")
D) Lines 20-22 ("no love...prosperity")

23

Which of the following sets of lines best identifies the author's central argument?

A) Lines 13-16 (In a...children")
B) Lines 26-29 ("It ought...community")
C) Lines 39-44 ("A great...duties")
D) Lines 50-53 ("The people...community")

24

As it is used in line 32, "means" most nearly means

A) equipment.
B) resources.
C) technique.
D) determines.

25

Under which of the following circumstances would the author agree that it is acceptable to enjoy life?

A) After one has fulfilled duties to home and country
B) While one is engaged in politics
C) After one has served in the military
D) Once one has started a family

26

According to the author, which of the following is something that many consider to be the hallmark of good citizenship but that the author believes is the minimum requirement of a good citizen?

A) Succeeding in business
B) Serving in the military
C) Reproducing
D) Voting

27

According to the author, why should American citizens feel duty bound to engage in political life?

A) We should not allow laziness to keep us from participating in politics.
B) We cannot complain of immorality in politics if we are unwilling to go into politics to fix things.
C) We must work to maintain the right to self-government by participating in government.
D) We must, at the very least, vote in order to be members of a free society.

28

Which of the following provides the best evidence for the answer to the previous question?

A) Lines 39-44 ("A great...duties")
B) Lines 50-53 ("The people...community")
C) Lines 53-57 ("If freedom...organization")
D) Lines 74-77 ("men...politics")

29

Within the context of the passage as a whole, the information in lines 59-67 ("We should...stamp") primarily serves to

A) provide an analogous situation in which the usual excuses for not participating in politics would be considered unacceptable.
B) illustrate why many businessmen choose not to join political life.
C) provide examples of areas of life other than politics in which people also make excuses for not fully participating.
D) show the author's contempt for the realm of business when compared with the realm of politics.

30

As it is used in line 73, "share" most nearly means

A) division.
B) experience.
C) claim.
D) interest.

Questions 31-40 are based on the following passage.

The following passage is excerpted from James Fenimore Cooper's *The Last of the Mohicans*.

The Indians silently repaired to their appointed stations, which were fissures in the rocks, whence they could command the approaches to the foot of the falls.
In the center of the little island, a few short and
5　stunted pines had found root, forming a thicket, into which Hawkeye darted with the swiftness of a deer, followed by the active Duncan. Here they secured themselves, as well as circumstances would permit, among the shrubs and fragments of stone that were
10　scattered about the place. Above them was a bare, rounded rock, on each side of which the water played its gambols, and plunged into the abysses beneath, in the manner already described. As the day had now dawned, the opposite shores no longer presented a
15　confused outline, but they were able to look into the woods, and distinguish objects beneath a canopy of gloomy pines.
　　A long and anxious watch succeeded, but without any further evidences of a renewed attack; and Duncan
20　began to hope that their fire had proved more fatal than was supposed, and that their enemies had been effectually repulsed. When he ventured to utter this impression to his companions, it was met by Hawkeye with an incredulous shake of the head.
25　"You know not the nature of a Maqua, if you think he is so easily beaten back without a scalp!" he answered. "If there was one of the imps yelling this morning, there were forty! and they know our number and quality too well to give up the chase so soon. Hist!
30　look into the water above, just where it breaks over the rocks. I am no mortal, if the risky devils haven't swam down upon the very pitch, and, as bad luck would have it, they have hit the head of the island. Hist! man, keep close! or the hair will be off your crown in the
35　turning of a knife!"
　　Heyward lifted his head from the cover, and beheld what he justly considered a prodigy of rashness and skill. The river had worn away the edge of the soft rock in such a manner as to render its first pitch less
40　abrupt and perpendicular than is usual at waterfalls. With no other guide than the ripple of the stream where it met the head of the island, a party of their insatiable foes had ventured into the current, and swam down upon this point, knowing the ready access
45　it would give, if successful, to their intended victims.
　　As Hawkeye ceased speaking, four human heads could be seen peering above a few logs of drift-wood that had lodged on these naked rocks, and which had probably suggested the idea of the practicability of the
50　hazardous undertaking. At the next moment, a fifth form was seen floating over the green edge of the fall, a little from the line of the island. The savage struggled powerfully to gain the point of safety, and, favored by the glancing water, he was already
55　stretching forth an arm to meet the grasp of his companions, when he shot away again with the shirling current, appeared to rise into the air, with uplifted arms and starting eyeballs, and fell, with a sudden plunge, into that deep and yawning abyss over
60　which he hovered. A single, wild, despairing shriek rose from the cavern, and all was hushed again as the grave.
　　The first generous impulse of Duncan was to rush to the rescue of the hapless wretch; but he felt himself
65　bound to the spot by the iron grasp of the immovable scout.
　　"Would ye bring certain death upon us, by telling the Mingoes where we lie?" demanded Hawkeye, sternly; "'Tis a charge of powder saved, and
70　ammunition is as precious now as breath to a worried deer! Freshen the priming of your pistols—the midst of the falls is apt to dampen the brimstone—and stand firm for a close struggle, while I fire on their rush."
　　He placed a finger in his mouth, and drew a long,
75　shrill whistle, which was answered from the rocks that were guarded by the Mohicans. Duncan caught glimpses of heads above the scattered drift-wood, as this signal rose on the air, but they disappeared again as suddenly as they had glanced upon his sight. A low,
80　rustling sound next drew his attention behind him, and turning his head, he beheld Uncas within a few feet, creeping to his side. Hawkeye spoke to him in Delaware, when the young chief took his position with singular caution and undisturbed coolness. To
85　Heyward this was a moment of feverish and impatient suspense; though the scout saw fit to select it as a fit occasion to read a lecture to his more youthful associates on the art of using firearms with discretion.

31

As it is used in line 1, "repaired" most nearly means

A) restored.
B) retired.
C) replaced.
D) recovered.

32

As it is used in line 18, "succeeded" most nearly means

A) replaced.
B) followed.
C) accomplished.
D) prevailed.

33

Which of the following best identifies the point of view in which the passage is written?

A) Third person omniscient
B) Third person limited
C) Second person
D) First person

34

According to the passage, the Indians might be able to approach the hidden group of men due to

A) a waterfall that is significantly less steep than the average waterfall.
B) the men's loud conversation and poor hiding place.
C) the unusually strong current of the stream, which carried them straight to the men's hiding place.
D) the Indian's incredible knowledge of the surrounding area.

35

What made the Indians' approach "hazardous" (line 50)?

A) The shallow waters
B) The driftwood that blocked their way
C) The chance of being shot by the hidden men
D) The risk of being carried over the edge of a waterfall

36

Duncan can best be described as

A) Unfortunately ignorant
B) Inexperienced but kind
C) Cruelly pragmatic
D) Bloodthirsty

37

Which of the following provides the best support for the answer to the previous question?

A) Lines 19-21 ("Duncan...supposed")
B) Lines 25-27 ("You...answered")
C) Lines 63-66 ("The first...scout")
D) Lines 67-69 ("Would...sternly")

38

Which of the following best summarizes the difference between Heyward and Hawkeye?

A) Heyward is afraid of Indians while Hawkeye prefers their company.
B) Heyward is very observant while Hawkeye is overly cautious.
C) Heyward is rash, but Hawkeye has a patience born of experience.
D) Heyward is patient, but Hawkeye is rash and thoughtless.

39

Which of the following provides the best evidence for the answer to the previous question?

A) Lines 36-38 ("Heyward...skill")
B) Lines 71-73 ("Freshen...rush")
C) Lines 82-83 ("Hawkeye...Delaware")
D) Lines 84-88 ("To Heyward...discretion")

40

Who is the leader of the group of hidden men?

A) Uncas
B) Hawkeye
C) Heyward
D) Duncan

The following passage is adapted from an article titled "Why There Aren't Yet Nanobot Doctors," written by Rose Eveleth and published in *The Atlantic*.

Nanobots have been promised by the cutting edge of medicine for many years. These nanobots are described as tiny machines that could navigate your body dispensing drugs, checking on arteries, and
5 keeping people healthy in general. However, these machines have not come to fruition to the degree that people thought they might. Creating a teeny tiny machine to not only navigate the complex infrastructure that is the human body, but also to do
10 the bidding of man is a colossal task.

Nanorobots in the medical field are nothing like the robots you're most likely thinking of. "A robot means a machine that can handle things automatically," says Aniket Margarkar, a researcher at the Centre for Drug
15 Research at the University of Helsinki in Finland. Nanorobot scientists are constructing small packages that can execute tasks in an automated way. "Sensing, responding, detecting friend or foe, delivering a payload, delivering cargo, these are tasks that we build
20 robots to do on the macro scale," adds Shawn Douglas, a researcher at the University of California in San Francisco.

Douglas confesses that calling this technology nanorobots is a bit of a PR move. He talks about his
25 own work on a nanorobot paper. "We're submitting this to Science and it's going to get a lot more attention if we call this something that will resonate with people," but that doesn't really bother him. "I don't begrudge anybody for overhyping their work,"
30 he says.

Although they may not be robots in the same sense that you or I might envision, the tiny molecules that can automate their tasks are very useful. Both Douglas and Margarkar are in the process of creating
35 nanorobots that can not only tell where they are, but also administer a drug in the right place. A bot carrying drugs that target liver-cancer cells would also be equipped with a sensor to identify those cells.

This type of targeted drug delivery has many
40 advantages: the body is not being saturated in poison in hopes that it will reach the smaller target, for example. However, it's not simple to design. The entire field of nanorobotics has come across all sorts of challenges since its invention, ones that keep us
45 from the promise of those predictors and science-

fiction writers.

One issue that arises when synthesizing nanorobots is the amount of work it takes to actually create enough material to test your ideas on. "It's a matter of
50 all the practical annoying steps of actually doing it," Douglas says. "The big thing that half of my lab is stuck on is making enough material that we can test. We could do a very small amount of material, we synthesize the DNA and we run a few experiments
55 and show in a petri dish and say 'Hey this looks promising. We made millions of little things and some of them do what we expect.'" However, the next step in the process means taking the few that work and testing them once more on a million other things. "We
60 need 100,000 times that much material, which would bankrupt the entire lab. So we have to invent a new way to make it, so that takes a couple of years. And then before you know it five years have gone by."

Once you have a hopeful candidate and enough
65 material, Margarkar says that oftentimes there is not a good way to test your idea. Pharmaceutical studies look for the end result to the illness. For example, if a drug for liver cancer reduces the amount of cancer in the liver, it is successful. However, nanoparticle
70 delivery requires researchers to know if the actual movement from the injection site to the target area is successful. Failure could be chalked up to detection failure, delivery failure, or even failure for the drug to operate the way it was intended. Initially, it was
75 difficult to figure it out but now, researchers are able to use computer models and scans to track the nanorobots throughout their entire journey.

After pinpointing both a system and a drug that works, researchers must then deal with the FDA. The
80 approval of the nanoparticle is not the main issue, but getting both the drug and robot approved can be tricky. Margarkar says that even if the researchers prove the individual safety of both the nanoparticle and the drug, the FDA may still require that they be
85 run as a combination through the entire approval process again. "So you're testing it again in the lab, then on animals, then on people. From the moment you enter that process it can take eight to ten years to finish," he says.

90 Ultimately, it is not a simple task to build and implement nanorobots. The first drug encapsulated in a nanoparticle was approved by the FDA in 1995. Since then, there have only be about thirty nanoparticle drugs approved and put on the market,
95 when there have been over 700 new drugs approved by the FDA in the same period of time

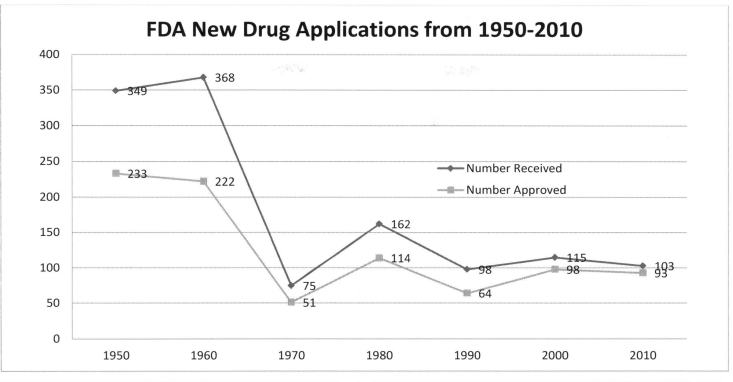

FDA New Drug Applications from 1950-2010

Number Received
Number Approved

1950: 349, 233
1960: 368, 222
1970: 75, 51
1980: 162, 114
1990: 98, 64
2000: 115, 98
2010: 103, 93

41

As it is used in line 6, "degree" most nearly means

A) severity.
B) extent.
C) grade.
D) credentials.

42

As it is used in line 17, "execute" most nearly means

A) assassinate.
B) complete.
C) prosecute.
D) achieve.

43

It can be inferred from the passage that nanobots are unlike the robots we imagine in that nanobots

A) are only molecules rather than the machines we typically associate with the term robot.
B) cannot handle tasks like delivering a payload or detecting an enemy automatically.
C) are merely a public relations stunt.
D) are very difficult to build.

44

Which of the following best supports the answer to the previous question?

A) Lines 17-22 ("Sensing...San Francisco")
B) Lines 23-24 ("Douglas...move")
C) Lines 31-33 ("Although...useful")
D) Lines 47-49 ("One...on")

According to the passage, why is it difficult to get medical nanobots approved by the FDA?

A) Because the FDA is likely to approve the drug but not the nanoparticle
B) Because the FDA has never before approved a nanoparticle drug
C) Because the FDA is notorious for approving only a small fraction of the drugs submitted each year
D) Because the FDA requires approval of the drug and the nanoparticle both separately and in combination

Which of the following best supports the answer to the previous question?

A) Lines 79-82 ("The approval...tricky")
B) Lines 82-86 ("Margarkar...again")
C) Lines 91-94 ("The first...market")
D) Lines 95-96 ("when...time")

Which of the following best describes the primary purpose of the fifth paragraph (lines 39-46) within the context of the passage as a whole?

A) It proves that the development of nanobot technology should be a priority for the medical community.
B) It illustrates the primary benefits of nanobot technology in the field of medicine.
C) It transitions from a discussion about the potential benefits of nanobots to the reasons why nanobots are not yet in common use.
D) It transitions from a comparison of nanobots and robots to an explanation of why nanobots are harder to build than robots are.

Which of the following is NOT a challenge to the implementation of nanobot technology discussed in the passage?

A) Locating test subjects
B) Obtaining FDA approval
C) Finding a means of testing nanobots
D) Creating enough nanobots to test

The evidence in the passage is primarily

A) expert testimony.
B) statistics.
C) personal experience.
D) hypothetical situations.

Based on information in the passage and the graph, it can best be inferred that

A) there are fewer scientific discoveries now than there were in the 1950s.
B) the FDA has made it much more difficult to apply for drug approval in recent decades.
C) it may become more difficult to obtain FDA approval in the future since the number of applications has declined in recent decades.
D) it may become easier to obtain FDA approval in the future since the percentage of approved applications is higher than it was in prior decades.

Questions 51-60 are based on the following passage.

The following passages, originally published by the *New York Times*, discuss the issue of women in the field of science.

Passage 1

Earlier in the day, dealing with an armful of files, a not-so-small computer, and a ten pound mega-purse, one of us got a heavy steel door to the face when an out-to-lunch undergraduate slammed it shut on us.
5   This leads to the question: Are Cornell students empty-minded fledgling sociopaths? No, and most male scientists are not inclined to belittle the talent of female scientists in their labs.

Tim Hunt, 2001 Nobel Prize recipient in
10 Physiology or Medicine, recently made some egregious remarks regarding female scientists in the work place. But his words represent an eroding minority – as is demonstrated by the national data on women in science, which shows continued progress.
15 Economists Donna Ginther and Shulamit Kahn demonstrated in large-scale analyses that the academic landscape has changed rapidly, with men and women being treated comparably in most domains. Although some differences still exist,
20 usually to the benefit of men if they do occur, these differences are exceptions, not the rule.

Female assistant and associate professors largely earn as much as their male counterparts, are tenured and promoted at similar rates, continue at their jobs
25 equally, and demonstrate comparable job satisfaction rates. Most importantly, women are hired at higher rates than men.

Women were less than one percent of professors in academic engineering in 1971. Today, women
30 populate roughly 25 percent of the demographic of assistant professors, with proportionate growth in all traditionally male dominated domains – physics, chemistry, geosciences, mathematics/computer science, and economics. In 1973, 15 percent or less of
35 assistant professors in these fields were women, whereas today, they comprise 20 percent to 40 percent of these fields.

While women prefer not to major in these fields while in college (choosing life sciences, premed,
40 animal science, social science, or law instead) and women do not apply to professional posts as often as men, female Ph.D.'s who apply for tenure-track jobs are offered these positions at a higher rate than their

male counterparts. Because the majority of both men
45 and women are not accepted to these positions when they apply, this statistic is not as obvious. But when the positions are filled, women are usually hired over men.

Recently, we reported the results of five national
50 experiments. The results showed that of 872 faculty members, male and female, employed at 371 different universities and colleges largely preferred, 2 to 1, to hire a female applicant rather than an identically qualified male applicant. When asked to evaluate just
55 one applicant, most faculty members rated the woman as stronger than the man. This pro-female hiring pattern of preference was found in all four fields that were studied.

Passage 2

Affirmative action, its original intents aside, can
60 now be described as two very different types of efforts. The first involves lowering the bar to meet diversity standards. The second does not lower the standards, but involves taking meaningful steps to reduce discrimination, including unconscious bias.
65 This type – I'll call it "affirmative effort" – is necessary to provide a level playing field for women who desire careers in the science, technology, engineering, and mathematics (STEM) fields. There is no other way that I can think of to challenge the
70 unconscious bias recently demonstrated in a Yale study.

Unconscious bias leads to the undervaluation of women and their work. This was discovered by psychologists over two decades ago, supported by
75 various studies documenting its negative impact on female advancement in STEM fields. Approximately 15 years ago, universities started to address the problem, particularly at the faculty level, but implementing more scrupulous data-driven
80 approaches to evaluate merit in hiring, promotion, and compensation.

Affirmative action, or "affirmative effort," has been vastly successful in increasing the number of women faculty members in STEM fields. While this
85 has helped diversify and ensure equity, it has not been as successful in removing the core problem, unconscious bias in the minds of both male and female faculty members, who still marginalize and undervalue women and their work in STEM fields.
90 People often ask, "But if a woman is really good enough, can't she make it on her own? And can't a conscious effort to help or support women even

exacerbate the problem?" Extensive inspection of the data on how women have advanced in STEM fields
95 answers both those questions with a resounding "no." It's like asking, "But couldn't a really great runner win an Olympic race even if he had a 10 pound (invisible) weight strapped to his back?" While women can make it by overcoming bias, the cost is
100 usually high and doesn't allow women to reach their full potential.

Affirmative action is now a derogatory term used to look down on women who advanced purely on merit. But we cannot let the delusion that bias no
105 longer exists stop us from using "affirmative effort" to overcome the unconscious bias that still holds many women back.

51

As it is used in line 7, "inclined" most nearly means

A) compelled.
B) skewed.
C) persuaded.
D) predisposed.

52

Which of the following best summarizes the central claim of Passage 1?

A) For the most part, discrimination against women in the sciences is no longer a common problem.
B) In the field of science, it is easier for a woman to find a job than for a man to find a job.
C) Gender discrimination still exists in the scientific fields.
D) There is still a long way to go before female scientists enjoy the same privileges as their male counterparts.

53

How would the author of Passage 1 most likely respond to the assertion that only a very small percentage of female applicants for tenure-track jobs are hired?

A) The claim is inaccurate since female applicants are generally preferred over male applicants.
B) Few applicants are hired for tenure-track positions, regardless of gender.
C) The small percentage of females in tenure-track positions is due to the fact that few females choose to study science in college.
D) This statistic is an exception to the rule.

54

Which of the following best supports the answer to the previous question?

A) Lines 19-21 ("Although...rule")
B) Lines 38-40 ("While...instead")
C) Lines 44-46 ("Because...obvious")
D) Lines 46-48 ("But...men")

55

As it is used in line 41, "posts" most nearly means

A) places.
B) panels.
C) jobs.
D) services.

56

Which of the following best summarizes the central claim of Passage 2?

A) Although discrimination against women in science may no longer be overt, action is still necessary to combat the more subtle discrimination that creates barriers for women.
B) Affirmative action has successfully increased the number of women in science, technology, engineering, and mathematics.
C) Universities have taken laudable steps to address discrimination against women in science.
D) Affirmative action merely harms women in science by creating the impression that they do not deserve their positions.

Which of the following provides the best support for the answer to the previous question?

A) Lines 76-81 ("Approximately..compensation")
B) Lines 82-84 ("Affirmative...fields")
C) Lines 90-93 ("People...problem")
D) Lines 104-107 ("But...back")

The authors of both passages would most likely agree with which of the following statements?

A) Universities show a marked preference for hiring women over men.
B) Women in STEM fields no longer face significant discrimination.
C) In recent decades, the number of women employed in STEM fields has increased dramatically.
D) Overt actions to combat discrimination against women in STEM fields will likely make the problem worse.

How would the author of Passage 1 most likely respond to the assertion made by the author of Passage 2 in lines 84-89 ("While...fields")?

A) Females in STEM show similar rates of job satisfaction as their male counterparts, suggesting a lack of concern over discrimination.
B) Women are hired for STEM positions at rates that are equal to or higher than men.
C) Women who feel unable to overcome such biases simply choose not to pursue STEM fields in college.
D) The unconscious bias against women is rare.

Which of the following statements best compares the use of evidence in the two passages?

A) Passage 1 relies primarily on recent studies while Passage 2 references personal anecdotes.
B) Passage 1 relies primarily on personal anecdotes while Passage 2 references a recent study.
C) Passage 1 references general trends while Passage 2 uses specific statistics.
D) Passage 1 uses specific statistics while Passage 2 references general trends.

This passage is adapted from an article titled "The Roanoke Island Colony: Lost, and Found?" published August 2015 in the *New York Times*.

Sweating in the blazing sun, Nicholas Luccketti swats at mosquitoes as he observes his archaeology team working in a shallow depression on a hillside above the glistening waters of Albemarle Sound. On
5 a shaded tabletop, a mound of plastic bags full of artifacts was rising.

On a dusty road zigzagging through soybean fields, the clearing is located amid two cypress swamps crawling with venomous snakes. This location,
10 known as Site X, may solve the enigma at the core of America's founding: the fate of the "lost colonists" who disappeared from a settlement on Roanoke Island in the late 16th century.

Over the course of three years, Mr. Luccketti and
15 his colleagues with the First Colony Foundation have been exhuming portions of the hillside, trying to locate evidence of the colonists. Soon, the foundation will publish its discoveries, including the theory that at least some of the missing colonists relocated to Site
20 X.

The publication is guaranteed to excite scholars. Numerous scholars who have examined the evidence agree with the findings, but at least one views the evidence as too trivial to make solid conclusions. All
25 are in concurrence that more excavating is necessary. The new findings are expected to incite a new series of questions: Why would some of the settlers have separated from the other colonists and headed to the inland site? Where did they go next? What happened
30 of the remaining Roanoke colonists?

The mystery of the Lost Colony of Roanoke is likely the most spooky American history stories studied by grade schoolers. In 1587, a valiant Englishman named John White brought over 100
35 settlers to Roanoke Island, which is located inside the barrier islands that are now known as the Outer Banks. This was Sir Walter Raleigh's second endeavor to colonize North Carolina, but the first involving civilians and families. White eventually
40 headed back to England on a resupply trip, but his return was delayed by a naval war with Spain.

When he did return three years later, the settlers were gone. All he could find were cryptic clues: the word "Croatoan" carved into a fence post, and the
45 letters "CRO" on a tree. Part tragedy, part mystery, part historic novelty, the destiny of the colony has produced a mix of serious scholarship, wild supposition, and at minimum one utter hoax. A commonly held theory — still unverified — is that
50 colonists slowly assimilated with the local tribes.

In 2012, when the British Museum reexamined one of White's coastal maps for the First Colony Foundation, the most enticing clue in centuries regarding the fate of the Lost Colonists surfaced. X-
55 ray spectroscopy and other imaging techniques discovered that a patch concealed a four-pointed blue and red star on the western end of Albemarle Sound. That site, near the outlets of the Chowan River and Salmon Creek, crudely paralleled White's implicit
60 allusion to a site 50 miles inland, which he cited in testimony he gave following his attempt to go back to the colony.

James Horn, a foundation board member, had written a book theorizing that this spot, with its
65 sheltered harbor and a neighboring Native American village, might have been a potential point of relocation. The problem is that this notion lacked tangible evidence; while the map seemed to support it, only digging could confirm it.

70 It was nothing short of a miracle that the property was untouched. Located in the economically depressed and mostly rural Bertie County, the plot had been slated as the site for more than 2,000 luxury condominiums, restaurants and, a marina, but those
75 plans dissolved after the financial crisis of 2008.

North Carolina law necessitates archaeological surveys prior to the start of large coastal developments. By happenstance, the developers had appointed Mr. Luccketti's team to examine the site in
80 2007. The excavation had uncovered various Native American artifacts, commonly found in the area — but also several European artifacts. At that point, Mr. Luccketti postulated that they had been abandoned by later European settlers from the mid-1600s.

85 But the latest outcomes from the British Museum's examination of the map caused the foundation to reevaluate the 2007 findings from Merry Hill and other dig sites in the area. The reassessment of the Site X relics led to a decision to conduct additional
90 surveys. With the landowner's agreement, archaeologists commenced sifting the soil for a second time in 2012.

Gradually, the site revealed its secrets. Surrey-Hampshire Border ware, which was a variety of
95 ceramic not imported to the New World after the

Virginia Company disbanded in the early 17th
century, has become a way of identifying the earliest
colonial life. Even with limited areas excavated, the
hillside has generated a remarkably high
100 concentration of Border ware and other colonial
artifacts, including a food-storage container called a
baluster, a hook meant for stretching hides, a buckle,
and fragments of early gun flintlocks known as
priming pans. Although there are no signs of a fort or
105 other structures, the aggregate of the artifacts were
enough to persuade the archaeologists that at least a
few of the colonists wound up in this location.

61

It is reasonable to conclude that the main goal of the
archaeologists described in the passage is to

A) disprove a popular theory regarding the missing
colonists of Roanoke.
B) assist developers in a rural town in relocating a
historical site.
C) test the reliability of new imaging techniques in
finding lost relics.
D) examine a site believed to have belonged to the
missing colonists of Roanoke.

62

Which of the following provides the best evidence for
the answer to the previous question?

A) Lines 48-50 ("A commonly...tribes.")
B) Lines 54-57 ("X-ray...Sound.")
C) Lines 67-69 ("The problem...it.")
D) Lines 76-78 ("North...developments.")

63

As used in line 3, "depression" most nearly means

A) cavity
B) crisis
C) dullness
D) failure

64

Which of the following best describes the purpose of
paragraphs 5 and 6 in the context of the passage as a
whole?

A) A detailed physical description of Site X
B) An explanation of how the Roanoke Colony become
lost
C) An account of the initial circumstances that
prompted the survey of Site X
D) A summary of the evidence found at Site X

65

The author suggests which of the following about the
Lost Colony of Roanoke?

A) It is one of many mysteries of the late 16th century
caused by failed endeavors to colonize the Americas.
B) The fate of the Lost Colonists could not be
determined until more advanced instruments became
available.
C) Pinpointing what happened to the Lost Colonists is a
rare, highly debated mystery in American history.
D) The Lost Colonists were never truly lost because it
was known that they relocated to be closer to a local
Native American tribe.

66

Which of the following provides the best evidence for
the answer to the previous question?

A) Lines 37-39 ("This was...families.")
B) Lines 45-48 ("Part...hoax.")
C) Lines 54-57 ("X-ray...Sound.")
D) Lines 64-67 ("this spot...relocation.")

67

As it is used in line 73, "slated" most nearly means

A) billed.
B) enlisted.
C) elected.
D) reserved.

68

The passage suggest that the published theory about Site X is likely to be

A) definitively accepted by the academic community.
B) accepted by many members in the academic community, with a few scholars in disagreement.
C) acknowledged by the academic community, but mostly viewed as irrelevant.
D) viewed as a joke by the whole academic community.

69

Which of the following caused Mr. Luccketti and his team to reexamine Site X in 2012?

A) The British Museum reexamined one of John White's coastal maps for the First Colony Foundation.
B) James Horn, a foundation board member, published a book positing that this site was the spot to which the Lost Colonists relocated.
C) Site X was abandoned after potential development plans fell through during a financial crisis.
D) North Carolina law necessitates that archaeological surveys be conducted before large developments can be built on the coast.

70

Which of the following ultimately persuaded the archaeologists that some of the Lost Colonists ended up at Site X?

A) The discovery of a fort and other building structures
B) Finding Native American and English artifacts together
C) The proximity of Site X to the original location of the Roanoke Colony
D) Dating of the type of materials used to produce various artifacts found at the site

The following passage from Dwight Eisenhower's Farewell Speech given on January 17, 1961.

We now stand ten years past the midpoint of a century that has witnessed four major wars among great nations. Three of these involved our own country. Despite these holocausts, America is today
5 the strongest, the most influential, and most productive nation in the world. Understandably proud of this pre-eminence, we yet realize that America's leadership and prestige depend, not merely upon our unmatched material progress, riches, and military
10 strength, but on how we use our power in the interests of world peace and human betterment.
Throughout America's adventure in free government, our basic purposes have been to keep the peace, to foster progress in human achievement, and
15 to enhance liberty, dignity, and integrity among peoples and among nations. To strive for less would be unworthy of a free and religious people. Any failure traceable to arrogance, or our lack of comprehension, or readiness to sacrifice would inflict
20 upon us grievous hurt, both at home and abroad.
Progress toward these noble goals is persistently threatened by the conflict now engulfing the world. It commands our whole attention, absorbs our very beings. We face a hostile ideology global in scope,
25 atheistic in character, ruthless in purpose, and insidious [insidious] in method. Unhappily, the danger it poses promises to be of indefinite duration. To meet it successfully, there is called for, not so much the emotional and transitory sacrifices of crisis,
30 but rather those which enable us to carry forward steadily, surely, and without complaint the burdens of a prolonged and complex struggle with liberty the stake. Only thus shall we remain, despite every provocation, on our charted course toward permanent
35 peace and human betterment.
Crises there will continue to be. In meeting them, whether foreign or domestic, great or small, there is a recurring temptation to feel that some spectacular and costly action could become the miraculous solution to
40 all current difficulties. A huge increase in newer elements of our defenses; development of unrealistic programs to cure every ill in agriculture; a dramatic expansion in basic and applied research — these and many other possibilities, each possibly promising in
45 itself, may be suggested as the only way to the road we wish to travel.

But each proposal must be weighed in the light of a broader consideration: the need to maintain balance in and among national programs, balance between the
50 private and the public economy, balance between the cost and hoped for advantages, balance between the clearly necessary and the comfortably desirable, balance between our essential requirements as a nation and the duties imposed by the nation upon the
55 individual, balance between actions of the moment and the national welfare of the future. Good judgment seeks balance and progress. Lack of it eventually finds imbalance and frustration. The record of many decades stands as proof that our people and their
60 Government have, in the main, understood these truths and have responded to them well, in the face of threat and stress.
But threats, new in kind or degree, constantly arise. Of these, I mention two only.
65 A vital element in keeping the peace is our military establishment. Our arms must be mighty, ready for instant action, so that no potential aggressor may be tempted to risk his own destruction. Our military organization today bears little relation to that known
70 of any of my predecessors in peacetime, or, indeed, by the fighting men of World War II or Korea.
Until the latest of our world conflicts, the United States had no armaments industry. American makers of plowshares could, with time and as required, make
75 swords as well. But we can no longer risk emergency improvisation of national defense. We have been compelled to create a permanent armaments industry of vast proportions. Added to this, three and a half million men and women are directly engaged in the
80 defense establishment. We annually spend on military security alone more than the net income of all United States corporations.
Now this conjunction of an immense military establishment and a large arms industry is new in the
85 American experience. The total influence — economic, political, even spiritual — is felt in every city, every Statehouse, every office of the Federal government. We recognize the imperative need for this development. Yet, we must not fail to
90 comprehend its grave implications. Our toil, resources, and livelihood are all involved. So is the very structure of our society.

71

The author indicates that which of the following could harm "America's adventure in free government" (lines 12-13)?

A) wealth, strength, and influence
B) freedom, self-respect, and honesty
C) spirituality, morality, and philosophy
D) overconfidence, ignorance, and greed

72

Which of the following provides the best evidence for the answer to the previous question?

A) Lines 7-11 ("America's...betterment.")
B) Lines 13-16 ("our basic...nations.")
C) Lines 17-20 ("Any...abroad.")
D) Lines 24-26 ("We face...method.")

73

The author suggests that in order to maintain "our charted course toward permanent peace and human betterment" (lines 34-35), America needs

A) to prepare to battle short, insignificant threats.
B) to be ready for an extended endeavor to defend liberty.
C) to assert our dominance by reacting to every threat with violence.
D) to avoid conflict by ignoring all threats, at home and abroad.

74

As used in line 23, "absorbs" most nearly means

A) ingests.
B) captivates.
C) understands.
D) grasps.

75

It can be inferred from the passage that America's military during this period of time was

A) being threatened by the economic, political, and spiritual influences within the country.
B) unprecedented due not only to its size, but the support it received from a newly formed arms industry.
C) budgeted with less money annually than the net income of all United States corporations combined.
D) constantly being challenged by new dangers that varied significantly in type and intensity.

76

Which of the following provides the best evidence for the answer to the previous question?

A) Lines 63 ("But...arise.")
B) Lines 80-82 ("We...corporations.")
C) Lines 83-85 ("Now...experience.")
D) Lines 85-88 ("The total...government.")

77

Which of the following best identifies the purpose of the fifth paragraph in the context of the passage as a whole?

A) It offers all concerns that must be addressed before executing any new government plans or programs during crises.
B) It lists all of the duties that the American people regularly put in the hands of the politicians they elect.
C) It provides a detailed description of the ideal methods for creating new government programs.
D) It implores the American people and the government to remain balanced by keeping the peace.

78

As it is used in line 60, "main" most nearly means

A) utmost.
B) channel.
C) primary.
D) major.

79

Which of the following government decisions would the author most likely deem acceptable?

A) Spending billions of taxpayer dollars funding research into genetically modified food in an effort to solve a temporary food shortage.
B) Ramping up production on hundreds of new fighter jets in response to rumors of a rival country's new military fleet.
C) Melting down or repurposing all military vehicles and equipment when the country is not at war.
D) Maintaining consistent production of military weaponry whether during wartime or peacetime.

80

Which of the following best identifies the main idea of the passage?

A) America has been concentrated on fighting wars for too long and now needs to try to focus on nurturing strong spirituality and rebuilding other weaker nations.
B) To promote our national goals, America needs to focus on not only being deliberate and consistent in decision making, but also continually maintaining a military force.
C) Faced with never ending threats, the world is no longer safe, so America must fight to isolate itself from the rest of the world to maintain peace and liberty.
D) America's reputation depends solely upon our unrivaled physical growth and wealth, which must be maintained by having the most advanced military in the world.

The following passage is excerpted from Jules Verne's
20,000 Leagues Under the Sea.

The Canadian paused in his work. But one word
twenty times repeated, one dreadful word, told me the
reason for the agitation spreading aboard the Nautilus.
We weren't the cause of the crew's concern.

5 "Maelstrom! Maelstrom!" they were shouting.

The Maelstrom! Could a more frightening name
have rung in our ears under more frightening
circumstances? Were we lying in the dangerous
waterways off the Norwegian coast? Was the Nautilus

10 being dragged into this whirlpool just as the skiff was
about to detach from its plating?

As you know, at the turn of the tide, the waters
confined between the Varrö and Lofoten Islands rush
out with irresistible violence. They form a vortex from

15 which no ship has ever been able to escape. Monstrous
waves race together from every point of the horizon.
They form a whirlpool aptly called "the ocean's
navel," whose attracting power extends a distance of
fifteen kilometers. It can suck down not only ships but

20 whales, and even polar bears from the northernmost
regions.

This was where the Nautilus had been sent
accidentally—or perhaps deliberately—by its captain.
It was sweeping around in a spiral whose radius kept

25 growing smaller and smaller. The skiff, still attached
to the ship's plating, was likewise carried around at
dizzying speed. I could feel us whirling. I was
experiencing that accompanying nausea that follows
such continuous spinning motions. We were in dread,

30 in the last stages of sheer horror, our blood frozen in
our veins, our nerves numb, drenched in cold sweat as
if from the throes of dying! And what a noise around
our frail skiff! What roars echoing from several miles
away! What crashes from the waters breaking against

35 sharp rocks on the sea floor, where the hardest objects
are smashed, where tree trunks are worn down and
worked into "a shaggy fur," as Norwegians express it!

What a predicament! We were rocking frightfully.
The Nautilus defended itself like a human being. Its

40 steel muscles were cracking. Sometimes it stood on
end, the three of us along with it!

"We've got to hold on tight," Ned said, "and screw
the nuts down again! If we can stay attached to the
Nautilus, we can still make it . . . !"

45 He hadn't finished speaking when a cracking sound
occurred. The nuts gave way, and ripped out of its

socket, the skiff was hurled like a stone from a sling
into the midst of the vortex.

My head struck against an iron timber, and with this

50 violent shock I lost consciousness.

We come to the conclusion of this voyage under the
seas. What happened that night, how the skiff escaped
from the Maelstrom's fearsome eddies, how Ned Land,
Conseil, and I got out of that whirlpool, I'm unable to

55 say. But when I regained consciousness, I was lying in
a fisherman's hut on one of the Lofoten Islands. My
two companions, safe and sound, were at my bedside
clasping my hands. We embraced each other heartily.

Just now we can't even dream of returning to

60 France. Travel between upper Norway and the south is
limited. So I have to wait for the arrival of a steamboat
that provides bimonthly service from North Cape.

So it is here, among these gallant people who have
taken us in, that I'm reviewing my narrative of these

65 adventures. It is accurate. Not a fact has been omitted,
not a detail has been exaggerated. It's the faithful
record of this inconceivable expedition into an
element now beyond human reach, but where progress
will someday make great inroads.

70 Will anyone believe me? I don't know. Ultimately
it's unimportant. What I can now assert is that I've
earned the right to speak of these seas, beneath which
in less than ten months, I've cleared 20,000 leagues in
this underwater tour of the world that has shown me

75 so many wonders across the Pacific, the Indian Ocean,
the Red Sea, the Mediterranean, the Atlantic, the
southernmost and northernmost seas!

But what happened to the Nautilus? Did it
withstand the Maelstrom's clutches? Is Captain Nemo

80 alive? Is he still under the ocean pursuing his frightful
program of revenge, or did he stop after that latest
mass execution? Will the waves someday deliver that
manuscript that contains his full life story? Will I
finally learn the man's name? Will the nationality of

85 the stricken warship tell us the nationality of Captain
Nemo?

I hope so. I likewise hope that his powerful
submersible has defeated the sea inside its most
dreadful whirlpool, that the Nautilus has survived

90 where so many ships have perished!

81

The passage is told from the point of view of

A) a captain who saw another ship pulled into a vortex.
B) a Canadian crewman who worked on the Nautilus.
C) the Maelstrom who was trying to sink the Nautilus.
D) a sailor who barely survived a maritime accident.

82

Which of the following best describes the main purpose of the third paragraph (lines 12- 21)?

A) It conveys various sailors' tales that have been told about this region of the ocean.
B) It describes a similar area with which the reader might be more familiar for the purpose of comparison.
C) It reiterates background information on the Maelstrom that the reader is already supposed to know.
D) It answers the questions that were poised by the crew in the prior paragraph.

83

The narrator indicates that he is unsure

A) exactly how he was knocked unconscious.
B) of the exact location and size of the Maelstrom.
C) whether the ship was purposely directed into the vortex.
D) of the accuracy of the account of his journey on the Nautilus.

84

Which of the following provides the best evidence for the answer to the previous question?

A) Lines 8-9 ("Were...coast?")
B) Lines 22-23 ("This was...captain.")
C) Lines 52-55 ("What...say.")
D) Line 70 ("Will...know.")

85

As used in line 30, "sheer" most nearly means

A) erect.
B) outright.
C) translucent.
D) slight.

86

Which of the following would best describe the relationship between the narrator, Conseil, and Ned Land?

A) brothers
B) strangers
C) accomplices
D) crewmates

87

As it is used in line 68, "element" most nearly means

A) material.
B) component.
C) environment.
D) chapter.

88

The narrator indicates that Captain Nemo's life story is

A) mysterious.
B) exaggerated.
C) heartbreaking.
D) dangerous.

89

It can be inferred from the passage that the narrator believes that the Nautilus was

A) resilient enough to escape when no other ship could.
B) drawn into the whirlpool after losing consciousness.
C) successful in getting revenge against the captain.
D) incapable of surviving the deadly Maelstrom.

Which of the following provides the best evidence for the answer to the previous question?

A) Lines 39-40 ("The Nautilus...cracking.")
B) Lines 52-55 ("What...say.")
C) Lines 80-82 ("Is he...execution?")
D) Lines 87-90 ("I likewise...perished")

The following passage is adapted from an article titled "What's the Difference Between Poisonous and Venomous Animals?," written by Helen Thompson and published in *Smithsonian Magazine*.

Corythomantisgreeningifrogs look pretty harmless amid an arid forest of cacti. These tree frogs' drab brown and green hues contrast sharply to the bright cautionary colors of poison dart frogs. So when Carlos
5 Jared of Brazil's Butantan Institute headed out into the forest to gather and study these frogs, he assumed they did not pose a threat – until he felt pain in his palm.

"It took me a long time to realize that the pain had a relationship with the intense and careless collection of
10 these animals hitting the palm of my hands," recalls Jared. He was a victim to a completely unique defense mechanism: The helmet-headed frogs have spikes along their lips which inject strong chemicals, causing predators to receive a mix between a head butt and a
15 toxic kiss. Jared and his team found, after careful study, that C. greening and a similarly related species of hylid frog, Aparasphenodonbrunoi, are the only venomous frogs discovered.

"This is very, very cool. Unprecedented would
20 actually be an understatement," says Bryan Fry, a molecular biologist at the University of Queensland who was not affiliated with the study. We already knew frogs could be poisonous, so why is this considered a big deal? The often-misunderstood
25 distinction between venom and poison is the key.

Both venom and poison affect the body similarly by attacking the heart, brain, or other vital organs. But their similar effects are caused by two very different modes of reception. A venomous creature bites, stings,
30 or stabs the target to inflict damage, while poisonous creatures must be bitten or touched to feel the effects. This is why venomous creatures need fangs or teeth or similar organs that puncture. All octopuses are venomous, along with several squid, loads of snakes,
35 spiders, and scorpions, a handful of lizards, vampire bats, and even the slow loris. Lionfish, as well as other similar fish, have spines on their bodies to sting attackers with venom. Iberian ribbed newts are another type of amphibian that is venomous. Iberian
40 ribbed newts will force their own ribs out of their bodies to use the spikes at the ends to stab predators with toxins.

Organisms that are poisonous are more passive in the way they disperse their toxins. They will often line
45 their skin or other surfaces with toxic chemicals. These animals get their poison two different ways: it can be created within the organism or acquired by what they eat. Cane toads naturally make poison in glands behind their ears and secrete the poison causing
50 harm and even death to predators that consume it. On the other hand, poison dart frogs create an extremely poisonous alkaloid skin coating they make from eating poisonous ants. Mother frogs pass the chemical on to their tadpoles using egg sacs that contain the alkaloid;
55 by taking young poison dart frogs out of its natural habitat and motherly care, the young frog will actually lose its toxicity.

Having to eat unpleasant foods to survive could potentially have driven some organisms to evolve
60 poisons used to defend against predators. "If this provided some protection against predation, you can see how this could favor the evolution of systems to actually concentrate the toxins in the skin rather than dispose of them," explains Kyle Summers who is an
65 evolutionary biologist at East Carolina University. Although this is true, venoms have also evolved for offensive needs as well. Some organisms, like the male platypus, use venom in mating. Male platypi will use tiny, prickly foot barbs to shoot out toxins and
70 paralyze rival male suitors.

Most venom is derived from simple, harmless hormones. Somewhere in the gene code of an organism, a common gene might get copied and present itself in another area where it should not be –
75 like the salivary glands in a snake. When attacked or attacking, the extra gene may be slightly toxic to the predator or prey, causing that specific gene code to be favored by evolution. Over time, the toxicity of those venoms and enzymes increases and evolves in
80 potency.

Because the toxins get delivered in different ways, venoms tend to be larger compounds that must be injected to break through skin, while poisons are usually smaller chemicals that can be absorbed. So is
85 one type of toxin fundamentally more potent than the other?

"The toxicity of both poisons and venoms varies dramatically across species in nature," says Summers, so it's impossible to say that one type of chemical
90 weapon is fundamentally more dangerous. The main takeaway is that both venom and poison can kill you in truly horrifying and painful ways.

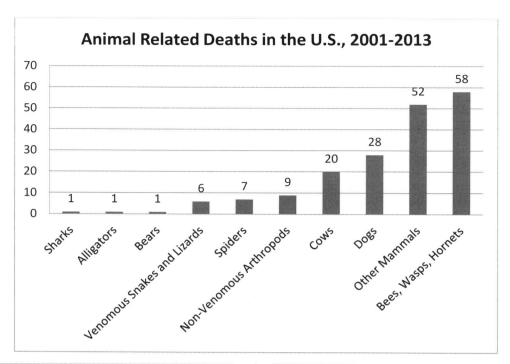

Animal Related Deaths in the U.S., 2001-2013

Sharks: 1
Alligators: 1
Bears: 1
Venomous Snakes and Lizards: 6
Spiders: 7
Non-Venomous Arthropods: 9
Cows: 20
Dogs: 28
Other Mammals: 52
Bees, Wasps, Hornets: 58

91

As it is used in line 29, "reception" most nearly means

A) party.
B) delivery.
C) reaction.
D) greeting.

92

According to the passage, which of the following is the difference between venomous and poisonous animals?

A) Venomous animals are dangerous to touch, while poisonous creatures bite or sting.
B) Venomous animals acquire their toxins from their diets, while poisonous animals create the toxins naturally.
C) Venomous animals are predators, while poisonous animals are prey.
D) Venomous animals bite, sting, or stab to deliver their toxins, while poisonous animals are dangerous if touched or bitten.

93

Which of the following best supports the answer to the previous question?

A) Lines 12-15 ("The helmet… toxic kiss.")
B) Lines 24-25 ("The… key.")
C) Lines 26-27 ("Both… organs.")
D) Lines 29-31 ("A venomous… effects.")

94

Which of the following is most strongly implied by the second paragraph?

A) The majority of dangerous frogs are poisonous.
B) Collecting animals with bare hands is often potentially dangerous.
C) Carlos Jared didn't understand the difference between venom and poison.
D) C. greeningi frogs use their venom to attack prey.

95

Which of the following, according to the passage, is NOT venomous?

A) the slow loris
B) the cane toad
C) octopi
D) the platypus

96

Which of the following best identifies the effect of the word choice found in lines 19-20?

A) It undermines the speaker's authority on the subject matter.
B) It utilizes colloquial language to help the reader relate to the information.
C) It establishes an informal and conversational tone that is maintained throughout the passage.
D) It is off-putting to the reader because it makes light of a very grave issue.

97

It can be inferred from the passage that most venoms and poisons are the result of

A) natural selection.
B) toxins ingested by animals' mothers.
C) secretions from glands located behind the ears.
D) passive response rather than active.

98

Which of the following provides the best support for the answer to the previous question?

A) Lines 43-44 ("Organisms...toxins.")
B) Lines 46-48 ("These… eat.")
C) Lines 53-57 ("Mother… toxicity.")
D) Lines 75-78 ("When… evolution.")

99

As it is used in line 63, "concentrate" most nearly means

A) collect.
B) centralize.
C) aggregate.
D) focus.

100

It can be inferred from the passage and the graph that

A) people in the United States are more likely to be killed by non-poisonous/non-venomous animals.
B) spiders are often more dangerous than bees, wasps, and hornets.
C) humans are more likely to die from venomous animals than from poisonous animals.
D) some mammals are poisonous.

Reading Practice Answer Keys

Explanations can be found online at http://www.tpgenius.com/

Practice Passage 1 – Kepler 452b	Practice Passage 2 – First Thanksgiving	Practice Passage 3 – Theodore Roosevelt	Practice Passage 4 – Last of the Mohicans	Practice Passage 5 - Nanobots
1. D	11. A	21. C	31. B	41. B
2. A	12. A	22. A	32. B	42. B
3. D	13. C	23. B	33. A	43. A
4. C	14. D	24. B	34. A	44. C
5. A	15. B	25. A	35. D	45. D
6. B	16. D	26. D	36. B	46. B
7. B	17. B	27. C	37. C	47. C
8. B	18. C	28. C	38. B	48. A
9. D	19. C	29. A	39. D	49. A
10. C	20. C	30. D	40. B	50. B
Practice Passage 6 – Women in Science	**Practice Passage 7 - Roanoke**	**Practice Passage 8 – Dwight Eisenhower**	**Practice Passage 9 – 20,000 Leagues Under The Sea**	**Practice Passage 10 – Poisonous vs. Venomous Animals**
51. D	61. D	71. D	81. D	91. B
52. A	62. C	72. C	82. C	92. D
53. B	63. A	73. B	83. C	93. D
54. C	64. B	74. B	84. B	94. A
55. C	65. C	75. B	85. B	95. B
56. A	66. B	76. C	86. D	96. B
57. D	67. D	77. A	87. C	97. A
58. C	68. B	78. A	88. A	98. D
59. B	69. A	79. D	89. A	99. A
60. D	70. D	80. B	90. D	100. A

Explanations can be found online at http://www.tpgenius.com/

Section 3
Evidence-based Writing

Organization
Word Choice
Development of Ideas
Sentences
Punctuation
Quantitative Information
Verb Errors
Pronoun Errors
Parallelism and Modifier Errors
Other Errors

Organization

Concept Introduction

The most common questions on the PSAT writing section deal with organization. This includes introductions, conclusions, transitions, and logical sequence. Well organized writing requires two important things: Logic and flow. When writing is logical, one ideas leads clearly to the next without creating confusion. When writing flows, it utilizes a variety of transitional strategies to help ideas flow smoothly.

Spotting Organization Questions

There are several different types of questions that test your understanding of organization.

Introduction and conclusion questions will almost always include the words "introduction," "introduce," "conclusion," or "conclude." This makes them pretty easy to spot. These questions will usually ask you which answer choice provides the best introduction or conclusion to the passage (or, sometimes, to a single paragraph in the passage).

Transition questions can take two forms. Transition questions that test more complex transitional strategies will usually ask which choice best transitions from one paragraph or idea to another. Usually, these questions use entire sentences to transition between paragraphs. Other transition questions will simply feature a transition word or phrase that is underlined in the passage and several alternative transitions as answer choices. These will not have a specific question; instead, when you see answer choices that are all transitional words or phrases, you will know that it is a transition question.

Finally, logical sequence questions will almost always have a question that includes a word like "logical" or "logically." The question will reference a paragraph in which the sentences have been numbered. Sometimes the question will ask where a specific sentence should be logically placed; other times the question will ask you to determine the most logical order for the sentences in the paragraph.

Answering Introduction and Conclusion Questions

First, it's important to know what makes a good introductory or concluding sentence. A good introductory sentence will introduce the main idea of the passage without giving away too many details. A good concluding sentence summarizes the main idea of the passage or restates the author's main claim. Both introductory and concluding sentences need to reflect the overall style and tone of the passage.

To answer introduction and conclusion questions, follow these steps:

1. Examine the answer choices, including the underlined sentence in the passage (if there is one). Eliminate any answer choices that do not seem to reflect the style and tone of the passage as a whole. For example, if the passage is generally formal, eliminate answer choices that use informal or colloquial language.
2. Eliminate any answer choices that reference information that is not related to the main idea or claim of the passage.
3. For an introduction question, read the first paragraph and eliminate any answer choices that are not related or only loosely related to the information in that paragraph.
4. Eliminate answer choices that make claims that are not supported by the passage.
5. Of the remaining answer choices, choose the one that best reflects the information and the style of the passage.

Answering Transition Questions

Let's begin with transition questions that focus on transition words and phrases. The error in these questions is usually in misidentifying the purpose of the transition. Use this chart to help clarify appropriate transitions for different situations:

Purpose	Transitions	
Sequence	First	Afterward
	Second	Before
	Third	Earlier
	Then	Currently
	Next	During
	After	Simultaneously
Position	Above	Behind
	Below	Beyond
	Next to	Nearby
	Adjacent	Here
	In front	There
	In back	
Emphasis	Indeed	Truly
	In face	Even
	Of course	
Example	For example	To illustrate
	For instance	Specifically
Support/Evidence	In addition	Equally Important
	Additionally	Furthermore
	As well as	Moreover
Cause/Effect	As a result	Hence
	Accordingly	Therefore
	Consequently	Thus
Similarity	Similarly	Just as...so too
	Also	Likewise
Difference	However	Nevertheless
	In spite of	In contrast
	Nonetheless	On the contrary
	Still	Yet
Conclusion	Finally	On the whole
	In conclusion	In summary
	In the end	To conclude

Keep in mind that there are many other transitional words and phrases other than those listed in this chart, but this should provide you will a good guide to help determine the intended purpose of a transition.

For questions that require that you choose the best transitional word or phrase for a particular context, follow these steps:

1. Determine which sentences are being connected by the transition.
2. Based on the content of those sentences, decide what the purpose of the transition should be -- which purpose best describes the relationship between the two sentences?
3. Eliminate any answer choices that do not reflect the purpose of the transition or that fail to accurately reflect the relationship between the sentences.
4. Of the remaining choices, choose the one that best reflects the relationship between the ideas in the two sentences.

An added layer of difficulty is introduced when transition questions focus on more complex transitional strategies. These questions will usually use a transitional sentence to link two paragraphs. When answering these questions, follow these steps:

1. Determine the main ideas of each of the two paragraphs being linked by the transition sentence. Eliminate any answer choices that disagree with or are completely unrelated to these main ideas.
2. Based on the main ideas, determine the relationship between the two paragraphs. Eliminate any answer choices that do not reflect the relationship between the two paragraphs.
3. Eliminate any answer choices that reference information found in paragraphs elsewhere in the passage.
4. Eliminate any answer choices that do not suit the style and tone of the passage.
5. Of the remaining choices, choose the one that most logically links the two paragraphs.

Answering Logical Sequence Questions

Most logical sequence questions of the PSAT will ask you where a particular sentence ought to be placed. To answer these questions, follow these steps:

1. Look at the sentence in question, then reread the paragraph without that sentence.
2. Use context clues to determine which sentence or sentences are most logically related to the sentence in question. The sentence should probably appear either immediately before, after, or between those sentences.
3. Decide where you believe the sentence best fits. Reread the paragraph with the sentence inserted in that spot. If the paragraph flows logically, this is likely the correct answer.

Other logical sequence questions will ask you to put the sentences of a paragraph in the most logical order. These questions are like puzzles. To solve the puzzle, follow these steps:

1. Closely examine the paragraph to determine which elements are out of place. In particular, look for transitions that don't make sense, sentences that contain related ideas but are not placed close together, or sentences that relate to other paragraphs but that are not near those paragraphs.
2. Rearrange the sentences to address the issues you identified in step 1. Ensure that transitions make sense, that related ideas are placed close together, and that sentences that seem to transition to or from other paragraphs are at the beginning or end of the paragraph.
3. Choose the answer that best reflects your chosen order.

Example Questions:

(1) On Thanksgiving, we like to eat foods that are historically accurate. Turkey, stuffing, mashed potatoes, cranberry sauce, and pumpkin pie come to mind. However, if you wanted to host a historically accurate feast, comprised of only those foods that historians are positive were eaten at the alleged "first Thanksgiving," you would be faced with slimmer pickings.

(2) Two chief sources -- the only remaining texts that mention the meal -- recount some of the staples served at the harvest celebration shared by the Pilgrims and Wampanoag at Plymouth Colony in 1621. An English leader in attendance, Edward Winslow, wrote of men sent "fowling, that so we might after a special manner rejoice together," of their Indian neighbors who "went out and killed five deer, which they...bestowed on our governor." This governor, William Bradford, also described the meal, adding, "And besides waterfowl there was great store of wild turkeys, of which they took many, besides venison, etc...besides Indian corn."

Unfortunately, determining any other fare that might have been present at the feast of the colonists and Wampanoag is more difficult. Because of a lack of first-hand accounts, historians must rely on documents such has period cookbooks and garden records to reveal what types of foods were available. (3) Despite this, knowledge of the produce that was available in North America at the time provides a revealing image of the First Thanksgiving.

1. Which of the following provides the best introduction to the passage?

A) NO CHANGE
B) What are the traditional Thanksgiving dishes of today?
C) The traditional Thanksgiving meal is based on the meal eaten at the First Thanksgiving.
D) Who doesn't love to eat a great Thanksgiving meal?

2. Which of the following provides the best transition between the first and second paragraphs?

A) NO CHANGE
B) Very few first-hand accounts exist of the harvest celebration shared by the Pilgrims and the Wampanoag at Plymouth Colony in 1621.
C) First-hand accounts of the harvest celebration shared by the Pilgrims and Wampanoag at Plymouth Colony in 1621 show that only meat and corn were available.
D) Thanks to first-hand accounts of the harvest celebration at Plymouth Colony in 1621, we know that it is likely that the Pilgrims and the Wampanoag enjoyed turkey, just as we do today.

3. A) NO CHANGE
B) Although
C) Luckily
D) Similarly

[1] Based on such sources, historians have determined that although the First Thanksgiving may have featured a turkey, few of our other modern staples would have been available. [2] Likewise, cranberries, wheat, and butter were absent. [3] For instance, neither white potatoes nor sweet potatoes were yet grown in North America. [4] Instead, seafood, nuts, beans, and squash likely featured heavily at any 1621 feast in Plymouth. **(4)**

So how did Thanksgiving become the feast of modern day? Our traditional recipes more closely resemble those of the mid-1800s than 1621 because Thanksgiving became a national holiday during the Civil War. **(5)** Any Civil War hero would feel right at home at our Thanksgiving meal.

4. Sentence two should most logically

A) remain where it is.
B) be placed after sentence 3.
C) be placed after sentence 4.
D) be eliminated.

5. Which of the following best concludes the passage?

A) NO CHANGE
B) Isn't it weird that a holiday celebrating the 1600s might be shaped by the 1800s?
C) The subsequent publication of Thanksgiving recipes and cookbooks shaped the feast that we share today.
D) Wartime deprivations made the Thanksgiving feast a particularly welcome respite from an unpleasant time.

The first question is an introduction question. First, we can eliminate choice D because its very informal style does not suit the passage as a whole. Choice C opposes the main claim of the passage, so we can eliminate choice C. Nothing in the passage argues that we should prefer or do prefer historically accurate foods, so we can eliminate choice A. Choice B suits both the introductory paragraph and the passage as a whole.

The second question is a transition question that focuses on transitional strategies. The first paragraph introduces the main idea of the passage -- that the meal at the First Thanksgiving was very different from our modern Thanksgiving feasts. The second paragraph discusses food items that were definitely served at the First Thanksgiving based on first-hand accounts. Choice B fails to address the discussion of food; choice C makes a claim that is negated by the rest of the passage; choice D side-steps the main claims of both paragraphs by narrowing the focus to turkey. Choice A is the best option.

The third question is a simpler transition question. The sentence that begins with the transition is adding similar information to that contained in the previous sentence. We need to find a transition that shows this. As such, we can eliminate choices A and B. Choice C, "luckily," is tempting because it seems to suit the context of the paragraph, but choice D more clearly shows the relationship between the two sentences.

The fourth question is a logical sequence question. The transition word "likewise" tells us that this sentence should go after a sentence that also tells us about foods that would not have been at the original Thanksgiving. Sentence three best fits this description, so choice B is the best answer.

The last question is a conclusion question. We can eliminate choice B because its informal style doesn't suit the rest of the passage. Choice D is unrelated to the main idea of the passage, so it can be eliminated. Choice A makes a claim that is unsubstantiated by the passage. Choice C is the best answer as it ties the information in the last paragraph back to the main claim of the passage.

Word Choice

Concept Introduction

Since writing is all about words, word choice is an important element of good writing. The PSAT tests your knowledge of word choice using several different types of questions. Every writing passage will include at least one question that focuses on precision or concision. Precision questions ask you to choose the most precise word for a particular sentence while concision questions ask you to choose the most concise (least wordy) way of phrasing something. Slightly less common are questions that test your mastery of frequently confused words. Finally, the PSAT will test word choice through questions that focus on writing style.

Spotting Word Choice Questions

Precision Questions

Precision questions can appear in one of two ways. Sometimes precision questions will be easy to spot because they will ask you to choose the most precise word for a given context. Other times, they may be harder to identify because they may simply include an underlined word and three similar alternatives.

Concision Questions

Like precision questions, concision questions can either be very easy to spot (by asking you for the most concise way of phrasing a part of the passage) or difficult to spot. When you see answer choices that all seem to be synonymous to the original phrasing but are different lengths, the question is likely a precision question.

Frequently Confused Words

These questions are usually fairly easy to spot because they offer several words that are spelled or pronounced very similarly to one another. These include possessive determiners like *they're/their/there* or *its/it's*.

Writing Style

These are the least common word choice questions, but they are usually fairly easy to spot because they usually include the words "style," "stylistically," or "tone."

Answering Precision Questions

Precision questions can seem difficult at first glance because the answer choices are almost always words that are very similar in meaning. After all, it can be tough to choose between words that are as similar as "aggressive" and "assertive." There are two key concepts to help eliminate incorrect answer choices with precision questions.

Connotation

The connotation of a word is the emotion or feeling engendered by the word. For instance, let's look at aggressive versus assertive. We usually think of someone who is aggressive as being pushy or angry; this word has a negative connotation. We usually think of someone who is assertive as being a leader; this word has a more positive connotation. The same can be seen with words like thin versus gaunt; both indicate that a person is skinny, but gaunt has a more negative connotation than thin.

Specificity

The very word "precise" means "exact" or "specific." With precision questions, it is important to achieve the appropriate level of specificity for the context of the passage. Words that are either too general or too specific won't work. Consider these examples:

Sentence 1: It poured today, so now my yard is flooded.

Sentence 2: It rained today, so now my yard is flooded.

Sentence 3: It precipitated today, so now my yard is flooded.

Each of these sentences is essentially saying the same thing, but with varying levels of specificity. Sentence 1 is most specific, sentence 3 is most general, and sentence 2 is somewhere in between. Given the context of the sentence as a whole, the most specific option would be the best option because "poured" indicates a level of rain that would lead to a flood. If the second part of the sentence were to say, "so my car got a little wet," then "poured" would be overly specific and "rained" would work better.

To answer precision questions, follow these steps:

1. Cover up the word in the passage. Using the context of the surrounding sentence(s), come up with a word that you think would best fit.
2. Look at all of the answer choices. Eliminate those answer choices that have a significantly different connotation from the word you chose in step 1.
3. Using your word choice from step 1 as a guide, eliminate those answer choices that are either too specific or too general for the context of the sentence.
4. If there is more than one answer choice remaining, reread the sentence filling in the blank with each remaining answer choice. Choose the one that seems most natural in the context of the sentence.

Answering Concision Questions

Concision questions focus on two different types of errors: wordiness and redundancy. Wordiness occurs when a writer uses more words than are necessary to convey a point. There are a few common mistakes that lead to wordiness.

One of the most common errors that leads to wordiness is **passive voice**. Passive voice occurs when the subject of the sentence is not performing the action. For example:

Passive: The treat was given to the cat by the child. (10 words)

Active: The child gave the cat a treat. (7 words)

In this example, you can easily see how passive voice leads to wordiness in a sentence. Both of these sentences say the exact same thing, but the active voice sentence is 3 words shorter.

Another error that leads to wordiness is beginning a sentence with a filler phrase like "this is...," "that is...," "there are...," "there is...," or "it is..." Let's look at an example:

Sentence 1: There are several reasons why people like to go to the beach. (12 words)

Sentence 2: People like to go to the beach for several reasons. (10 words)

The second sentence is shorter and more to the point, making it a better option than the first sentence.

When addressing wordiness, be sure to pay attention to the content of the answer choices rather than simply choosing the shortest option. You need to ensure that the answer you choose doesn't lose any of the original meaning.

Finally, concision questions will test your ability to eliminate redundancy. Sentences often become longer than necessary through the needless repetition of words, phrases, or ideas. For example:

Sentence 1: Each year, millions of people who were once students drop out of college.
(13 words)

Sentence 2: Each year, millions of people drop out of college.
(9 words)

Both of these sentences share the same information, but sentence 1 contains redundant information. After all, people who drop out of college MUST have once been students; non-students can't drop out.

By eliminating the redundant phrase ("who were once students"), we can create a much more concise sentence.

To answer concision questions, follow these steps:

1. Read the underlined sentence *and* the sentences immediately before and after that sentence. Identify any redundancies in the underlined portion and eliminate answer choices that do not eliminate those redundancies.
2. Eliminate any answer choices that use passive voice or that begin with an unnecessary phrase.
3. Of the remaining answer choices, choose the shortest answer that still maintains the ideas presented in the original sentence.
4. Plug your chosen answer into the sentence to ensure that it doesn't introduce any new redundancies.

Answering Frequently Confused Words Questions

Unfortunately, there are no secret strategies for answering frequently confused words questions other than to be familiar with frequently confused words.

Some of the most common frequently confused words are sometimes known as possessive determiners. These include:

Its/It's/Its'	**Its:** The possessive form of "it." **It's:** A contraction of "it is." **Its':** Not really a word. This is NEVER correct.
Their/They're/There	**Their:** The possessive form of "they." **They're:** The contraction of "they are." **There:** Refers to a place or used with a "to be" verb.
Your/You're	**Your:** Possessive form of "you." **You're:** Contraction of "you are."

Other frequently confused words can be a bit more difficult to master because there are *a lot* of them! The following chart provides a sample of some of the most frequently confused words:

Accept/except	**Accept:** to take willingly. *I **accept** your apology.* **Except:** excluding. *I forgive everything **except** that joke about my mom.*
Adapt/adept/adopt	**Adapt:** to adjust. *I will have to **adapt** to college life.* **Adept:** skilled. *I am **adept** at soccer.* **Adopt:** to accept as your own. *I will **adopt** the persona of an Englishman.*
Advice/advise	**Advice:** an opinion intended to be helpful. *The guidance counselor provides good college application **advice**.* **Advise:** to give advice. *The guidance counselor's job is to **advise** students.*
Affect/effect	**Affect:** to influence. *I will not let your opinion **affect** my decision.* **Effect:** usually means "a result." *A lack of sleep can have an **effect** on your test score.*
Assure/ensure/insure	**Assure:** to guarantee. *I **assure** you that I will ace this test.*

	Ensure: to make sure. *I studied for hours to **ensure** my high score.* **Insure:** to provide insurance against loss. *The law requires that you **insure** your car.*
Bare/bear	**Bare:** to expose. *He prefers not to **bare** his soul to the world.* **Bear:** to carry. *I cannot **bear** the weight of the fridge by myself.*
Breadth/breath/breathe	**Breadth:** width or extent. *The **breadth** of the security breach was only recently discovered.* **Breath:** the air that you breathe. *I got a hug that took my **breath** away.* **Breathe:** the act of breathing. *I could not **breathe** after running for five miles.*
Censor/censure/sensor	**Censor:** to prohibit free expression (or one who prohibits free expression). *The library chose to **censor** all fantasy books.* **Censure:** to criticize. *They will likely **censure** her for her poorly thought out comments.* **Sensor:** something that interprets stimulation. *The temperature **sensor** on the oven was broken.*
Elicit/illicit	**Elicit:** to draw out. *Her sad expression was intended to **elicit** sympathy.* **Illicit:** illegal or illegitimate. *He was suspended from school for **illicit** activities.*
Emanate/eminent/imminent	**Emanate:** to issue or spread. *There was a noticeable smell **emanating** from his locker.* **Eminent:** prestigious. *An **eminent** painter visited our art class today.* **Imminent:** about to happen. *The tornado represents an **imminent** threat to the Cincinnati area.*
Peek/pique/peak	**Peek:** to look quickly without someone knowing. *I **peeked** under the bed to see if my presents were hidden there.* **Pique:** to provoke or resentment. *My parents exchanged a look that **piqued** my curiosity.* *OR Anne felt a bit of **pique** at the harsh criticism written on her essay.* **Peak:** the highest point. *My family decided that it would be a bad idea to visit the amusement park during **peak** summer season.*
Than/then	**Than:** used to compare. *My dog is smarter **than** your dog.* **Then:** a time that is not now. *First, add the eggs, and **then** add the milk.*

To answer frequently confused words questions, follow these steps:

1. Quickly define each answer choice. By looking at their definitions, you can help eliminate the confusion of similarly spelled words.
2. Look at the sentence. Cover up the underlined word and replace it with a word of your own choosing.
3. Choose the answer that is most similar in meaning to the word you chose in step 2.

Answering Style Questions

An author's style and tone is determined primarily by word choice. While reading look for the following clues to help you determine the style and tone of the passage:

- Does the author use first or second person in the passage? This typically suggests a less formal style than a passage that uses third person.
- Is the author trying to persuade, perhaps by using emotional language, or to inform, perhaps by using more academic language? The language should remain fairly consistent throughout the passage.
- Are the adjectives and adverbs vibrant or dull?

Once you've observed the writer's style, use these steps to answer style questions:

1. Eliminate answer choices that introduce a change of point of view. For instance, if most of the passage is written in the first person, a sudden switch to second person is likely incorrect.
2. Eliminate answer choices that introduce a notably different choice of words. For instance, if most of the passage is rather dry and academic, an answer choice that is passionate and emotional is likely incorrect. Likewise, in a passage filled with vibrant adjectives, an answer choice featuring dull adjectives is likely incorrect.
3. Of the remaining answer choices, choose the one that seems to best match the author's use of language throughout the rest of the passage.

Example Questions:

The park service has played an important role in shaping and reshaping popular historical awareness. During the past two decades, **(1)** Civil War sites have been overhauled by the park service, which has incorporated material on slavery into exhibits that had long been **(2)** exonerated by scholars for avoiding discussion of the root causes of the conflict.

1. A) NO CHANGE
   B) there are several Civil War sites that have been overhauled by the park service, which has incorporated
   C) it has overhauled Civil War sites, incorporating
   D) Civil War sites have incorporated

2. Which is the most precise replacement for the underlined word?

   A) NO CHANGE
   B) nit-picked
   C) blasted
   D) criticized

The first question doesn't have a clear indication (like the word "concise") that it is a concision question. However, if we examine the underlined portion, we see that there are no grammatical errors and that it is written in passive voice. We can, therefore, assume that it is a concision question. First, we can eliminate choice A because of its use of passive voice. Choice B uses "there are," which we know often unnecessarily lengthens a sentence; we can eliminate choice B. Choices C and D both look good at first glance, but choice D eliminates the reference to the park service. As a result, choice D loses some significant meaning since it is the park service, not the sites, that took action. Choice C is the best answer.

The second question is clearly a precision question. Let's ignore the underlined word and try to come up with a replacement. Based on the context of the sentence, we know that the scholars probably weren't happy that the sites ignored slavery; we need a negative word like critiqued. Based on this, we can easily eliminate choice A because exonerated is similar to forgiven; this has the opposite connotation as the word we are looking for. All of the remaining answer choices are negative, but choice B doesn't suit the style of the rest of the paragraph since nit-picked is a colloquialism. Choice C seems too extreme in connotation; it seems unlikely that scholars would have blasted something. Choice D is the best answer.

Development of Ideas

Concept Introduction

Good writing isn't simply about grammar, mechanics, and organization. The writer's ideas matter, too. The PSAT tests your ability to evaluate and improve the development of a writer's ideas through four types of questions. Among the most common of these questions are main idea questions. These questions require that you provide the best thesis statement for the passage or topic sentence for a paragraph. Development of ideas questions also include support questions, which test your ability to identify appropriate support for an argument, and focus questions, which test your ability to eliminate unnecessary information to streamline writing.

Spotting Development of Ideas Questions

Main Idea Questions

Main idea questions will sometimes specifically ask you for the main idea of the passage or the paragraph. Other words to look for include "thesis" or "topic sentence."

Support Questions

Support questions will often include the words "support" or "evidence." Alternatively, a support question may ask whether the author should add a given supporting sentence.

Focus Questions

These questions will generally either ask you whether or which sentence should be eliminated from a given paragraph.

Answering Main Idea Questions

Main idea questions require that you be able to identify thesis statements and topic sentences. The thesis statement is a statement of the primary idea of the passage as a whole. It is usually found in the introduction of the passage and is often either the first or the last sentence of the introduction. Topic sentences state the main idea or claim of a paragraph. The topic sentence is often, but certainly not always, one of the first sentences of a paragraph.

Main idea questions either require that you add a sentence that identifies the main idea of the passage or paragraph or that you choose whether to replace an existing thesis statement or topic sentence. Regardless of the form the question takes, follow these steps to arrive at the correct answer:

1. In your own words, summarize the main idea or claim of the paragraph or passage. If the question asks about the passage as a whole, pay particular attention to information in the introduction and conclusion as these paragraphs often summarize main ideas.
2. Examine the answer choices. Eliminate any that negate or are unrelated to your summarized main idea.
3. Eliminate any answer choices that focus on smaller details or supporting ideas.
4. Eliminate any answer choices that do not suit the style and tone of the passage.
5. Of the remaining answer choices, choose the one that best reflects your assessment of the main idea and the style of the passage.

Answering Support Questions

Support questions will generally ask which sentence provides the best support for an argument or whether an author should add a possible supporting sentence. In either form, the question requires that you identify appropriate support for a given argument. To answer support questions, follow these steps:

1. Determine the argument or main idea of the paragraph referenced by the question.
2. If the question asks whether a supporting sentence should be added, evaluate whether that sentence adds new, pertinent information to the author's argument.

3. If the question asks for the best support of the given options, consider whether each answer choice is specific to the paragraph's main idea or argument. Eliminate those answers that are not directly related to the main idea or argument.
4. Eliminate any answer choices that contradict the main idea or argument.
5. Of the remaining answer choices, choose the one that most strongly and meaningfully develops the main idea or argument.

Answering Focus Questions

Paragraphs that contain a lot of irrelevant or loosely related information are unnecessarily confusing. Focus questions ask us whether we should eliminate sentences that might not suit the paragraph in which they appear. To answer focus questions, follow these steps:

1. Determine the main idea or argument of the paragraph referenced by the question. Without looking at the answer choices, try to determine whether one of the sentences in the paragraph does not meaningfully develop the argument or main idea.
2. If you were able to identify a sentence in step 1, and if that sentence is listed as a possible answer choice, that is most likely the correct answer.
3. If you were unable to identify a sentence in step 1, or if that sentence is not a possible answer choice, reread the paragraph eliminating each answer choice with each rereading. Choose the answer that results in the clearest and most concise paragraph.

Example Questions:

In 2015, Georgetown joined Stanford in its promise to stop investing in coal companies, under pressure from student groups seeking widespread college divestment from the fossil fuel industry. Unfortunately, this student activism is sorely misplaced. **(1)** <u>Only by investing in fossil fuels can colleges and students hope to make a difference in the fight against global warming.</u>

1. Which of the following best functions as the thesis of this passage?

A) NO CHANGE
B) Divestment is really a rather stupid solution to a very serious global problem, and only college students could possibly think it would make a real difference.
C) Divestment makes no dent in the industry and doesn't make renewable energy more affordable or reliable, thus it tackles none of the presumed causes or effects of global warming.
D) It is the leaders of universities who should be taking an active role in leading divestment movements.

Those who advocate for divestment say shareholder advocacy has failed to change the fossil fuel industry's behavior, so schools should sell their stocks. The first part of that statement is true: Shell and Exxon are not going to quit drilling because some shareholders tell them to stop. But if the aim is to persuade the industry to convert to renewables, divestment is a worse strategy. **(2)** Capital markets aren't punishing fossil fuel companies — they have plenty of investors willing to buy up shares — and corporations have no incentive to heed ex-investors.

So why has a call to divest achieved traction on some college campuses? Emotional appeal. Divestment is one of those campaigns that stir up people who want to feel like they are doing something, when, in truth, they are doing nothing.

[1] As political psychology, co-opting universities as PR machines if they divest, or oppressive adversaries if they don't, is clever. [2] Global warming activists aim to build a long-term constituency that despises fossil fuels and is primed to pursue every alternative no matter the cost. [3] Divestment sidelines real debates about energy and climate policy by condensing them into polarized yea-or-nay decisions about finances. [4] One divestment organizer deems the movement important specifically for its ability to "politicize" and "radicalize" students. **(3)**

That thinking reflects more about desired outcomes of future presidential elections than about next year's S&P 500 Energy Index, which is, incidentally, down 28 percent on one-year annual returns — due, not to divestment, but to an oil glut.

2. The author is considering adding the following sentence here:

   Shares sold by universities will simply be purchased by another investor.

   Should the author make this addition?

   A) No because it creates a redundancy within the paragraph without adding meaningful information.
   B) No because it is more closely related to the information in the next paragraph than to this paragraph.
   C) Yes because it meaningfully develops the claim made in the previous sentence.
   D) Yes because it provides an important explanation of how capital markets work.

3. Which sentence should be eliminated in order to improve the focus of the paragraph?

   A) Sentence 1
   B) Sentence 2
   C) Sentence 3
   D) Sentence 4

The first question uses the word "thesis," so we know it is a main idea question. If we look only at the introduction and the concluding sentence, we can summarize the passage's primary claim as "divestment doesn't work." Based on this summary, we can eliminate choice D because it seems to claim that divestment *does* work. Choice A makes a claim that is not substantiated anywhere in the passage, so we can eliminate A. Choice B does not suit the style or tone of the passage as it takes a disparaging, insulting attitude toward college students in general. Choice C is the best answer.

The second question asks whether we should add a supporting sentence, so we know it's a support question. We need to figure out if it adds new and important information. The very next sentence in the paragraph tells us that fossil fuel companies have plenty of investors, which is very similar to the information provided by the sentence in the question. Based on this, we'll keep choice A as a possible answer. The sentence in question has nothing to do with the next paragraph, so we can eliminate choice B. The sentence in question adds little that is not already addressed in the following sentence, so it isn't really developing the idea that "divestment is a worse strategy." We can eliminate choice C. The sentence in question may tangentially address the concept of a marketplace, but it doesn't explain how capital markets work, so we can eliminate choice D. Choice A is the best answer.

Finally, question three offers a focus question. The main idea of the paragraph is that the divestment debate is a political strategy used to blindly turn students against fossil fuels. Of the four sentences in the paragraph, only sentence 3 fails to develop this idea, so choice C is the best answer.

Sentences

Concept Introduction

One of the grammar concepts that is most frequently tested on the PSAT writing section involves identifying sentence errors and combining sentences. Questions that test this concept include identifying and correcting run-on sentences, correcting fragments, and using coordination or subordination to combine sentences.

Sentence Boundary Review

A complete sentence must contain a subject and a verb and must express a complete idea. A sentence that fails to meet this standard is a sentence fragment. Sentences that meet this standard but that are not properly connected are run-on sentences. For example:

> **Sentence Fragment:** On Kepler-452b, humans would weigh twice as much as they do on Earth. <u>Because Kepler's gravity is stronger than the gravity on Earth.</u>

> **Run-On Sentence:** On Kepler-452b, humans would weigh twice as much as they do on <u>Earth, Kepler's gravity</u> is stronger than the gravity on Earth.

> **Correct Sentence:** On Kepler-452b, humans would weigh twice as much as they do on <u>Earth because Kepler's gravity</u> is stronger than the gravity on Earth.

In the first example, the underlined portion is an example of a fragment. Although it contains both a subject (Kepler's gravity) and a verb (is), the word "because" makes this an incomplete idea -- because what?

The second example eliminates the problem with "because," but improperly connects the two sentences with a comma, making the sentence a run-on.

The third example correctly combines the two sentences into a single correct sentence using subordination.

Subordination Review

Subordination is one means of combining sentences using conjunctions. With subordination, we make one of the two sentences a dependent clause. A dependent clause cannot stand on its own as a sentence. In the example of a sentence fragment, the fragment is a dependent clause thanks to the subordinating conjunction "because."

There are many subordinating conjunctions. Some of the most commonly used subordinating conjunctions include:

Used to show...	Conjunction
Contrast	Although Even though While
Condition	If Even if
Time	When After Before Until Since
Place	Where Wherever

Cause/Effect	Because
	Since
	So that
	In order to
	As a result of

When using subordination, there are two important concepts to master. The first is choosing a conjunction that reflects the correct relationship between the two clauses. For example:

Incorrect: Although Kepler-452b orbits a solar star at about the same distance at which Earth circles the sun, the day-night cycle is likely similar.

Correct: Since Kepler-452b orbits a solar star at about the same distance at which Earth circles the sun, the day-night cycle is likely similar.

The conjunction "although" does not properly describe the cause and effect relationship between the two sentences. As a result, the incorrect sentence simply makes no logical sense. This is corrected by the use of the conjunction "since," which properly identifies the relationship between the two sentences.

The second important concept to master regarding subordination is proper punctuation of the sentence. There are two rules governing punctuation with subordination:

1. If the subordinating clause comes first (as in this sentence), use a comma after the subordinating clause.
2. Do not use a comma if the subordinating clause comes last (as in this sentence).

Coordination Review

The other means of combining sentences using conjunctions is **coordination**. Coordination is somewhat simpler than subordination because there are only 7 coordinating conjunctions. You may know them as **FANBOYS**:

For **A**nd **N**or **B**ut **O**r **Y**et **S**o

Unlike with subordination, coordination combines two independent clauses. Independent clauses are clauses that could stand as sentences on their own. Using coordination does not create a dependent clause in the way that subordination does.

Also unlike subordination, there is only one correct way of punctuating a sentence that uses coordination: When combining sentences with coordination, always use a comma and a coordinating conjunction.

Coordination errors are most likely to occur when the sentence is improperly punctuated (usually by missing the comma) or when the chosen conjunction does not logically reflect the relationship between the two sentences. For example:

Incorrect: Kepler-452b's solar star is in a more energetic phase of its life cycle than our sun so the sunlight on Kepler would be slightly different than that on Earth.

Incorrect: Kepler-452b's solar star is in a more energetic phase of its life cycle than our sun, but the sunlight on Kepler would be slightly different than that on Earth.

Correct: Kepler-452b's solar star is in a more energetic phase of its life cycle than our sun, so the sunlight on Kepler would be slightly different than that on Earth.

The first sentence is missing its comma, making it incorrect. The second sentence uses a conjunction that does not identify the cause and effect relationship between the two sentences. Only the third sentence is both properly punctuated and uses a logical conjunction.

Answering Sentences Questions

To answer sentences questions, you must have a good understanding of the basic rules of sentences. Let's review the rules covered in this lesson:

1. A complete sentence requires a subject and verb and must express a complete idea. Sentences that don't meet these criteria are sentence fragments.
2. Two complete sentences that are combined by either a comma without a conjunction or nothing at all create a run-on sentence.
3. Both fragments and run-ons can often be solved by properly combining sentences.
4. Subordination is one means of properly combining sentences. When using subordination:
   a. Choose a subordinating conjunction that expresses a logical relationship between the two sentences.
   b. Use a comma after the dependent clause when the subordinating conjunction comes at the beginning of the sentence.
   c. Do not use a comma when the subordinating conjunction is in the middle of the sentence.
5. Coordination is another means of properly combining sentences. When using coordination:
   a. Choose a coordinating conjunction (FANBOYS) that expresses a logical relationship between the sentences.
   b. Always use a comma before the coordinating conjunction.

These steps may help you to answer questions regarding sentences:

1. If the underlined portion includes the juncture where two sentences meet, check to be sure that neither sentence is a fragment. If one sentence is a fragment, look for an answer choice that properly connects the fragment and the other sentence using subordination.
2. If the answer choices include coordinating or subordinating conjunctions, choose the answer choice that is properly punctuated and uses a conjunction that reflects a logical relationship between the two sentences being combined.

Punctuation

Concept Introduction

It is safe to assume that every passage on the PSAT writing section will include at least one punctuation error. The PSAT tests your knowledge of punctuation through a wide variety of possible punctuation errors, including within sentence punctuation such as commas and semicolons, the correct use of apostrophes in possessives, items in a series, parenthetical elements, and the use of unnecessary punctuation. It is important to understand punctuation rules in order to succeed on these questions.

Items in a Series

When three or more items occur in a series, they must be properly punctuated. Most of the time, they will be punctuated using commas, as in this example:

> **Commas in a Series:** Our travel plans include San Francisco, Los Angeles, and Las Vegas.

Notice that the list of cities is separated by commas. The final comma in the series, the one that comes before the word "and," is called an Oxford comma. Some style guides require the use of the Oxford comma while others do not; because of this grammar controversy, it is highly unlikely that the use of the Oxford comma will be tested on the PSAT. If, however, a question seems to test the use of the Oxford comma, you are safest selecting the answer choice that includes the Oxford comma.
Items in a series can also be separated by semicolons. If even one of the items in the series already contains a comma, then you should use semicolons to separate the items, as in this example:

> **Semicolons in a Series:** Our travel plans include San Francisco, California; Los Angeles, California; and Las Vegas, Nevada.

Because the items in the series now have commas separating the cities and states, the list needs to be separated by semicolons. The same rule applies no matter why a comma appears in the series items. For example:

> **Semicolons in a Series:** Our travel plans include seeing the Golden Gate Bridge, Ghirardelli Square, and Fisherman's Wharf in San Francisco; Hollywood and Disney in Los Angeles; and the Strip in Las Vegas.

In this case, the first item (the list of sights in San Francisco) contains commas, yet the series as a whole must still be separated by semicolons -- do not mix punctuation marks when separating items in a series.

Finally, colons can also have a role to play in items in a series. If the list follows an independent clause that could stand on its own as a sentence, use a colon to introduce the list. For example:

> **Colons before a Series:** We will be visiting cities in the west on our vacation: San Francisco, Los Angeles, and Las Vegas.

Let's look at some common errors regarding items in a series and how to fix them:

> **Colon Misuse:** Our travel plans include: San Francisco, Los Angeles, and Las Vegas.

In this sentence, the colon is not used after an independent clause -- "Our travel plans include" cannot stand on its own as a sentence, so a colon should not be used. There are two ways to correct this error:

Correction #1: Our travel plans include San Francisco, Los Angeles, and Las Vegas.

Correction #2: Our travel plans include **some very interesting cities**: San Francisco, Los Angeles, and Las Vegas.

In the first correction, we simply remove the offending colon; this is the easiest correction. In the second correction, we added "some very interesting cities" to make the introductory clause an independent clause, which makes the use of a colon correct.

Comma Overuse: I can't wait to visit foggy, hilly San Francisco, sunny, bustling Los Angeles, and bright Las Vegas.

Because some of the items in the series have adjectives that are separated by commas, this sentence has so many commas that it becomes confusing. To clarify the sentence, we should limit the number of commas.

Correction: I can't wait to visit foggy, hilly San Francisco**;** sunny, bustling Los Angeles**;** and bright Las Vegas.

In the corrected sentence, we replaced the commas that were separating the items with semicolons. This clarifies the separation between each item, making the sentence easier to read.

Mixed Punctuation: I can't wait to visit foggy, hilly San Francisco; sunny, bustling Los Angeles, and bright Las Vegas.

In this sentence, the writer separated the items that contain commas using a semicolon -- he was on the right track. But then he used a comma to separate the final two items. Whichever type of punctuation is used to separate items in a series must be used consistently.

Correction: I can't wait to visit foggy, hilly San Francisco; sunny, bustling Los Angeles; and bright Las Vegas.

This corrected sentence changes the final comma to a semicolon, making the punctuation consistent throughout. We could not have changed the first semicolon to a comma because two of the items already contain commas -- remember that if even one item has a comma in it, you must separate the items with semicolons.

Punctuating Quotations

Errors regarding within sentence punctuation often arise with quotes. Both commas and colons can play a role in introducing quotations:

Comma: When I showed my mother the room I had painted, she said, "I like the new color."
Colon: When I showed my mother the room I had painted, she said: "I like the new color."

Although these sentences use two different punctuation marks to introduce the quotation, both sentences are grammatically correct. It will be rare for you to need to choose between using a comma or a colon to introduce a quotation, but should such a situation arise, there is a simple guide: It is advisable to only use a colon to introduce longer quotations that are more than seven words long. Using this guide, we should use a comma in the samples above. A better example of colon usage would be:

Better Colon Usage: When I showed my mother the room I had painted, she said: "I like the new color, but now the chair rail and base boards need to be repainted."

This is a more traditional example of colon usage when introducing quotations.
Another common punctuation issue with regard to quotations is whether the punctuation at the end should go inside or outside of the quotation marks. When the quotation comes first, the comma goes inside the quotation marks:

Comma: "I like the new color," my mother said.

The rules can be slightly more complicated when it comes to terminal punctuation -- the punctuation that ends a sentence. If the terminal punctuation is part of the quotation, it goes inside the quotation marks. If the terminal punctuation is *not* part of the quotation, it goes outside the quotation marks. For example:

Inside: Susan asked, "Do we have homework?"
Outside: Do I need to learn to play "The Entertainer"?

In the first sentence, the question mark is part of the quotation, so we place it inside the quotation marks. In the second sentence, the question mark is part of the sentence as a whole, not the quotation. In this case, the question mark goes outside of the quotation marks. The same rule applies to any terminal punctuation, including question marks, exclamation points, and periods.

Commas: Paired Adjectives

When more than one adjective is used to describe something, those adjectives should often (but not always!) be separated by commas:

With Comma: He enjoyed the **decadent, rich** dessert.
Without Comma: He enjoyed the **decadent baked** dessert.

Both of the above sentences are correct, but you may not see why at first glance. The general rule of thumb is that if you can switch the adjectives and the sentence still sounds just as good, the adjectives should be separated with a comma.
The sentence with the comma would still make perfect sense if we switched the adjectives: "He enjoyed the rich, decadent dessert." The sentence without the comma doesn't make quite as much sense if we switch the adjectives: "He enjoyed the baked decadent dessert." This is because the adjective "baked" is describing the dessert, while the adjective "decadent" is describing the "baked dessert."

Nonessential Elements

The term "nonessential elements" refers to clauses or phrases that are not essential to the meaning of a sentence. If you can remove a clause or phrase and retain the same meaning, that clause or phrase is a nonessential element. For example:

Essential: The man **who is wearing the ridiculous sweater** is my dad.
Nonessential: The soccer coach**, who is wearing the ridiculous sweater,** is my dad.

In the first sentence, the only thing that helps us to identify "my dad" is the phrase "who is wearing the ridiculous sweater." If we remove the phrase, the sentence loses important meaning. In the second sentence, "my dad" is already identified as "the soccer coach," so the phrase "who is wearing the ridiculous sweater" is much less necessary.
Notice that the nonessential element is set off using commas, and the essential element is not. Nonessential elements need to be set apart from the sentence using punctuation. Commas can usually be used to set apart nonessential elements, but sometimes we use parentheses or hyphens instead.

Commas: Fred, who purchased a tiller last week, prepared his backyard for a garden bed.
Parentheses: Fred used tiller (a machine that breaks up the ground) to prepare his backyard for a garden bed.
Hyphens: Fred used a tiller -- and almost took his foot off -- to prepare his backyard for a garden bed.

Let's look at the subtle reasons for why one type of punctuation might work better than another. Commas don't interrupt the flow of the sentence, so they get used the most frequently. We use commas to offset information that feels like a natural part of the sentence. They are sort of the all-purpose punctuation for nonessential elements. In the first sentence, the nonessential element gives us useful information that isn't necessary to the meaning of the sentence. The information is relevant to the sentence, so we used commas to set it apart.

Parentheses are used to deemphasize information or to include information that is a bit out of place in a sentence (an aside, a clarification, a definition, a commentary, etc.). In the second sentence, the nonessential element tells us what a tiller is; although this is useful information, it isn't necessary to the sentence and would feel out of place if we tried to make it a more natural part of the sentence. Thus parentheses are the idea punctuation.

Hyphens actually emphasize information. We use hyphens for information that is surprising or particularly interesting. In the third sentence, the nonessential element is certainly not necessary to the meaning of the sentence, but it provides a very interesting note.

Combining Sentences

In the last lesson, we discussed coordination and subordination. There are special punctuation rules for both methods of sentence combining. Let's review.

With subordination, we use a comma after the subordinate dependent clause if the clause comes at the beginning of the sentence. If the subordinate dependent clause comes at the end of the sentence, we do not use a comma. For example:

Correct: Even though she likes to read**,** she did not like that particular book.
Correct: She did not like that particular book **even though** she likes to read.
Incorrect: Even though she likes to read she did not like that particular book.
Incorrect: She did not like that particular book**, even though** she likes to read.

With coordination, we always use a comma before the coordinating conjunction. For example:

Correct: She likes to read**, but** she did not like that particular book.
Incorrect: She likes to read **but** she did not like that particular book.
Incorrect: She like to read **but,** she did not like that particular book.

Another common way of combining sentences is to use a semicolon or a colon. We can use a semicolon to combine two sentences without the use of a conjunction. Because there is no conjunction to clarify the relationship between the sentences, the sentences should be very clearly related to one another. For example:

Semicolon: She likes to read**;** she does not like to watch television.

In this sentence, we know that both independent clauses share information about someone's preferences. Even though there are no conjunctions, we can easily understand the sentence.
We can use colons to combine sentences when the second sentence summarizes or clarifies the first sentence. For example:

Colon: She goes to the library almost every day: she really likes to read.

Notice that, as with semicolons, we don't use a conjunction with a colon. If we only use colons when one sentence clarifies the other, we shouldn't need a conjunction to clarify the relationship. In this example, the second sentence clearly tells us why she goes to the library; we don't need a conjunction to make this clear.

Apostrophes

Apostrophes are used in contractions (such as "can't") and in possessives. An apostrophe with the letter *s* almost always means possession, not plurality. This is a common error. For example:

> **Incorrect:** The manager wrote out a sign that said, "Apple's On Sale."
> **Correct:** The manager wrote out a sign that said, "Apples On Sale."
> **Correct:** The apple's color was vibrant.

In the first sentence, the apostrophe is misused. The context of the sentence tells us that the intention was to make "apple" plural; the second sentence accomplishes this correctly. The final sentence shows us possession.

There is an exception to the rule regarding *'s*. When a noun already ends in *s*, it is acceptable to make the noun possessive using only an apostrophe. For example: *Texas' statute, Charles' house, the dogs' collars.*

Unnecessary Punctuation

The most frequently abused punctuation mark is the comma. Writers often mistakenly add commas here they aren't necessary. Some of the most common unnecessary comma errors include:

> **Before a subordinating conjunction:** She decided to sell her house**,** because it was too small.
> **Separating a compound predicate:** She went to the store**,** and bought some bananas.
> **Because it feels right:** The most important thing teachers do**,** is to inspire students.

Each of these sentences should not have a comma. In the first sentence, the comma breaks the rules we learned about subordination. In the second sentence, the comma comes before the word "and," which can be used as a coordinating conjunction. In this sentence, "and" does not function as a coordinating conjunction; it separates two predicates (went and bought). In the final sentence, the comma seems to be placed where there is a natural pause in the sentence, but there is no grammatical reason for this comma.

Answering Punctuation Questions

To answer sentences questions, you must have a good understanding of the basic rules governing punctuation use. Let's review the rules covered in this lesson:

1. When items occur in a series, they should be separated by commas or semicolons.
   a. If even one of the items already contains a comma, use semicolons.
   b. Be sure the punctuation remains consistent throughout the list.
2. A colon can be used to introduce items in a series if the colon comes after an independent clause.
3. Quotations can be introduced using commas or colons.
4. Terminal punctuation that is part of a quotation should be inside the quotation marks; terminal punctuation that is not part of the quotation should be outside the quotation marks.
5. When using more than one adjective, try flipping the order of the adjectives. If the adjectives can be flipped and the sentence still sounds good, use a comma between the adjectives. If the sentence no longer makes as much sense when the adjectives are flipped, do not use a comma.

6. Nonessential elements are phrases or clauses that are not necessary to the meaning of the sentence. They must be set off by punctuation marks.
    a. Use parentheses to set off nonessential elements that should be deemphasized or that interrupt the flow of the sentence.
    b. Use hyphens to set off nonessential elements that are surprising or unexpected.
    c. Use commas to set off most nonessential elements, especially those that feel like a natural part of the sentence.
7. Punctuation is usually, but not always, needed to combine sentences.
    a. With subordination, use a comma after the subordinating clause if it comes at the beginning of the sentence. Do not use a comma if the subordinating clause comes at the end of the sentence.
    b. With coordination, use a comma before the coordinating conjunction.
    c. Semicolons combine sentences that are clearly related to one another. Do not use a conjunction with a semicolon.
    d. Colons combine sentences when the second sentence clarifies or summarizes the first sentence.
8. Apostrophes typically indicate contractions or possession, not plurality. Use an apostrophe followed by the letter *s* to make most nouns possessive; nouns that already end in *s* can simply receive an apostrophe.
9. Avoid using commas simply because it feels right. Keep the rules for comma use in mind to spot unnecessary punctuation.

Quantitative Information

Concept Introduction
Each PSAT writing section will include at least one passage that is accompanied by a graphic such as a graph, table, or chart. Quantitative information questions will require us to draw connections between the graphic and the passage.

Recognizing Quantitative Information Questions
Quantitative information questions will often reference the graphic. These questions will often ask you to add information to the passage based on the graphic. Other quantitative information questions may not reference the graphic; for example, a quantitative information question may simply include an underlined portion of the passage that includes data related to the graphic. In such cases, you are usually required to correct inaccurate information in the graphic.

Regardless of the form the question takes, any quantitative information question will require that you be able to accurately interpret the information in the graphic. Pay very close attention to any titles and axis labels on the graphic.

Answering Quantitative Information Questions
The best way to approach quantitative information questions is to eliminate answer choices that disagree with the graphic. Here is a strategy to answer quantitative information questions:

1. Read the question and carefully examine the graphic.
2. Eliminate any information that clearly disagrees with the graphic .
3. Take a second look to eliminate answers that misinterpret the graphic or that make major assumptions that cannot be supported by the graphic.
4. Eliminate any answer choices that disagree with information found elsewhere in the passage.
5. After carefully examining the remaining answer choices, choose the one that most clearly and accurately reflects the information in the graphic.

Verb Errors

Concept Introduction

Among the most common verb errors are verb tense errors. A verb's tense tells us when an action occurred. Other verb errors include verb mood errors. A verb's mood can be indicative (statements of fact, opinion, and question); imperative (used to issue commands); or subjunctive (used to express states of unreality).

Verb Tense Errors

Beyond the basic "past," "present," and "future," there are several other degrees of verb tenses. Look at the table below to review verb tenses:

	Past	Present	Future
Simple	*Simple past:* Actions that took place at a specific time in the past. I **ran** to practice yesterday.	*Simple present:* Actions that take place at the present moment. I **run** to practice every day.	*Simple Future:* Actions that will happen at a point in time in the future. I **will walk** to practice tomorrow.
Progressive	*Past progressive:* Actions that occurred over a period of time in the past and were interrupted by another action. I **was running** to practice when I pulled a calf muscle.	*Present Progressive:* Actions that occur over a period of time including the present moment. I **am running** to practice right now.	*Future Progressive:* Actions that will occur over a period of time in the future. I **will be running** to practice for about half an hour after school tomorrow.
Perfect	*Past perfect:* Actions that occurred before another event in the past. I **had run** to practice before I realized I left my cleats at home.	*Present perfect:* Actions that occurred in the past and include the present moment. I **have run** to practice every day since last year.	*Future perfect:* Actions that will occur in the future but before another event in the future. By the time practice begins, I **will have run** a mile and a half.

The context of the sentence will provide us with the details we need to determine the appropriate verb tense. For example:

> **Incorrect:** My brother wants to go to the park, but I was doing my homework.
> **Correct:** My brother **wanted** to go to the park, but I was doing my homework.
> **Correct:** My brother wants to go to the park, but I **am doing** my homework.

In the first sentence, the two verbs don't make logical sense. In the first clause, the verb is in the present tense; in the second clause, the verb is in the past progressive tense. The second sentence corrects this by bringing the first verb into the past; the third sentence corrects this by bringing the second sentence into the present. Remember to pay attention to context to be sure that verb tenses make sense with one another.

Verb Moods

A verb's mood can be indicative, imperative, or subjunctive. Let's review what each of these moods means:

Imperative: I **am going** to the park with my brother.
Imperative: Go to the park with your brother.
Subjunctive: I wish he **were going** to the park by himself.

The indicative mood is used for most writing. It indicates a statement of fact, opinion, or question. If a sentence's context doesn't suit one of the other moods, it should be in the indicative mood.

The imperative mood indicates an order to a command. The subject of the sentence is assumed to either be "you" or the person being addressed in the sentence.

The subjunctive mood can be the most difficult. This mood indicates a situation of unreality, such as a wish, hope, hypothetical situation, suggestion, or request. A common error with subjunctive mood involves *was* versus *were*. When a sentence expresses something that is not true, the verb should be *were* rather than *was*.

Answering Verb Error Questions

Here is a strategy to answer verb error questions:
1. If there is a verb in the underlined portion of the sentence, examine the rest of the sentence and the sentences immediately surrounding it for clues that suggest a verb tense or mood error.
2. Determine the appropriate verb tense based on the context of the sentence. Eliminate any answer choices that are in the wrong tense.
3. Determine the appropriate mood based on the context of the sentence. Eliminate any answer choices that are in the wrong mood.
4. Look for any other verb-related errors, such as subject-verb disagreement (for a quick review of subject-verb agreement, see lesson 10). Eliminate these answer choices.
5. Choose the answer that best suits the context of the sentence.

Pronoun Errors

Concept Introduction

There are two common pronouns errors that are frequently tested on the PSAT: agreement errors and ambiguity. Agreement errors occur when the pronoun does not agree with the antecedent (the noun to which the pronoun refers). Ambiguity occurs when it is unclear to whom or to what the pronoun refers.

Pronoun-Antecedent Agreement

Just as subjects and verbs must agree, so must pronouns and their antecedents. Pronouns and antecedents must agree in number and in person.

Agreement in number means that a singular antecedent gets a singular pronoun, and a plural antecedent gets a plural pronoun. This seems simple enough, but certain sentences can make spotting pronoun-antecedent agreement errors more difficult. For example:

> **Incorrect:** Each of the team members must undergo a physical; **they** must provide the coach with a signed form from the doctor.
> **Correct:** Each of the team members must undergo a physical; **he or she** must provide the coach with a signed form from the doctor.

One of the most common errors regarding agreement in number is the use of "they" as a gender-neutral singular pronoun. Remember that in proper writing -- the type tested on the PSAT -- "they" is a plural pronoun. In this example sentence, the pronoun is referring to "each of the team members," which is singular. As such, we must use the singular "he or she" rather than "they."

Agreement in person means that the pronoun needs to maintain the same point of view as the rest of the sentence. Here are the pronouns for each person:

	Pronouns
1st Person	I, we, me, us
2nd Person	You
3rd Person	He, she, it, one, they, him, her, them

The writer needs to maintain the same point of view throughout the sentence. These errors typically occur with the use of multiple pronouns. For example:

> **Incorrect:** When *you* take the PSAT, *one* should bring several pencils and a calculator.
> **Correct:** When *one takes* the PSAT, *one* should bring several pencils and a calculator.
> **Correct:** When *you* take the PSAT, *you* should bring several pencils and a calculator.

This represents one of the most common pronoun person errors -- the combination of "one" and "you." In this error, we have both the 3rd person and the 2nd person in the same sentence. To correct the error, both pronouns must either be in the 3rd person or in the 2nd person.

Pronoun Ambiguity

For a sentence to make sense, it's important that the reader be able to clearly understand to what each pronoun refers. An ambiguous pronoun happens when it's difficult to figure out the antecedent for a pronoun.

Pronoun ambiguity often occurs when a pronoun could refer to two different nouns in the sentence. For example:

> **Incorrect:** Brian and Greg loved *his* new video game.

Correct: Brian and Greg loved *Greg's* new video game.

In the incorrect sentence, we don't know who the video game belongs to -- Brian or Greg. The second sentence replaces the pronoun with a possessive noun, which clarifies the sentence.

Pronoun ambiguity is often common when the pronoun has no antecedent. This commonly occurs with the pronouns "they" and "it." For example:

Incorrect: *They* said the video game was the highest rated game to be released in the last five years.

Correct: *The salespeople* said the video game was the highest rated game to be released in the last five years.

In the first sentence, "they" has no antecedent. Who are they? The second sentence clarifies this by telling us who "they" are.

Answering Pronoun Error Questions

Here is a strategy to answer pronoun error questions:

1. If there is a pronoun in the underlined portion of the sentence, examine the sentence for pronoun errors.
2. Identify the pronoun and its antecedent. If the antecedent is unclear, then there is a pronoun ambiguity error. Eliminate any answer choices that fail to address this error by clarifying the pronoun reference.
3. If the antecedent is clear, check to be sure that the pronoun agrees with the antecedent in number and in person. Eliminate any answer choices that do not create agreement between the pronoun and the antecedent.
4. If there is more than one pronoun in the sentence, be sure the pronouns maintain the same point of view. Eliminate any answer choices that fail to maintain agreement in person.
5. Choose the answer that best suits the context of the sentence.

Parallelism and Modifier Errors

Concept Introduction

Some of the trickiest grammar errors to spot can be errors in parallelism and modifiers, yet these errors are fairly common throughout the PSAT writing section. Parallelism errors occur when similar elements of a sentence do not occur in the same form; for example, in a sentence that contains a list of actions, the verbs should all be in the same tense and mood in order for the sentence to be parallel. Modifier errors occur when a modifying phrase (usually an adjective or adverb) is out of place.

Parallelism Errors

There are three common issues that lead to parallelism errors: parts of sentences combined with coordinating conjunctions, items in a series, and comparisons. In all of these instances, pieces of a sentence need to be in the same form.

Although coordinating conjunctions are typically used to combine sentences, they can also be used to combine parts of sentences such as predicates. When this occurs, those parts of the sentence must be in the same form. For example:

>   **Incorrect:** I would prefer to take the train or driving.

>   **Correct:** I would prefer to take the train or **to drive**.

>   **Correct:** I would prefer **taking** the train or driving.

In the incorrect sentence, the verbs "to take the train" and "driving" are connected by the coordinating conjunction "or." These verbs are not in the same form. Both the second and third sentences solve this error by making the verbs follow the same form.

Items in a series must also appear in the same form. Let's look at an example:

>   **Incorrect:** When I couldn't find my homework, I looked in my backpack, my desk, and under the bed.

>   **Correct:** When I couldn't find my homework, I looked in my backpack, **in** my desk, and under the bed.

In the incorrect sentence, the items in a series don't match. Two of the items, "in my backpack" and "under the bed," are prepositional phrases; "my desk" is a noun. To solve the error, we simply make "my desk" into a prepositional phrase. The same error can occur with other parts of speech. For example:

>   **Incorrect:** For her birthday, she asked for a puppy, a new computer, and to go to the beach.

>   **Correct:** For her birthday, she asked for a puppy, a new computer, and **a trip** to the beach.

In the incorrect sentence, the first to items are nouns and the third item is a verb. To make the sentence parallel, we have to make that verb into a noun.

The final issue that commonly leads to parallelism errors is comparisons. When two or more items are compared, they must be in the same form in order to be parallel. For example:

>   **Incorrect:** I would rather be reading than watch television.

>   **Correct:** I would rather be reading than **watching** television.

>   **Correct:** I would rather **read** than watch television.

In the first sentence, the items being compared are both verbs, but they are in different forms. This is corrected in both the second and third sentences.

Answering Parallelism Error Questions

Here is a strategy to answer questions that include parallelism errors:

1. Identify which items should have parallel structure. Remember that items connected by coordinating conjunctions, items in a series, and items in comparisons need to be parallel.
2. If all of the items are contained in the underlined portion, eliminate any answer choices that contain more than one form or structure.
3. If one or more items are not in the underlined portion, these items will determine the correct form for the remaining item(s). Eliminate any answer choices that do not match that form.
4. Choose the answer that seems to best address the parallelism error. Reread the sentence with your chosen answer to ensure that you have not introduced a new parallelism error.

Modifier Errors

Modifier errors tend to take two forms: misplaced modifiers and dangling modifiers.

A misplaced modifier occurs when a modifying phrase is not placed near the object being modified. When this happens, sentences can become confusing. For example:

> **Incorrect:** Waving in a strong wind, we watched the trees bend and snap as the hurricane approached.

> **Correct:** We watched the trees, **which were waving in a strong wind,** bend and snap as the hurricane approached.

In the first sentence, the modifying phrase is "waving in a strong wind." As the sentence is originally written, the phrase seems to be modifying "we," but that makes very little sense. To correct the error, we need to decide which noun is being modified. If it isn't "we," it could be either "trees" or "hurricane." Since hurricanes typically create wind rather than wave in wind, we can assume the modifier should be modifying trees. To make this correction, we have to move the modifier so that it comes immediately before or after the object being modified.

Misplaced modifiers can change the entire meaning of the sentence. In fact, there are some very funny examples of misplaced modifiers. For instance:

> **Incorrect:** With his tail held high, my father led his prize poodle around the arena.

> **Correct:** My father led his prize poodle, whose tail was held high, around the arena.

In the first sentence, "with his tail held high" seems to be modifying "my father." My father (hopefully) doesn't have a tail, so this sentences is illogical. We can correct it by moving the modifier where it belongs, near "poodle."

A dangling modifier occurs when a modifying phrase is included in a sentence but the object being modified does not. For example:

> **Incorrect:** Driving like a maniac, the car was completely ruined.

> **Correct:** Driving like a maniac, **Mike completely ruined the car.**

In the first sentence, the modifier "driving like a maniac" seems to be modifying "the car." This is illogical since cars don't generally drive themselves like maniacs. To correct the error, we need to provide something for the modifying phrase to modify.

Answering Modifier Error Questions

Here is a strategy to answer modifier error questions:

1. Identify the modifier in the sentence.
2. Identify what the modifier is modifying as currently written and what it should be modifying. Based on this information, determine whether you have a misplaced modifier (not near enough to the item being modified) or a dangling modifier (the item being modified does not appear in the sentence).
3. If the error is a misplaced modifier, eliminate any answer choices that fail to place the modifier near the item that should be modified.
4. If the error is a dangling modifier, eliminate any answer choices that fail to introduce the object that should be modified or that fail to place that object near the modifier.
5. If more than one answer choice remains, examine the remaining answer choices for new errors (such as punctuation errors). Eliminate these answer choices.
6. Choose the answer that best suits the context of the sentence.

Other Errors

Concept Introduction

There are several other errors that could potentially appear on the PSAT. In this lesson, we'll focus on the two that are the most likely to be included in the PSAT writing section: subject-verb agreement and preposition errors.

Subject-Verb Agreement

Subject-verb agreement is, in principle, a simple concept: plural subjects get plural verbs, and singular subjects get singular verbs. The PSAT can complicate subject-verb agreement questions by utilizing sentences that contain several nouns that might be the subject. To help identify the correct subject and verb, which makes identifying and solving subject-verb agreement errors easier, follow these steps:

1. Cross out word groups contained inside commas.
2. Cross out prepositional phrases (phrases that start with prepositions like "to," "of," "on," "near," "for," or "like").
3. Cross out word groups from "either" to "or" (or from "neither" to "nor").
4. Identify the action taking place. This is the verb.
5. Identify who or what is performing the action. This is the subject.

Let's look at an example:

> One of the students, the girl with the ponytail, will stay in Mrs. Smith's class after school to review for the big test.

> 1. One of the students, ~~the girl with the ponytail,~~ will stay in Mrs. Smith's class after school to review for the big test.
>   *We can cross out the modifier contained inside commas.*
> 2. One ~~of the students~~ will stay ~~in Mrs. Smith's class after school to review for the big test.~~
>   *There are a lot of prepositional phrases in this sentence. All of these can be eliminated.*
> 3. One will stay.
>   *This sentence does not contain an either/or or neither/nor construction.*
> 4. One will stay.
>   *The action here is "will stay." This is the verb.*
> 5. One will stay.
>   *"One" is performing the action. This is the subject.*

In the example above, there were a lot of nouns or pronouns that could have been the subject: One, students, girl, ponytail, Mrs. Smith, class, school, and test. By following the steps, we were able to clearly identify the subject.

These steps help you to avoid the most common subject-verb agreement pitfalls. Let's look at some of those common errors.

> **Prepositional Phrases:** Each of the students are going on the field trip.

In this case, the sentence is functioning as if "students" were the subject. "Students" is the object of the prepositional phrase "of the students;" "each" is the subject. This makes spotting the subject-verb agreement error a bit easier. "Each are going..." is incorrect. To correct the error, we need to change "are" to "is."

> **Compound Subject Connected by "Or" or "Nor":** The students or the teacher are going to clean the classroom.

When a compound subject is connected by "or" or "nor," the subject closest to the verb determines whether the verb should be singular or plural. At first glance, the sentence above might seem correct, but in this case, it is "the teacher" that determines whether the verb should be singular or plural. As such, the verb should be "is going" instead of "are going" even though "the students" is plural.

> **Inverted Word Order:** Among the Botanical Gardens' flower beds hide a beautiful edible garden.

Most sentence follow a subject - verb - object word order. Sometimes a writer flips this word order around, as in the sentence above. By following the steps we outlined for finding subjects and verbs, we can avoid getting tricked by inverted word order. Using these steps on this sentence, you would find that the verb "hide" goes with the subject "garden." This creates a subject-verb agreement error; the verb should be the singular "hides."

Answering Subject-Verb Error Questions

Here is a strategy for addressing subject-verb error questions:

1. Identify the subject and the verb. If it is not immediately obvious, use the steps outlined in this lesson to eliminate unnecessary parts of the sentence.
2. Check to see if the subject and the verb agree.
3. If the subject and verb do not agree, eliminate any answer choices that fail to solve the problem.
4. Choose the answer that best suits the context of the sentence.
5. Check to be sure your chosen answer does not create new errors (such as verb tense errors).

Preposition Errors

Prepositions tell us when, where, and how things occurred. Because prepositions can achieve so many functions, there are a lot of nuances regarding different prepositions and their uses. This provides fertile ground for possible errors. Two common preposition errors include:

> **At, On, and In with Time:** We will plant a new garden at the springtime.

At, on, and in can all be used as part of prepositional phrases that indicate time. We use "at" to indicate a precise time, such as "at 5 pm." We use "on" to indicate a specific date, such as "on Monday." And we use "in" to indicate longer, more generalized times, such as months, seasons, years, or decades. By this rule, the sentence above should read "in the springtime" rather than "at the springtime" because "springtime" is a season.

> **At, On, and In with Place:** He stopped in the red light.

In addition to time, prepositional phrases containing at, on, or in can also indicate location. We usually use "at" to indicate a specific point or place, such as "at home" or "at the intersection." "On" usually indicates a surface, such as "on the wall." "In" usually indicates an enclosed space, such as "in the car." In the case of the sentence above, unless he was physically inside the light, the sentence should read "at the red light."

Other preposition errors tend to occur when a preposition is simply misused within the context of the sentence. To address these errors, you must know the most frequently used prepositions and their uses. These include (but are definitely not limited to):

Time		
Preposition	Use	Example
On	Specific dates/days	On Monday On my birthday On July 6th
In	Longer periods of times (seasons, months, years, etc.)	In June In the summer In the 1980s

At	Specific times	At night
		At 6 am
Since	From a certain time until now	Since last year
For	Over a certain period of time	For three years
Before	Earlier than a certain point in time	Before the test
		Before 1990
Until	When something will end	Until Monday
Place		
Preposition	Use	Example
In	An enclosed space	In *Huck Finn*
	A book or piece of art	In the taxi
At	Specific point or place	At the intersection
	An event	At the concert
	A place where you do a specific thing	At school
On	A surface	On the floor
	A certain side	On the left
	A floor in a building	On the second story
Under	Covered by something else	Under the carpet
Below	Lower than something else, but not necessarily covered	Below the sink
Above	Higher than something else, but not directly on it	Above the sink
To	Movement toward something	To New York
From	Movement from something	From New York
Towards	Movement in the direction of something but not directly to it	Towards the house
Other		
Preposition	Use	Examples
Of	Who/what it belongs to	A page of the book
	What it shows	The picture of the lake
By	Rising or falling or something	Prices fell by five percent
	Mode of travel	Traveled by car
About	Topic (of conversation, of a book, etc.)	We talked about him

Answering Preposition Error Questions

Here is a strategy to answer questions that include preposition errors:

1. If the underlined portion contains a preposition, look at the context of the sentence to see if the preposition used makes logical sense.
2. Eliminate any answer choices that use an inaccurate or incorrect preposition.
3. Choose the answer that best suits the context of the sentence.
4. Reread the sentence to be sure your chosen answer doesn't introduce any new errors.

Questions 1-10 are based on the following passage.

From Afar; An Indomitable Man, an Incurable Loneliness

To most Americans born prior to World War II, the passing of Richard Milhous Nixon seemed barely believable, despite the fact that he was 81 years old and had appeared frail during his most recent trip to Russia. For those born before the 1940s, he had played an **1** implausibly large – at times undesirable -- role in **2** they're lives as part of a public career that spanned almost 50 years after his election to Congress in 1946.

This obstinate political figure returned over and over again to prominence even after losses and a scandal that would have sent other politicians into permanent exile. **3** At the time of his death, he had fought hard to overcome the Watergate scandal that had forced him out of the White House in 1974 and **4** have managed to attain a relatively respected position as elder statesman, political analyst, author, and commentator. He had been such a familiar figure in American politics, so often in the midst of controversy, that it was unfathomable that the nation would not "have Nixon to kick around anymore."

1

All of the following words can be used here EXCEPT

A) astonishingly
B) remarkably
C) unbelievably
D) unexceptionally

2

A) NO CHANGE
B) there
C) their
D) its

3

The author is considering placing the following sentence at this point:

Nixon was given the nickname "Tricky Dick" by his election opponents for his campaign tactics.

Should the author make this addition?

A) Yes, because it gives insight on how Nixon is perceived by his colleagues.
B) Yes, because it provides an idea that supports the main idea of the paragraph.
C) No, because the information is not relevant.
D) No, because the information does not support the ideas presented in the paragraph.

4

A) NO CHANGE
B) had managed
C) having managed
D) has managed

That infamous statement, aimed at the press with which he so frequently battled, was the departure line in a self-proclaimed "last press conference" after his loss in the race for governor of California in 1962. That setback was only two years after Nixon had lost to John F. Kennedy in one of the most famous, and the closest, Presidential elections of the modern era.

5 Despite those devastating upsets, he was elected as the 37th President of the United States in 1968 in yet another nail-biter. Four years later, Richard M. Nixon secured a second term in one of the largest landslides ever recorded.

At the time, America's youth born after 1972 likely thought of Nixon primarily as the first President forced to resign the nation's highest office. Richard Nixon's distinctive—even comical—features and mannerisms, **6** such as his jowly, beard-shadowed face, with the ski-jump nose and the widow's peak, and the arms extended displaying the peace sign, made him a prime subject for caricatures. Those depictions are true and perhaps **7** fair enough, but they ignores so much about the only American other than Franklin D. Roosevelt to have been nominated on five national tickets, to run for President or Vice President.

5

To best transition from the first part of the essay to the second, which of the following should be inserted here?

A) NO CHANGE

B) Nonetheless,

C) Therefore,

D) However,

6

A) NO CHANGE

B) such as: his

C) such as, his

D) such as – his

7

Which of the following would be the most precise word choice to replace the underlined word?

A) NO CHANGE

B) candid

C) adequate

D) decent

8 To characterize Richard Nixon only as a President forced to resign would say little about a career and a character steeped in controversy long before Watergate. He was a tough and ruthless competitor who seldom hesitated to cut corners or engage in questionable tactics, and many opponents never forgave what they regarded as his smears and trickery.

Nixon was a rare case of a lonely **9** introvert who successfully made his way to the pinnacle of the extroverted world of politics. The assiduous effort to do so -- to persuade the public that a shy and reserved man was an amiable backslapper -- **10** must have to come at a price psychologically; he was left with an enduring mistrust that he never permitted Americans to see the "real Nixon."

8

Which of the following, if added here, would best identify the main idea of the paragraph?

A) NO CHANGE

B) Nixon was undoubtedly one of the most disliked politicians in history.

C) His contributions as president and politician will always be marred by his public scandals.

D) Nixon's attitude towards others affected the policies he was able to implement.

9

A) NO CHANGE

B) introvert, which successfully

C) introvert that successfully

D) introvert who's success

10

A) NO CHANGE

B) would have come

C) must have come

D) must come

Questions 11-21 are based on the following passage.

Dark Matter

[1] In high school, students are taught that the universe is made of atoms and molecules, **11** protons and electrons and stars and galaxies, and so forth. [2] Many students learn this in physics class, while others learn the information in chemistry or astronomy. [3] However, astronomers have unhappily concluded over the last few decades that all of this is just a thin backdrop overlying a boundless shadowy domain of invisible "dark matter" whose gravity rules the composition of the cosmos. [4] Dark matter is essentially an enigmatic something that occupies a quarter of the universe and holds galaxies together. **12**

Scientists now have **13** the Alpha Magnetic Spectrometer a device that may be able to prove that the mysterious signals previously recorded by satellites and balloons are effusions from the dark matter. This evidence would **14** let slip whether particles and forces that have only been theoretical dreams are actually a reality.

11

Which choice most closely matches the stylistic pattern established earlier in the sentence?

A) NO CHANGE

B) protons, electrons, stars, galaxies,

C) protons and electrons, stars and galaxies,

D) protons or electrons, or stars and galaxies

12

To make this paragraph most logical, sentence 2 should be placed where?

A) NO CHANGE

B) After sentence 3.

C) After sentence 4.

D) It should be deleted from the paragraph.

13

A) NO CHANGE

B) the Alpha Magnetic Spectrometer –

C) the Alpha Magnetic Spectrometer; however

D) the Alpha, Magnetic Spectrometer

14

A) NO CHANGE

B) reveal

C) blurt out

D) leak

Prior to the creation of the Alpha Magnetic Spectrometer, Pamela, a European satellite, recorded a surplus of [15] anti-electrons or positrons, in space. This surplus could have potentially been caused by collisions of dark matter particles. [16] However, the satellite had no idea how to differentiate the positrons, which are rare, from protons, which are commonly found the nuclei of hydrogen and everywhere. [17] The Alpha spectrometer can make the distinction. It is one of the most ambitious and complex experiments ever to set out for space; an eight-ton assemblage of wires, magnets, aluminum, iron, silicon, and electronics. [18] This piece of equipment pales in the comparison of size and is in fact a miniature version of the cathedral-sized particle detectors that now line the Large Hadron Collider.

15

A) NO CHANGE

B) anti-electrons; or positrons

C) anti-electrons or positrons

D) anti-electrons, or positrons

16

A) NO CHANGE

B) Although

C) Additionally

D) Moreover

17

At this point, the author of the passage is considering starting a new paragraph with this sentence. Should he do it?

A) Yes, because the passage moves on from discussing the problem to discussing the solution.

B) Yes, because the material that precedes this sentence needs to the material that follows to make sense.

C) No, because the material following the sentence is too short to need its own paragraph.

D) No, because the tone of the entire paragraph is consistent.

18

A) NO CHANGE

B) This piece of equipment is a miniature version of the cathedral sized particle detectors that now line the Large Hadron Collider.

C) This small piece of equipment is a miniature version of the gargantuan, cathedral-sized particle detectors that now line the Large Hadron Collider.

D) This piece of equipment pales in size next to the gargantuan, cathedral-sized particle detectors that now line the large Hadron Collider.

The Alpha spectrometer is designed to comb through the high-energy particles hurtling through space known as cosmic rays. The space shuttle Endeavor is scheduled to transport the spectrometer to a permanent dock on the space station in February 2011. However, **19** it's real destination is the shadow universe.

20 Knowing the nature of dark matter and what it is made of could be useful someday in ways that people cannot even imagine. Curved spacetime, one of Einstein's many theories, was a theory that was just as indefinable as dark matter, but eventually proved critical to the function of GPS devices that were invented decades after Einstein's death.

Positrons from dark matter have been speculated to have a unique spectral signature by some physicists. These signatures should be picked up and measured by the cosmic ray spectrometer. The scientific community may be able to fully embrace dark matter if the signal follows the model.

Other scientists are more skeptical, stating that it would be difficult, if not impossible, to differentiate the dark matter signal from the background noise of pulsars and black holes. Many physicists go as far as stating that they will not be mollified that dark matter **21** exists or have been found until there is proof from particle accelerators and underground experiments that seek to detect the particles directly.

19

A) NO CHANGE

B) its

C) its'

D) their

20

Which sentence provides the best transition to the rest of the passage?

A) NO CHANGE

B) Another theory that previously stumped scientists was eventually solved by noted physicist Albert Einstein.

C) Perhaps one day, dark matter might be used to power a new form of Global Positioning System, or GPS.

D) When scientists work on new and exciting theories, they could be affecting outcomes that happen years in the future.

21

A) NO CHANGE

B) exists or has been found

C) exist or has been found

D) exist or have been found

Questions 22-32 are based on the following passage.

Gandhi and Civil Disobedience

Mohandas K. Gandhi was born in 1869 to a Hindu merchant family. His mother was deeply religious and influenced him through the ways of Hinduism and Jainism. **22**

Gandhi studied in England to be a lawyer in the late 1880s. He found himself stationed in South Africa for his first job. South Africa was **23** shaped with discrimination against all people of color. During this time, Gandhi faced a life changing moment when he faced true **24** discrimination. He was forced off of a train by police for refusing to ride in third-class coach when he had purchased a first-class ticket.

[1] South Africa's discrimination policies were growing with injustice; a new law required all Indians in South Africa to register with the police and also provide fingerprints. [2] Gandhi, alongside many Indians, rebuffed the law and did not comply. [3] This was the first of many instances in which Gandhi was jailed. [4] Does spending time in jail make someone a bad person, or can jail teach a valuable lesson? **25**

22

The author is considering replacing the period with a comma and adding the following information here:

pressing the beliefs in fasting for purification, non-violence, and respect for all religions.

Should the author make this change?

A) Yes, because the information gives a truthful description of these religions.

B) Yes, because the information helps the readers understand the origin of some of Gandhi's beliefs.

C) No, because the information is irrelevant to the rest of the passage.

D) No, because the information is not an accurate description of Gandhi's belief system.

23

A) NO CHANGE

B) wrought

C) fashioned

D) molded

24

Which choice most effectively combines the sentences at the underlined portion?

A) NO CHANGE

B) discrimination, he

C) discrimination and he

D) discrimination - he

25

For the sake of unity and cohesion of the passage, sentence 4 should be placed where?

A) NO CHANGE

B) After sentence 1.

C) After sentence 2.

D) Delete it from the paragraph.

Gandhi read Henry David Thoreau's "Civil Disobedience" while in **26** jail, and adopted the term "civil disobedience" to define his way to non-violently being uncooperative with injustice. After his release, he continued his protest of the registration law, becoming the spearhead of many labor strikes and massive non-violent marches. Ultimately, the government cut out the most objectionable parts of the law.

Gandhi spent 20 years in South Africa and returned to India in 1914, where he was met with fanfare and hero-status. Gandhi spent the rest of his life battling what he saw as the three great evils tormenting **27** India: British rule, the terrible relations between Hindus and Muslims, and the Hindu caste system which labeled millions of Indians as "untouchables."

After World War I, Gandhi **28** called out the British for acts of peaceful civil disobedience when Britain did not grant India its independence. Some protests were met with British violence, while in other instances, Indians started rioting. Gandhi maintained that he would only lead a non-violent movement and would cancel protests to demand peaceful order.

After India gained independence, Gandhi faced the next of the three evils – how Hindus and Muslims would share power. In the midst of distrust and violence, he continued to preach peace and forgiveness and opposed dividing the country into two nations. **29** Ruling political leaders agreed in May 1947 to a Hindu-dominated India and a separate

26

A) NO CHANGE
B) jail adopting
C) jail and adopted
D) jail, after which he began adopting

27

A) NO CHANGE
B) India - British
C) India, British
D) India; British

28

A) NO CHANGE
B) called for acts of peaceful civil disobedience when
C) called out the British for peaceful and civil acts of disobedience when
D) called out to the British for civil, yet peaceful, acts of disobedience when

29

A) NO CHANGE
B) However, ruling
C) Fortunately, ruling
D) Although, ruling

Muslim Pakistan. Within months, Hindu and Muslim looting, murder, and violence **30** heightened throughout the country, causing many to flee.

Gandhi pledged to fast until "a reunion of hearts of all communities" had been attained. His health weakened rapidly in his old age, but he **31** holds strong until Hindu and Muslim leaders came pledging peace. A few days later, a Hindu assassin killed Gandhi, believing that Gandhi had sold out to the Muslims.

32 Gandhi confronted injustice with non-violent methods. "It is the acid test of non-violence," Gandhi once said, "that in a non-violent conflict, there is no rancor left behind and, in the end, the enemies are converted into friends."

30

A) NO CHANGE
B) accelerated
C) excited
D) excavated

31

A) NO CHANGE
B) held strongly
C) holds strongly
D) held strong

32

Which choice most strongly starts the concluding passage with a restatement of one of the author's claims?

A) NO CHANGE
B) Gandhi remained a religious man until his death.
C) Occasionally, Gandhi allowed violent protest if it obtained the desired results.
D) Gandhi led a full life and traveled to many different countries in his work.

Waiting for the Bomb to Drop

33 <u>My mother was born in Hawaii in 1941.</u> Hardly two months old, she spent the attack in the grasp of her fearful mother in an makeshift bomb shelter, where the two of them had joined 34 <u>there</u> Honolulu neighbors. My grandmother, however, 35 <u>vividly and powerfully remembered the intensely powerful events of that day the rest of her life:</u> the sound of the planes, the screaming of the alarms, and the feelings of panic. Most of all, she recalled the paralyzing uncertainty she felt, waiting in the dark and questioning whether the subsequent explosion would take her life or her baby's.

Forty years later, she recounted the story to me, her 11-year-old panic-stricken grandson. I had just discovered that Soviet ICBMs, or intercontinental ballistic missiles, could discharge nuclear weapons to objectives in the United States, including the military town 36 <u>at which I lived.</u> In relaying her memories of Pearl Harbor, my grandmother intended to soothe my fears.

33

The writer wants to include an introductory sentence to set the stage for the rest of the passage. Which of the following best serves this purpose?

A) NO CHANGE

B) My mother doesn't recall Pearl Harbor even though she was there.

C) I remember the stories my mother would tell me when I was a young child.

D) Pearl Harbor was one of the frightening times in history for Hawaiians.

34

A) NO CHANGE

B) their

C) they're

D) her

35

A) NO CHANGE

B) vividly and powerfully remembered the events of that day the rest of her life.

C) vividly and powerfully remembered and reminisced about the events of that day the rest of her life.

D) vividly remembered the events of that day the rest of her life.

36

A) NO CHANGE

B) at which I was living

C) where I lived

D) that I lived

37 Nevertheless, my mind fused her account of Pearl Harbor with my trepidation of nuclear weapons. After all, my country had deployed nuclear weapons against the citizens of Japan, the country from which my grandfather's family had emigrated. **38** As long as these weapons are in existence, I thought, we are all essentially down in that shelter, in eternal suspense.

[1] As I got further into my teenage years, normal occurrences could make nuclear war seem unavoidable. [2] Abrupt disruptions in TV or radio programs, especially tests of the Emergency Broadcast System, left my heart in my throat. [3] Since then, I've spoken with numerous children of the Cold War era on both sides of the Iron Curtain who were similarly certain that nuclear weapons would end their lives prematurely. [4]When a low-flying plane went over, I anxiously awaited the blinding blaze of a detonating warhead. [5] I eventually discovered that I wasn't alone. **39**

Luckily, nuclear war didn't **40** transpire, or hasn't as of yet. Few American civilians have personally witnessed aerial assaults. Though we may fear terrorist attacks, we are less concerned about death raining from the skies. However, civilians in other countries have felt an increase of that anxiety due to policies carried out by our country. In every country where United States drones regularly operate, civilians are subjected to the full assortment of the

37

A) NO CHANGE

B) Therefore,

C) In spite,

D) After awhile,

38

The author of the passage is considering adding the following sentence at this point:

That information rendered reassurances useless.

Should he make this change?

A) Yes, it gives information to the reader about why the author is still scared of the weapons; despite being told not to worry.

B) Yes, the information afterwards is irrelevant and confusing without this sentence included.

C) No, the information adds nothing to the passage and should be left out.

D) No, the information is different in tone from that of the rest of the passage and does not fit the passages' topic.

39

For the logic and clarity of the paragraph, sentence 3 should be placed where?

A) NO CHANGE

B) Before sentence 1.

C) After sentence 2.

D) After sentence 5.

40

A) NO CHANGE

B) emerge

C) come to light

D) leak out

41 weapons outcomes. **42** When a strike happens, civilians are frequently among the dead. If they live, they may endure physical harm, property or job loss, and the emotional trauma of witnessing the death of those close to them. In addition, the survivors and witnesses of drone strikes often demonstrate symptoms of post-traumatic stress disorder, or PTSD.

For those on the ground, drone flyovers are a heinous fusion of air raids and the terror of the Cold War. In essence, the suspense and uncertainty my grandmother **43** remembered is prolonged over weeks, months, even years. Like the threat of nuclear weapons, drones turn the possibility of death from above into a circumstance of daily life.

41

A) NO CHANGE

B) weapon's outcomes

C) weapons' outcomes

D) weapons's outcomes

42

The author of the passage is considering starting a new paragraph at this point. Should he do so?

A) Yes, because it moves on from talking about weapons to talking about how to use those weapons.

B) Yes, because the paragraph is too long to stay focused on one topic

C) No, because it is giving the natural result of what happens in the previous sentence.

D) No, because the tone of the material after the point is identical to the tone of the material before the point.

43

A) NO CHANGE

B) remembered are

C) was remembering is

D) was remembering are

Questions 44-53 are based on the following passage.

Stuck at the Airport? Why Not Take in an Art Exhibit

Airports are naturally hectic and chaotic spaces, filled with planes **44** contending for runway space as passengers mull about from terminal to terminal. In a space of unending motion, it is easy to disregard the space you are in and focus more on the **45** destination, but as more airports integrate art into their terminals, it is now possible to stop and enjoy the view before departing on a jet.

46 "Art can make a space feel more human," says Laura Greene of Heathrow Airport's award-winning T5 Gallery. "It can evoke emotions and provide something that is often overlooked in large spaces such as airports."

Art has been integrated into some airports that have dedicated permanent space for exhibits. Although the Denver International Airport's public art displays may not be on the top of the list for many travelers, **47** but it has been deemed one of the most acclaimed public displays in the country. This airport is **48** so well renowned and known for its public art that it offers a walking tour for people who are not flying, featuring the airport's permanent and temporary exhibits.

44

Which of the following words could be used most precisely to replace the underlined word?

A) NO CHANGE

B) litigating

C) vying

D) striving

45

A) NO CHANGE

B) destination. But as

C) destination. However,

D) destination. Therefore,

46

The author is considering removing or moving this entire paragraph from the passage. How should the author proceed?

A) The paragraph is fine where it is.

B) The paragraph should be moved and placed before the fourth paragraph.

C) The paragraph should be integrated into the end of the first paragraph.

D) The paragraph should be removed from the passage altogether.

47

A) NO CHANGE

B) but has been deemed

C) it has been deemed

D) it is deemed

48

A) NO CHANGE

B) so renowned

C) so well renowned

D) well renowned and known

London's Heathrow airport has an entire commercial art gallery, T5, from which passengers can purchase pieces of art. T5 emphasizes exhibiting work from both professional and amateur artists. Throughout the year, the gallery showcases groups of **49** exhibits; ranging from a wood sculptures of animals to pastel paintings

Creating art programs **50** have become as important as an array of other customer service features to some airports. "The art program does help to provide meaningful things for passengers to do when they have layovers and when they get to the airport early," says David Vogt, airport art program manager at Atlanta's Hartsfield-Jackson International airport. **51** But these art programs offer much more. They offer passengers an opportunity to explore the city while remaining inside the airport's terminals. "This may be some passengers' only experience of Atlanta," Vogt says. "[The art] helps to tell the story of who we are." Hartsfield-Jackson has a permanent exhibit titled "A Walk Through Atlanta's History". **52** This exhibit depicts the history of Atlanta, ranging from thousands of years ago - during the time it was settled by native people – to present day history.

49

A) NO CHANGE

B) exhibits – ranging

C) exhibits that are ranging

D) exhibits, which are ranging

50

A) NO CHANGE

B) was becoming

C) has became

D) has become

51

The author is considering creating a new paragraph at this sentence. Should the author make the change?

A) No, because it further discusses the ideas presented at the beginning of the paragraph.

B) No, because the beginning of the paragraph is not long enough to stand alone as a paragraph.

C) Yes, because it is a supporting example for the theme presented in the beginning of the paragraph.

D) Yes, because the whole paragraph is too long to sustain the focus of the main topic of the paragraph.

52

At this point, the author wants to add this sentence to the end of the previous sentence. Which of the following best combines the two sentences?

A) NO CHANGE

B) History," which depicts the history of Atlanta, ranging from thousands of years ago – during the time it was settled by native people – to present day history.

C) History;" This exhibit depicts the history of Atlanta, ranging from thousands of years ago- during the time it was settled by native people- to present day history.

D) History": which depicts the history of Atlanta, ranging from thousands of years ago to present day history.

Whether it's an elegantly-suspended mobile or a world-class museum, remember to keep your eyes open when traveling. **53**

The author is considering altering the ending the passage with the following sentence:

traveling—a lengthy layover or missed flight might be the perfect excuse to take in an art show.

Should the author make the change?

A) Yes, because the original conclusion is too concise and short to be considered a conclusion.

B) Yes, because this ending neatly sums up the main focus of the entire passage

C) No, because it is an unnecessary addition to the sentence.

D) No, the conclusion is fine the way it is.

In Hawaii, Old Buses Are Being Turned Into Homeless Shelters

54 One thing you may not know about the 50th state is that it has one of the highest rates of homelessness in America. **55** In fact, the number of homeless in Hawaii per 100,000 people is almost twice as high as the national average. High rents, displacement from development, and income inequality **56** has resulted in approximately 7,000 people in Hawaii without a roof over their heads.

Now, architects at the Honolulu-based firm Group 70 International have developed an innovative solution to the homelessness **57** problem. The group wants to turn a fleet of retired city buses into temporary mobile shelters.

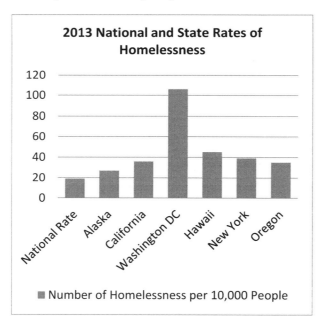

2013 National and State Rates of Homelessness

■ Number of Homelessness per 10,000 People

54

Which of the following sentences, if inserted here, provides the best introduction to the passage?

A) The thought of Hawaii usually brings to mind surfers, shaved ice, and sleek beach resorts.

B) Hawaii is a state of both vacationers and the homeless, much to the embarrassment of some of its residents.

C) Hawaii is one of the most expensive states in the United States of America according to recent economic trends.

D) Few U.S. states have more poor people than Hawaii does.

55

A) NO CHANGE

B) In fact, there are more homeless people in Hawaii than in any place in America.

C) In fact, the number of homeless in Hawaii per 100,000 people is over twice as high as the national average.

D) In fact, there are more homeless people in Hawaii than in any other state in America.

56

A) NO CHANGE

B) have resulted

C) have been resulting

D) has been resulting

57

Which of the following is the best way to combine the two sentences at this point?

A) problem: turn

B) problem, the group wants to turn

C) problem; because the group wants to turn

D) problem, so the group wants to turn

[1] The buses are still **58** efficient, but cannot be used by the city of Honolulu due to their high mileage. [2] The architects expect to be able to rework them into a multiplicity of spaces to assist the homeless populace. [3] Some buses will be sleeping accommodations, with folding origami-inspired beds that can be hidden when being used. [4] The buses will be utilized on the island of Oahu where they are most necessary. [5] Others will be equipped with showers to assist the homeless population with their hygiene needs. [6] The whole initiative depends on donated resources, including the buses and volunteer manpower. [7] U.S. Navy service members have volunteered, as have local builders and volunteers for Habitat for Humanity. [8] The first two buses are slated to be ready by summer's end. **59**

Architect Ma Ry Kim and **60** her friend Jun Yang, executive director of Honolulu's Office of Housing, devised the idea after attending a discouraging assembly of Hawaii's legislature. Although the issue of homelessness was deliberated, few solutions were proposed.

The initiative arose from a recent debate about new laws inhibiting the homeless from sleeping in public. Advocates say the laws, which make sitting or sleeping on Waikiki sidewalks illegal, are an empathetic method of relocating the homeless from the streets into shelters. Opponents say the laws are simply criminalizing vagrancy and making life tougher for Hawaii's most destitute populace in order to ensure vacationers feel **61** most comfortable.

58

A) NO CHANGE
B) handy
C) purposeful
D) functional

59

For the logic and cohesion of the paragraph, sentence 5 should be placed where?

A) After sentence 2.
B) After sentence 3.
C) After sentence 5.
D) The sentence should be deleted

60

A) NO CHANGE
B) her friend, Jun Yang executive director of Honolulu's Office of Housing,
C) her friend, Jun yang, executive director of Honolulu's Office of Housing,
D) her friend, Jun Yang executive director of Honolulu's Office of Housing,

61

A) NO CHANGE
B) most comforting
C) more comforting
D) more comfortable

The requirements of the homeless **62** varies. Though **63** a small portion of the homeless are habitually adrift, most are individuals facing tough transitions—losing a house to foreclosure, escaping domestic violence, being dislocated by natural disaster. Progressively, designers and architects are attempting to satisfy these needs through innovative design-based solutions.

But transitory shelters are still unable to resolve the conundrum of chronic homelessness. It's gradually thought that merely giving homeless people homes—a philosophy called Housing First—is more successful than trying to solve the underlying reasons for homelessness as they're still living in shelters. Housing First is also budget friendly, since people with homes end up requiring less public support and are less prone to end up in prisons or emergency rooms. **64**

62

A) NO CHANGE

B) vary

C) is varying

D) will vary

63

A) NO CHANGE

B) a small region of the homeless people of Hawaii are habitually adrift, never settling in one place, most are individuals facing tough transitions.

C) a small portion of the homeless never stay in one place for too long a period of time, most are individuals facing tough transitions.

D) a small portion of the homeless are wandering aimlessly from location to location, most are individuals facing tough transitions.

64

Which of the following sentences, if inserted here, best concludes the passage?

A) Nevertheless, the fact remains that with homelessness on the upsurge in America, we'll surely be in need of more innovative solutions, whether tiny, rolling, or otherwise.

B) Maybe all cities should commandeer their busses and turn them into rolling towns for the homeless.

C) The homeless in every city need our help; when possible, you should offer food, drink, or any other help they require.

D) If people don't start banding together to affect a change, soon Hawaii will become the U.S. state with the most homeless people.

Questions 65-75 are based on the following passage.
The Makeup Tax

65 There is no such thing as a "makeup tax". Women spend a lot of time and money doing their makeup and emphasizing their physical attributes **66** because it affects not only their relationships, but also their paychecks. While both men and women invest in things like haircuts, shaving cream, and moisturizer, men generally are not concerned with the price of makeup.

Studies show that the average woman will spend about $15,000 on makeup in her lifetime. **67** As a collective, the cosmetics industry generates about $60 billion a year. Not only does makeup cost money, but also time. If a **68** women's makeup routine ranges from ten minutes to an hour, she could be spending up to two full weeks a year on makeup alone.

65

Which of the following provides the most compelling introduction to the passage?

A) NO CHANGE

B) For most women, the "makeup tax" is a very real issue.

C) The "makeup tax" is something that only women are forced to pay.

D) Life charges a "makeup tax" on all women.

66

A) NO CHANGE

B) because its affects

C) because it effects

D) because it's affects

67

At this point, the author is considering inserting the following sentence:

Obviously men aren't spending this kind of money on their own grooming products.

Should the author make this change?

A) Yes, because it adds a little humor to a more serious paragraph.

B) Yes, because it supports the statements from the introduction paragraph.

C) No, because the information is redundant from the first paragraph and irrelevant to the second.

D) No, because it is not statement supported by evidence in the passage.

68

A) NO CHANGE

B) womens'

C) womans'

D) woman's

I'll pause now to address the most common response to this issue: "Just don't wear makeup!" For women, showing up to work or a social event without some blush, shadow, mascara, or lipstick could result in a **69** hailstorm of questions regarding our health or sleeping patterns. What it comes down to is the "just free yourself from makeup!" crowd, mostly men, have no idea how women look without the makeup.

So why wear makeup? **70** Makeup enhances facial contrast to your facial features to create the color distinctions in your face between your skin tone, lips, nose, and eyes. These traits are mostly associated with femininity. In a 2014 study, male and female participants agreed that women look best with a moderate amount of **71** makeup. Another study found that women seem more competent, likable, and attractive with subtle makeup.

[1] According to the polls given as part of these studies, the truth is that most women wear some sort of makeup, some of the time. [2]Although the accuracy of these polls may be biased – since they are generally sponsored by beauty related companies – they show that approximately 50 to 80 percent of women use makeup at least occasionally. [3]More notably, women that are paraded in front of us, intentionally and unintentionally, are all wearing some makeup: Our moms, actresses, and school teachers. [4] The media is covered with tips on how to "look flawless", imbedding in female minds that this is what women must look like: perfect skin, dark eyes, and shiny lips. **72**

69

Which of the following most accurately replaces the underlined portion?

A) sleet

B) pelting

C) barrage

D) drizzle

70

A) NO CHANGE

B) Makeup enhances facial contrast to create the color distinctions between your skin tone, lips, nose, and eyes.

C) Makeup enhances the contrast in your face like your skin tone, lips, nose, and eyes.

D) Facial contrast is caused by makeup creating color distinctions between the facial features that are your skin tone, lips, nose, and eyes.

71

Which of the following is the best way to combine these two sentences at this point?

A) NO CHANGE

B) makeup; whereas,

C) makeup - whereas,

D) makeup, whereas

72

Which of these sentences identifies the main idea of the paragraph?

A) Sentence 1.

B) Sentence 2.

C) Sentence 3.

D) Sentence 4.

73 It is hard for men to relate to the idea of how women feel being without makeup when they normally wear makeup and men do not wear it at all. One good analogy is being forced to wear a dirty, wrinkled, or stained shirt to a meeting. It may be ok to run errands in a shirt with a little mustard stain on the front, but if a man were to show up to an important business meeting with a glaring red or yellow stain on **74** their otherwise clean white shirt, and forced to present in front of the 'hard to impress' boss, he'd probably feel super uncomfortable and self-conscious. That's how many women feel without their makeup essentials.

75 All of these factors correlate to years of research, that concludes: attractive people get paid higher wages. Thus, the makeup tax: Good-looking men and women both excel, but men don't need makeup to look good.

73

A) NO CHANGE

B) It is hard for men to relate to the idea of how it feels for a woman who normally wears makeup to not wear any.

C) It's hard for men, who never wear makeup, to relate to the feelings of not wearing makeup that a woman might have when she normally wears makeup.

D) Men find it hard to relate to women's hatred of makeup when they themselves do not wear makeup at all.

74

A) NO CHANGE

B) they're

C) his

D) there

75

A) NO CHANGE

B) All of these factors correlate to years of research, that concludes, that attractive people get paid higher wages.

C) All of these factors correlate to years of research which concludes that: attractive people get paid higher wages.

D) All of these factors correlate to years of research that concludes that attractive people get paid higher wages.

Taxidermy

76 She does regular commission work—similar to what she is working on currently, preparing roosters for the display at a Los Angeles floral boutique. Markham also provides taxidermy courses on nights and weekends at Prey, her taxidermy shop, and volunteers in her free time at the Natural History Museum of Los Angeles, **77** where she used to spend much of her time hard at work.

Markham is part of a contemporary resurgence in the practice of taxidermy. At 32, she is a prosperous and **78** notorious representative of the new group of taxidermists, who are predominantly young, educated females. In May, Markham participated in the World Taxidermy & Fish Carving Championship, or the WTC, in Springfield, Missouri. With over 1,200 attendees, this year's WTC was bigger than it has ever been. Approximately 20 percent **79** of them at the event were women. Markham and ten of her female students submitted work at WTC that caused a stir at the three-decade-old tournament. Their attendance was met with enthusiasm, esteem, and optimism.

Taxidermy originated in Europe in the 16th and 17th centuries as a way of conserving **80** specimen's brought back by explorers. In most cases, these specimens became a component of a wealthy collector's "cabinet of curiosities," meant to provoke a sense of wonder and mystery in observers who knew very little of the distant regions of the world. By the late 19th century, taxidermy was so widespread in both America and England that there was a taxidermist in nearly

---

76

Which of the following sentences makes the most effective introduction to the passage?

A) Although taxidermy was once a dying art, Allis Markham is trying to change this fact.

B) Allis Markham has more jobs than she knows what to do with.

C) Allis Markham, if she keeps things up, could one day become one of the most popular taxidermists in America, if not the world.

D) Allis Markham is an extremely busy taxidermist.

77

A) NO CHANGE

B) where she used to work

C) where she used to work hard for her employer

D) where she previously worked for the benefit of others, as well as herself

78

A) NO CHANGE

B) tarnished

C) infamous

D) renowned

79

A) NO CHANGE

B) of these

C) of those

D) of which

80

A) NO CHANGE

B) specimen'

C) specimens

D) specimens'

every town. Frequently, **81** there was multiple, all competing for clients.

[1] After the end of the Great War, the practice of taxidermy began to decline due to multiple factors, but primarily the demand dissolved as new technologies were developed. [2] By the turn of the 20th century, the rise of amateur photography, thanks to George Eastman and his Brownie camera, meant that mantles once decorated with colorful taxidermy birds were now decorated **82** more cheaply with photographs. [3] Photography brought on the development of birding guides, which added to the taxidermy's diminishing popularity. [4] Lastly, big game hunting was no longer as socially acceptable following the end of World War II. **83**

81

A) NO CHANGE
B) there were
C) there are
D) there is

82

A) NO CHANGE
B) cheaper
C) cheapest
D) most cheaply

83

The author of the passage wants to add the following sentence to the passage:

Moreover, most of the large American museums – such as the Field Museum in Chicago and the American Museum of Natural History in New York – had already completed their elaborate habitat dioramas by the 1940s.

Where is the best place for this sentence?

A) Before sentence 1.
B) After sentence 1.
C) After sentence 2.
D) After sentence 3.

Still, taxidermy did not fully die off. Modern times have seen taxidermy resurge as contemporary practitioners view it as a hip and trendy art form, with everybody striving to discover new means to **84** stand out. Taxidermy also has scientific uses, such as restoring **85** museum exhibits or extracting DNA from the preserved bodies of long-lost or endangered species. The focus of modern taxidermy is to balance the art and science. While each creation may be viewed as art by the taxidermist, there is a scientific necessity to keep the work anatomically correct and an ethical necessity to ensure the specimens do not die specifically for the purposes of taxidermy. **86** Thus, the practice of taxidermy is still very much alive and kicking.

84

A) NO CHANGE

B) show up

C) bulge out

D) be proud of

85

A) NO CHANGE

B) museum exhibits or the extraction of DNA

C) or extracting museum exhibits or DNA

D) or extracting museum exhibits and DNA

86

The author of the passage wants to conclude the passage with a sentence that captures the irony of the passage's contents. Does this sentence succeed?

A) No, because the practice of taxidermy promotes cruelty to animals.

B) No, because the taxidermists do not actually kill the animals they work on.

C) Yes, because the practice of taxidermy involves dead animals, which cannot be alive or kicking.

D) Yes, because most animals kick before they die at the hands of taxidermists.

Questions 87-97 are based on the following passage.
America is Even Less Socially Mobile Than Most Economists Thought

Sociologists and economists are glad to see that <u>87 there decades'</u> worth of work on inequality and social mobility is finally in the spotlight in the eyes of the average American. However, the saturation of this message in the media leads to people taking the findings for granted, which can sometimes <u>88 cloud</u> what is true of any data-based work: Researchers are constantly learning new things, always trying to better map the degree of a phenomenon.

A recent Pew report alerts us of things about American social mobility that are <u>89 new and also</u> very familiar. Many reports have recognized the effects and correlations between parents' income and the potential financial success of their children. But this report suggests that the effects are higher than previously estimated. "One might think we'd have nailed it by now, but there was some uncertainty," says David Grusky, director of Stanford's Center on Poverty and Inequality and an author of the report. **90** Grusky and Pablo Mitnik, his co-author and colleague, have been using new data sets provided by the IRS to demonstrate that approximately half of parental income advantages are passed onto the next generation in the form of higher earnings.

87

A) NO CHANGE
B) their decades
C) there decades
D) their decades'

88

Which of the following words would not be a suitable replacement for the underlined word based on the tone and context of the passage?

A) muddy
B) obscure
C) spoil
D) muddle

89

A) NO CHANGE
B) new, but also
C) new, so also
D) new, and as a result are also

90

The author is considering starting a new paragraph at this point. Should he do so?

A) Yes, because the material after this point discusses a particular study in greater detail.
B) Yes, because the material after this point is no longer about American social mobility.
C) No, because the material after this point still pertains to American social mobility.
D) No, because the material after this point provides supporting details that are essential to understanding the information prior to this point.

This probability **91** decreases for the wealthier: People whose parents are in the 50th to 90th percentiles of earners receive about two-thirds of this parental edge.

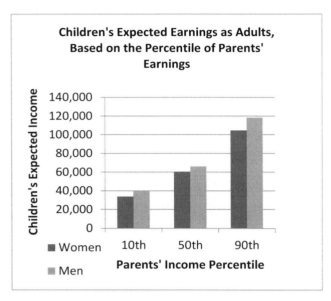

Children's Expected Earnings as Adults, Based on the Percentile of Parents' Earnings

[1] Grusky and Mitnik are formulating what is called intergenerational elasticity (IGE) to substantiate their claims. [2] In the past, estimates of IGE in the U.S. have ranged from 0.34 to 0.6, but Grusky and Mitnik's estimates are closer to 0.6. [3] IGE ranges from 0 to 1; 0 represents total economic **92** mobility and 1 represents the absence of it. [4] To simplify how IGE works, by comparing two children whose parents have a certain percent difference in their wages, IGE will determine how much of that certain percent edge the children tend to retain when they start earning their own income. **93**

91

A) NO CHANGE

B) is consistent

C) increases

D) is variable

92

A) NO CHANGE

B) mobility, and 1

C) mobility, but 1

D) mobility but 1

93

For the sake of clarity and cohesion of the paragraph, sentence 2 should be placed where?

A) NO CHANGE

B) Before sentence 1.

C) After sentence 3.

D) After sentence 4.

This effect is interestingly much stronger for males than females. Individually, men have an IGE of 0.56, retaining much more of their parents' advantages than women, whose IGE is 0.32. But rich women are more likely to marry and to marry rich. Therefore, children with rich parents tend to grow into households **94** who brought in similar amounts of money.

Can changes be made **95** to promote and encourage economic mobility in the U.S.? The authors of the report do not give up much when it comes to policy changes – "It's really a 'just the facts' report," Grusky states – but the subtext of the study strongly suggests that what we are currently **96** doing and planned on doing will not be enough to change the pace of economic mobility.

So, the main take away from this report: Take whatever extreme, politically unfeasible changes we thought would be necessary to increase economic mobility and make them even more extreme and unfeasible—that might be enough. **97** It seems the solution to economic mobility will not happen without drastic change.

94

A) NO CHANGE
B) who bring
C) which brought
D) which bring

95

A) NO CHANGE
B) promote
C) encourage the promotion of
D) promote the encouragement of

96

A) NO CHANGE
B) doing and have planned on doing
C) doing and are planning on doing
D) doing and plan on doing

97

The author of the passage is considering deleting the passage's concluding sentence. Should he do so?

A) Yes, the sentence provides a weak closing argument even though it introduces some material for the reader to dwell on.

B) Yes, the line simply repeats the previous sentence in a simpler manner.

C) No, the sentence is integral to the reader's understanding of the final paragraph.

D) No, the sentence accurately and succinctly sums up the entire passage.

Questions 98-108 are based on the following passage.

Linking Multiple Minds Could Help Damaged Brains Heal

If an individual has an injured kidney, a donor's spare organ can be transplanted into the injured individual, allowing both individuals to live. What if it was possible to do something **98** comparable for a friend with a deteriorating brain?

In his latest lab research, Miguel Nicolelis and his colleagues connected the brains of multiple monkeys to operate as **99** "brainets". These are shared networks capable of working together to manipulate a cybernetic arm and make deliberations and decisions. Nicolelis is hopeful that linking human brains in this manner will make possible a collection of new neurological instruments that could assist people with conditions from Parkinson's disease to paralysis.

Brain-machine interfaces **100** has been employed for the last two decades as a treatment option for numerous medical conditions. **101** However, prior work involved only one person. Nicolelis wanted to determine if more than one person could come together using a shared brain-machine interface to boost neural activity.

98

Which of the following words is a suitable replacement for the underlined word?

A) NO CHANGE

B) symmetrical

C) proportionate

D) analogous

99

At this point, the author is considering joining these two sentences together. Which of the following most effectively combines these two sentences?

A) NO CHANGE

B) "brainets" – shared networks

C) "brainets" are shared networks

D) "brainets"; shared networks

100

A) NO CHANGE

B) has employed

C) have employed

D) have been employed

101

The author is considering inserting the following sentence at this point::

> For example, some devices use the brain's electrical signals, deciphered by a computer, to allow people to manipulate prosthetics or even a wheelchair.

Should the author make this addition?

A) Yes, because it supports the main idea of the paragraph with a tangible example.

B) Yes, because the paragraph is too short to stand alone without the addition.

C) No, because the example is not essential to the reader's ability to understand the paragraph.

D) No, because the example is not relevant.

102 His team implanted electrodes in the brains of three monkeys where the implants would be used to monitor and document neural activity, which would subsequently be linked by a computer. [1] The monkeys were placed in separate rooms, each of which included a digital display that allowed the monkey to control its brain-machine interface to operate a virtual arm to get a reward.[2] In some of the experiments, the monkeys jointly controlled the arm, but in others, each monkey only had command of the arm when it was moving in a specific direction. [3]None of the animals were aware that they were working together to maneuver the arm. [4]Astonishingly, they not only completed the task, but they also improved with repetition. **103**

In another similar experiment **104** as it is described in Scientific Reports; four rats were physically connected with a microwire to discover how their brains collaborated as a linked unit when undertaking various puzzles. The rats were supplied with information via electrical pulse and rewarded when their brains synchronized. The information they received included data on temperature and barometric pressure. The rats were able to store, retrieve, and communicate this data—allowing **105** its combined brainet to make analyses that were superior to those of a single rat.

Nicolelis proposes that humans may already unconsciously participate in an instinctive method of brain sharing when **106** they exposed collective feedback. "The interesting thing is that this probably happens all the time with us. When we're watching a movie in a theater, this type

102

Which of the following would be the most effective replacement for the underlined portion?

A) NO CHANGE

B) Using electrodes, his team would use them to monitor and document neural activity and implant them into three monkeys' brains,

C) By implanting electrodes, his team monitored three monkeys'' brains,

D) His team implanted electrodes in the brains of three monkeys to monitor and document neural activity,

103

For the sake of continuity and cohesion in this paragraph, sentence 4 should go where?

A) NO CHANGE

B) Before sentence 1.

C) Before sentence 2.

D) After sentence 2.

104

A) NO CHANGE

B) (described in Scientific Reports)

C) as described in Scientific Reports,

D) described in Scientific Reports,

105

A) NO CHANGE

B) their

C) it's

D) they're

106

A) NO CHANGE

B) collective feedback is exposed.

C) they are exposed to collective feedback.

D) their collective feedback is exposed.

of feedback is probably synchronizing brains in the audience so that we have those group reactions, laughing or crying at the same moments," he says.

107 His team is currently attempting to translate the findings of this study to noninvasive clinical trials that could test whether brainets could effectively assist paralyzed humans with rehabilitation. 108

107

Which of the following is the best transition from the previous paragraph and creates a cohesive introduction to the conclusion of this passage?

A) NO CHANGE

B) Following the success of the monkey study,

C) Continuing to study the way brains work,

D) Brainets will change the way the world thinks; therefore,

108

The author is considering adding the following sentence to the end of the passage:

If his research is successful, brainet technology could provide millions of people around the world with a second chance they probably thought they would never get.

Should the author make this addition?

A) Yes, because the previous paragraph is too concise and does not properly conclude the entire passage.

B) Yes, because it supports the ideas presented in this paragraph and serves as a thought provoking conclusion to the passage.

C) No, because the information is irrelevant and does not match the tone of the passage.

D) No, because the passage's focus is on the work done on animals and not on humans.

TEST PREP GENIUS

THIS PAGE IS LEFT INTENTIONALLY BLANK

Writing Practice Answer Keys

Explanations can be found online at http://www.tpgenius.com/

Practice Passage 1	Practice Passage 2	Practice Passage 3	Practice Passage 4	Practice Passage 5
1. D	11. C	22. B	33. B	44. C
2. C	12. D	23. B	34. B	45. A
3. D	13. B	24. D	35. D	46. B
4. B	14. B	25. D	36. C	47. C
5. A	15. D	26. C	37. A	48. B
6. A	16. A	27. A	38. A	49. B
7. C	17. A	28. B	39. D	50. D
8. C	18. B	29. B	40. A	51. A
9. A	19. B	30. A	41. C	52. B
10. C	20. A	31. D	42. C	53. B
	21. B	32. A	43. B	

Practice Passage 6	Practice Passage 7	Practice Passage 8	Practice Passage 9	Practice Passage 10
54. A	65. B	76. D	87. D	98. D
55. C	66. A	77. B	88. C	99. B
56. B	67. C	78. D	89. B	100. D
57. A	68. D	79. C	90. A	101. A
58. D	69. C	80. C	91. C	102. D
59. B	70. B	81. B	92. B	103. A
60. A	71. D	82. A	93. D	104. D
61. D	72. A	83. D	94. D	105. B
62. B	73. B	84. A	95. B	106. C
63. A	74. C	85. A	96. D	107. B
64. A	75. D	86. C	97. B	108. B

Explanations can be found online at http://www.tpgenius.com/

Section 4
Math

Pre-Algebra Review

The following reminders, tips, and tricks review many of the topics covered in Pre-Algebra. Carefully read each topic and then try the problems on the next pages for extra practice.

Operations on Integers

- Instead of subtracting two numbers, change the subtraction sign to an addition sign and then change the sign of the second number: $2 - -4 = 2 + +4 = 6$.
- When multiplying or dividing two numbers with the same signs, you will get a positive answer: $-5 \times -4 = 20$.
- When multiplying or dividing two numbers with different signs, you will get a negative answer: $-2 \times 12 = -24$.

Fractions

- To add or subtract fractions, you must have a common denominator. $\frac{1}{3} + -\frac{1}{4} = \frac{4}{12} - \frac{3}{12} = \frac{1}{12}$
- You do not need a common denominator to multiply fractions. $\frac{3}{4} \times -\frac{2}{5} = -\frac{3}{10}$
- To divide one fraction by another, change the division sign to a multiplication sign and then take the reciprocal of the second number: $\frac{2}{3} \div -\frac{2}{5} = \frac{2}{3} \times -\frac{5}{2} = -\frac{5}{3}$.

Decimals

- To change a decimal to a percentage, move the decimal point two places to the right (or multiply it by 100 and add a percent sign): $0.69 = 69\%$.
- To change a percentage to a decimal, move the decimal point two places to the left (or divide it by 100 and remove the percent sign): $216\% = 2.16$.
- To change a fraction into a decimal, divide the denominator into the numerator. $\frac{2}{5} = 0.4$

Percentages

- $\frac{\text{part}}{\text{whole}} \times 100 = \%$
- $\frac{\text{final} - \text{initial}}{\text{initial}} \times 100\% =$ percent increase (positive answer) or percent decrease (negative answer)

Exponents and Radicals

- An exponent is like a repeated multiplication: $x^4 = x \times x \times x \times x$.
- When multiplying exponents, add the powers: $c^2 \times c^4 = c^6$.
- When dividing exponents, subtract the powers: $\frac{f^5}{f^2} = f^3$.
- When raising an exponent to a power, multiply the powers: $(a^3)^4 = a^{12}$.
- Any number raised to the first power is equal to itself: $s^1 = s$
- Any number raised to the zero power is equal to 1: $s^0 = 1$
- A number raised to a negative power is equivalent to the reciprocal of that number: $v^{-1} = \frac{1}{v}$
- Fractional exponents can be rewritten as follows: $\sqrt[7]{y^4} = y^{\left(\frac{4}{7}\right)}$
- The product of two or more numbers, each raised to the same power, is equivalent to the product of those numbers, raised as a collective to that power: $a^c b^c = (ab)^c$

Order of Operations

- **PEMDAS**
- **P**arentheses
- **E**xponents
- **M**ultiply / **D**ivide (From left to right)
- **A**dd / **S**ubtract (From left to right)

Absolute Value

- Treat absolute value bars as parentheses for the purpose of PEMDAS.
- After performing all of the operations inside the absolute value bars, change the final answer to a positive number: $|2 - 7| = |-5| = 5$

Coordinate Geometry

- The **midpoint** between two points, (x_1, y_1) and (x_2, y_2), can be found by using the midpoint formula: $\left(\frac{x_1 + x_2}{2}, \frac{y_1 + y_2}{2}\right)$.
- The **distance** between two points, (x_1, y_1) and (x_2, y_2), can be found by using the distance formula: $d = \sqrt{(x_2 - x_1)^2 + (y_2 - y_1)^2}$.

Reference Formulas and Information

The following formulas and information will be given to you on the SAT. While you don't necessarily have to memorize this, the more of it you know by heart, the better you will do:

1. The use of a calculator [is / is not] permitted.
2. All variables and expressions used represent real numbers unless otherwise indicated.
3. Figures provided in this test are drawn to scale unless otherwise indicated.
4. All figures lie in a plane unless otherwise indicated.
5. Unless otherwise indicated, the domain of a given function f is the set of real numbers x for which $f(x)$ is a real number.

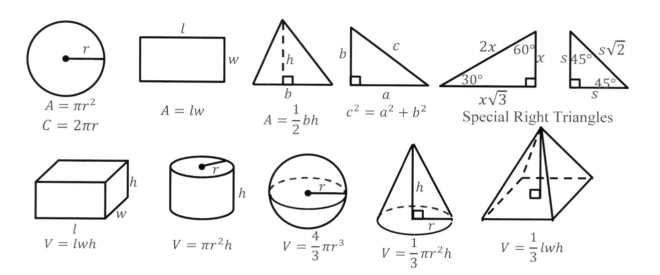

$A = \pi r^2$
$C = 2\pi r$

$A = lw$

$A = \frac{1}{2}bh$

$c^2 = a^2 + b^2$

Special Right Triangles

$V = lwh$

$V = \pi r^2 h$

$V = \frac{4}{3}\pi r^3$

$V = \frac{1}{3}\pi r^2 h$

$V = \frac{1}{3}lwh$

The number of degrees of arc in a circle is 360.

The number of radians of arc in a circle is 2π.

The sum of the measures in degrees of the angles of a triangle is 180.

1

The temperature in Juneau, Alaska, is currently –20.3°F. Yesterday, the high temperature in Juneau was –15.7°F. What is the absolute difference between the two temperatures?

A) –36.0°F
B) –4.6°F
C) 4.6°F
D) 36.0°F

2

Over one summer, Jeff's height increased from 4 foot 3 inches to 4 foot 9 inches. By what percentage did his height increase over the summer?

A) 89.47%
B) 13.95%
C) 11.76%
D) 10.53%

3

The price of a meal is $12.50, and Kyung wants to tip 15%. How much money should he leave?

A) $1.88
B) $10.63
C) $14.00
D) $14.38

4

$3.2 \times 10^2 + 4.6 \times 10^3 =$

A) 7.80×10^5
B) 7.80×10^3
C) 4.92×10^3
D) 3.66×10^2

5

$(1.2 \times 10^{-3})(-2.3 \times 10^{-3}) =$

A) -2.76×10^{-6}
B) -1.20×10^{-6}
C) -2.76×10^{-3}
D) -1.20×10^{-3}

6

$$\frac{x^5 y^3}{x^1 y^{-2}} =$$

A) $x^4 y^5$
B) $x^4 y$
C) $x^5 y^5$
D) $x^5 y$

7

The population of sea urchins off the coast of an Asian city is increasing by 2.5% each year. If there were y sea urchins at the beginning of 2012, how many sea urchins would there be at the end of 2015?

A) $y(2.5)^4$
B) $y(2.5)^3$
C) $y(1.025)^4$
D) $y(1.025)^3$

8

What is the midpoint of the line segment with endpoints $(3, 4)$ and $(-2, -5)$?

A) $(-0.5, -0.5)$
B) $(-0.5, 0.5)$
C) $(0.5, -0.5)$
D) $(0.5, 0.5)$

9

What is the length of the line segment with endpoints $(5, -3)$ and $(-2, 3)$?

A) $\sqrt{13}$
B) $3\sqrt{5}$
C) $\sqrt{85}$
D) $\sqrt{130}$

$$|20 - 4|^{\frac{3}{4}} =$$

A) 4
B) 8
C) 12
D) 24

Algebra

Solving Linear Equations

- To solve an equation, you must isolate the variable.

$$3x - 3 = 5 \;\rightarrow\; 3x = 8 \;\rightarrow\; x = \frac{8}{3}$$

- First, simplify both sides of the equation by using the distributive property, eliminating fractions, or combining like terms.

$$7(x - 2) = 3 \;\rightarrow\; 7x - 14 = 3 \;\rightarrow\; 7x = 17 \;\rightarrow\; x = \frac{17}{7}$$

$$\frac{1}{3}x - 2 = \frac{1}{2} \;\rightarrow\; 6\left(\frac{1}{3}x - 2\right) = 6\left(\frac{1}{2}\right) \;\rightarrow\; 2x - 12 = 3 \;\rightarrow\; 2x = 15 \;\rightarrow\; x = \frac{15}{2}$$

$$7x - 3x = 4 + 2 \;\rightarrow\; 4x = 6 \;\rightarrow\; x = \frac{3}{2}$$

- To solve a one-variable equation, add or subtract all of your variable terms to one side of the equation and all of your constant terms to the other side.

$$2x - 4 = 5x - 12 \;\rightarrow\; 12 - 4 = 5x - 2x \;\rightarrow\; 8 = 3x \;\rightarrow\; \frac{8}{3} = x$$

- When solving an equation, whatever you do to one side of the equation you must do to the other as well.

$$3x = -12 \;\rightarrow\; 3x \div 3 = -12 \div 3 \;\rightarrow\; x = -4$$

> What is the value of a if $(2a + 3) - (4a - 8) = 7$?

Since we're given a linear equation, let's start by simplifying both sides of the equation:

$$(2a + 3) - (4a - 8) = 7$$
$$2a + 3 - 4a + 8 = 7$$

Next, we can combine like terms:

$$-2a + 11 = 7$$

All of the variable terms are on the left-hand side of the equation, so we can move 11 to the right-hand side by subtracting:

$$-2a + 11 - 11 = 7 - 11$$

$$-2a = -4$$

Now we can divide both sides by -2 to get our answer.

$$-2a \div -2 = -4 \div -2$$

$$a = 2$$

Use these rules whenever you see a one-variable equation on the PSAT!

Solving Linear Inequalities

- Linear inequalities should be solved just like linear equations.

$$3x - 9 > 18 \;\rightarrow\; 3x - 9 + 9 > 18 + 9 \;\rightarrow\; 3x > 27 \;\rightarrow\; x > 9$$

- Whenever you multiply or divide both sides of the inequality by a negative number, you MUST flip the inequality sign (so $<$ becomes $>$, or $\geq$ becomes $\leq$).

If $-\frac{9}{5} < -3t + 1 < -\frac{7}{4}$, what is one possible value of $9t - 3$?

We're given a linear inequality, and everything seems to be simplified, but this inequality seems to have three "sides" instead of the usual two. However, the pattern still remains: whatever we do to one "side", we must do to all of them. Let's begin by subtracting 1 from each side.

$$-\frac{9}{5} < -3t + 1 < -\frac{7}{4}$$

$$-\frac{9}{5} - 1 < -3t + 1 - 1 < -\frac{7}{4} - 1$$

$$-\frac{14}{5} < -3t < -\frac{11}{4}$$

Next, we'll divide each "side" by -3. Remember to flip the inequality signs since we're dividing by a negative number!

$$-\frac{14}{5} \div -3 < -3t \div -3 < -\frac{11}{4} \div -3$$

$$\frac{14}{15} > t > \frac{11}{12}$$

So, we know that the value of t must be between $\frac{14}{15}$ and $\frac{11}{12}$. Wait! We're not looking for a possible value of t, we're looking for a possible value of $9t - 3$. So, we can just take any value of t, for example $\frac{23}{25}$, and plug it into $9t - 3$ for a possible answer. $9\left(\frac{23}{25}\right) - 3 = \mathbf{5.28}$.

There is another way to solve this problem though. If you compare $9t - 3$ and $-3t + 1$, you'll notice that we can just multiply $-3t + 1$ by -3 to get $9t - 3$! Let's try this:

$$-\frac{9}{5} < -3t + 1 < -\frac{7}{4}$$

$$-3\left(-\frac{9}{5}\right) < -3(-3t + 1) < -3\left(-\frac{7}{4}\right)$$

Don't forget to flip the signs.

$$\frac{27}{5} > 9t - 3 > \frac{21}{4}$$

Always be on the lookout for shortcuts like this. They can really cut down the time needed to solve the easy problems, giving you more time to work on the more difficult ones that show up later in the test.

Solving Systems of Linear Equations and Inequalities

- There are three common ways to solve a system of equations: Substitution, Elimination, and Graphing.
- Substitution requires you to solve one of the two equations for a variable, then to plug that variable's value into the second equation. You will use substitution most often.

$$\begin{matrix} 2x - 3y = 7 \\ y - 2x = 7 \end{matrix} \rightarrow \begin{matrix} 2x - 3y = 7 \\ y = 2x + 7 \end{matrix} \rightarrow 2x - 3(2x + 7) = 7 \rightarrow -4x - 21 = 7 \rightarrow x = -7$$

$$y - 2(-7) = 7 \rightarrow y = -7 \rightarrow \textbf{Solution: } (-7, -7)$$

- Elimination requires you to multiply one of the two equations by a constant (if necessary), then to add the two equations together to eliminate a variable. Elimination is the fastest method when variables are easily eliminated.

$$\begin{matrix} 2x - 3y = 7 \\ y - 2x = 7 \end{matrix} \rightarrow \begin{matrix} 2x - 3y = 7 \\ 3y - 6x = 21 \end{matrix} \rightarrow -4x = 28 \rightarrow x = -7$$

$$2(-7) - 3y = 7 \rightarrow y = -7 \rightarrow \textbf{Solution: } (-7, -7)$$

- Graphing requires you to graph each of the two equations then find the point of intersection of the two lines. Graphing is the most time consuming of the three methods, especially if you do not get to use a calculator, and you should avoid using it if at all possible.
- Sometimes, two equations never intersect. In this situation, the system has no solution. These systems of equations occur when the two lines are parallel, as shown below:

$$2x - 5y = 16 \rightarrow 2x - 5y = 16$$
$$4x = 10y - 24 \rightarrow 2x - 5y = -12$$

(We can tell the two lines are parallel because the coefficients for x and y are in the same ratio for both equations, but the constants are different)

- Sometimes, two equations overlap each other. In this situation, the system has an infinite number of solutions. These systems of equations occur when both lines are the same line, as shown below:

$$3x - 2y = 7 \rightarrow 3x - 2y = 7$$
$$0 = 4y - 6x + 14 \rightarrow 3x - 2y = 7$$

(We can tell the two lines overlap because they can be manipulated by multiplication or division to be the exact same equation)

Creating and Interpreting Equations and Inequalities

- Word problems on the PSAT will focus primarily on real-world situations like people getting paid for doing a job or a relationship that exists in science or economics.

  For every ounce of iron that is added to a vat of hydrochloric acid, the vat's temperature decreases by 1.2°F. If the initial temperature of the hydrochloric acid is 88.3°F, how many ounces of iron, x, need to be added to the vat to bring the temperature to 65.5°F?

- The PSAT will usually tell you which quantity you are solving for and occasionally assign it a variable.

  For every ounce of iron that is added to a vat of hydrochloric acid, the vat's temperature decreases by 1.2°F. If the initial temperature of the hydrochloric acid is 88.3°F, **how many ounces of iron, x, need to be added to the vat to bring the temperature to 65.5°F?**
  $$88.3 - 1.2x = 65.5 \rightarrow 88.3 - 65.5 = 1.2x \rightarrow 22.8 = 1.2x \rightarrow x = 19$$

- The PSAT will also ask you to interpret the meaning of part of an equation or to translate a situation into an equation.

  For every ounce of iron that is added to a vat of hydrochloric acid, the vat's temperature decreases by 1.2°F. If the initial temperature of the hydrochloric acid is 88.3°F, write an equation that can be used to determine the number of ounces of iron, x, that need to be added to the vat to bring the temperature to T°F?

  $$88.3 - 1.2x = T$$

- Always be aware of keywords for addition, subtraction, multiplication, division, equality, and each of the inequality signs.

Algebraic Term	Key Words
+	more than, increased by, greater than, additional, exceeds, sum
−	less than, decreased by, fewer than, difference
×	of, each, product, per
÷	per, ratio of, for every
=	is, equals, is equivalent to
<	less than, fewer than
>	more than, greater than
≤	at most, no more than, no greater than
≥	at least, no less than, no fewer than

A babysitter earns $8 an hour for babysitting 2 children and an additional $3 tip when both children are put to bed on time. If the babysitter gets the children to bed on time, what expression could be used to determine how much the babysitter earned?

A) $8x + 3$, where x is the number of hours
B) $3x + 8$, where x is the number of hours
C) $x(8 + 2)$, where x is the number of children
D) $3x + (8 + 2)$, where x is the number of children

In this problem, we need to translate a situation into an expression. We know that the babysitter earns $8 per hour for babysitting 2 children. In this case, per means we need to multiply: for every hour the babysitter works, he or she makes $8. The number of children seems to make no difference, so we know that the number of hours must be our variable, x, and we need to multiply that variable by $8, 8x$. Lastly, we know that the babysitter gets a $3 bonus if the kids are put to bed on time, and the babysitter achieves that goal, so we can add 3 to our previous expression. Our answer must be **A, $8x + 3$**.

In a certain game, a player can solve easy or hard puzzles. A player earns 30 points for solving an easy puzzle and 60 points for solving a hard puzzle. Tina solved a total of 50 puzzles playing this game, earning 1,950 points in all. How many hard puzzles did Tina solve?

A) 10
B) 15
C) 25
D) 35

First, we must realize that we're solving for the number of hard puzzles that Tina solved, so let's give that a variable: h. We also know that Tina solves easy puzzles as well; let's call those e. We know she gets 1950 points in all, and that she gets 30 points per easy puzzle and 60 points per hard puzzle.

$$30e + 60h = 1950$$

We also know that Tina solved a total of 50 puzzles, so the number of easy puzzles plus the number of hard puzzles must be equal to 50.

$$e + h = 50$$

We have a system of equations with two variables and two equations; let's use substitution to solve:

$$e = 50 - h$$
$$30(50 - h) + 60h = 1950$$
$$1500 - 30h + 60h = 1950$$
$$30h = 450$$
$$h = 15$$

So, our answer must be **B**.

1

A daycare employee gets paid $12.00 an hour for watching 25 children and an additional $15.00 bonus if all the children finish their homework. If the employee gets the children to finish their homework, what expression could be used to determine how much the babysitter earned?

A) $15x + 12$, where x is the number of hours worked
B) $12x + 15$, where x is the number of hours worked
C) $15x + 12$, where x is the number of children
D) $12x + 15$, where x is the number of children

2

$$\frac{1}{5}x + \frac{1}{3}y = 3$$
$$\frac{1}{15}x - \frac{1}{15}y = 1$$

Which ordered pair (x, y) satisfies the system of equations above?

A) $(0, 15)$
B) $(15, 0)$
C) $(30, -6)$
D) $(30, 15)$

3

To rent a kayak, Kaleigh's Kayaking charges a fee of $5 for the rental and $2.25 per hour spent using the kayak. Bob's Boats charges a fee of $8 for the rental and $1.50 per hour spent using the kayak. If x represents the number of hours spent using a kayak, what are all the values for x for which Kaleigh's Kayaking's total charge is greater than Bob's Boats' charge?

A) $x > 4$
B) $2 \le x \le 4$
C) $4 \le x \le 6$
D) $x < 6$

4

$$a = 158 + 4T$$

The equation above is used to model the relationship between the number of alligator snapping turtles, a, found in a 1-mile length of a stream and the average daily tempaerature, T, in degrees Fahrenheit. According to the model, what is the meaning of the 4 in the equation?

A) For every increase of 4°F, one more alligator snapping turtle will be found.
B) For every decrease of 4°F, one more alligator snapping turtle will be found.
C) For every increase of 1°F, four more alligator snapping turtles will be found.
D) For every decrease of 1°F, four more alligator snapping turtles will be found.

5

$$x - 3y > 6$$
$$x < 2 - 6y$$

Which of the following points is a solution to the system of inequalities above?

A) $(0, -2)$
B) $(4, -1)$
C) $(5, 1)$
D) $(6, 2)$

6

Maurice and Delmon are playing a game in which each player gets a certain number of points per minor objective he or she completes and a certain number of points per major objective he or she completes. If Maurice completed 3 minor objectives and 7 major objectives and scored 47 points, while Delmon completed 10 minor objectives and 3 major objectives and scored 55 points, how many points is completing a major objective worth?

A) 3
B) 4
C) 5
D) 6

7

Jamey is putting a fence around her entire rectangular backyard. If the perimeter of her backyard is 3750 yards and the width of her backyard is twice the length of her backyard, how wide is her backyard?

A) 312.5 yards
B) 625 yards
C) 937.5 yards
D) 1250 yards

8

$$2x = 3y$$
$$x - 2y = -2$$

Which ordered pair (x, y) satisfies the system of equations shown above?

A) $(2, 3)$
B) $(3, 2)$
C) $(4, 6)$
D) $(6, 4)$

9

What is the value of b if $6 - \frac{b}{3} = 3$?

10

What is the value of f if $(5f - 3) - (2f + 6) = 12$?

%s, Rates, Unit Conversions

Solving Ratios, Proportions, and Rate Problems

- A ratio is a relationship between two or more values and can generally be written as a fraction:

$$2 \text{ boys for every 3 girls} = 2 \text{ boys} : 3 \text{ girls} = \frac{2 \text{ boys}}{3 \text{ girls}}$$

- Proportions occur when ratios are set equal to each other. Proportions can be solved by cross multiplying:

$$\frac{7}{9} = \frac{21}{x} \rightarrow 7x = 189 \rightarrow x = 27$$

- The most basic rate questions involve the equation below:

$$\text{distance} = \text{rate} \times \text{time}$$

- Rates are used to show a "distance" that happens over a period of time, for example, miles per hour. Note, however, that the distance does not have to be a physical distance. A pay rate, such as dollars per hour, is another common rate.

> A car traveled at an average speed of 80 miles per hour for 3 hours and consumed fuel at a rate of 34 miles per gallon. Approximately how many gallons of fuel did the car use for the entire 3-hour trip?
>
> A) 2
> B) 3
> C) 6
> D) 7

In this problem, we seem to have two different rates: 80 miles per hour and 34 miles per gallon. Let's attack them separately:

Since we are traveling at a rate of 80 miles per hour for 3 hours, we can easily figure out how many miles we traveled:

$$\frac{80 \text{ miles}}{\text{hour}} \times 3 \text{ hours} = 240 \text{ miles}$$

Since we are looking for the number of gallons of fuel we used, we need to divide our distance by our fuel rate:

$$240 \text{ miles} \div \frac{34 \text{ miles}}{\text{gallon}} =$$

$$240 \text{ miles} \times \frac{1 \text{ gallon}}{34 \text{ miles}} = \textbf{7.06 gallons}$$

So, our answer must be **D**.

Solving Percentage Problems

- The most common types of percentage problems on the PSAT will be word problems.

  The price of a $350 television has decreased by 7%. What is the new price of the television?

  $$\$350.00 \times 0.07 = \$24.50$$
  $$\$350.00 - \$24.50 = \mathbf{\$325.50}$$

- **Tax** is a percentage added to the cost of a purchase – it works the same as a percent increase.

  A $30.00 meal is purchased in a state with a 6% tax rate. How much is the meal after tax?

  $$\$30.00 \times 0.06 = \$1.80$$
  $$\$30.00 + \$1.80 = \mathbf{\$31.80}$$

- **Commission** is a percentage used in calculating how much money certain salespeople make. A 10% commission means that 10% of a salesperson's sales will be added on to his or her salary.

  Jason made $30,000 in sales this month. If Jason gets 7.5% commission on all of his sales, how much money does he make through commission?

  $$\$30,000.00 \times 0.075 = \mathbf{\$2,250}$$

> A high school basketball team won exactly 65 percent of the games it played during last season. Which of the following could be the total number of games the team played last season?
>
> A) 22
> B) 20
> C) 18
> D) 14

Since a basketball team can only play an integer number of games, we need to figure out which of the above numbers provides an integer when you calculate 65% of it:

$0.62(22) = 14.3$ $0.65(20) = 13$ $0.65(18) = 11.7$ $0.65(14) = 9.1$

So, the answer must be **B**, 20.

Unit Conversion Problems

- In many word problems, we'll be required to change the units of information.

  If a dog can run 12 miles per hour, how fast can it run in feet per seconds?

- The easiest way to convert one unit to another unit is to use a table like the one below.

- Put your initial term in the top left corner. Then place unit conversions in subsequent columns in such a way that units cross out (in the top and bottom of the table).

12 miles	1 hour	1 minute	5,280 feet
1 hour	60 minutes	60 seconds	1 mile

Now multiply the numbers across the top of the table, then the bottom of the table, crossing out units that appear on both the top and bottom of the table. Divide the final result of the top row of the table by the bottom row of the table for your answer.

12 miles ×	1 hour ×	1 minute ×	5,280 feet =	63360 feet
1 hour ×	60 minutes ×	60 seconds ×	1 mile =	3600 seconds

$$\frac{63360 \text{ feet}}{3600 \text{ seconds}} = 17.6 \frac{\textbf{feet}}{\textbf{second}}$$

> A soda company is filling bottles of soda from a tank that contains 500 gallons of soda. At most, how many 20-ounce bottles can be filled from the tank? (1 gallon = 128 ounces)
> A) 25
> B) 78
> C) 2,560
> D) 3,200

Let's start by filling in our initial unit, 500 gallons, in the leftmost column of the table, then convert until we get to bottles:

500 gallons	128 ounces	1 bottle
	1 gallon	20 ounces

After multiplying across the top and dividing by the bottom, we get **3,200 bottles, D**.

A car gets on to the Interstate at an elevation of 200 meters. The incline of the Interstate at that level is such that for every 100 meters traveled along the length of the road, the elevation increases by 5 meters. If the car is traveling at a rate of 15 meters per second along the road, what is the elevation of the road, in meters, at the point where the car passes p seconds after entering the Interstate?

A) $200 + 0.75p$
B) $200 + 1.33p$
C) $200 + 33.33p$
D) $200 + 300p$

2

A sporting goods store sells golf balls individually and in packs of 4. On a certain day, the store sold 315 golf balls, 19 of which were sold individually. Which equation shows the number of packs of golf balls, g, sold that day?

A) $g = \frac{315 - 19}{4}$
B) $g = \frac{315 + 19}{4}$
C) $g = \frac{315}{4} - 19$
D) $g = \frac{315}{4} + 19$

A construction company is filling 50-pound bags of sand from a container of sand that contains 1000 gallons of sand. If the density of sand is approximately 13 pounds per gallon, at most how many bags of sand can be filled from the tank? (Density is equivalent to mass divided by volume.)

A) 150
B) 260
C) 650
D) 3846

A small plane flew at an average speed of 150 miles per hour for 2 hours and consumed fuel at a rate of 85 miles per gallon. Approximately how many gallons of fuel did the plane use for the entire 2-hour trip?

A) 2.5
B) 3.0
C) 3.5
D) 4.0

5

A business is required to give 17% of an employee's salary to the government for tax reasons. If the employee makes $15.50 per hour and works 70 hours in a two-week period, how much money will the employee bring home after taxes?

A) $184.45
B) $716.10
C) $900.55
D) $1085.00

6

A new type of protein bar is 40% protein, 24% fat, and 15% carbohydrates by weight. If the bar costs $3.09 and weighs 50 grams, what is the ratio of grams of protein per dollar for the protein bar?

A) 0.02
B) 0.15
C) 6.47
D) 40.45

7

Last year, Jameson grew 100 bushels of onions and 75 bushels of garlic on his farm and was able to sell a bushel of either at the same price. This year, he was able to grow 10 percent more onions and 10% less garlic by volume. If the price he was able to sell each bushel of onion or garlic at increased by 5%, by what percentage did his total amount of money earned increase?

A) 5%
B) 6.5%
C) 9%
D) 10.5%

8

The ratio of juniors to seniors in a chemistry class is 4 to 7. Which of the following could be the number of students in the chemistry class if each student is either a junior or senior?

A) 16
B) 28
C) 32
D) 33

9

A 100 liter vat of liquid metal is 30% tin and 70% copper, by volume. How many liters of tin should be added to the vat to so that the liquid metal inside the vat is 60% tin?

10

The price of a suit is decreased by 10% because of a sale. If a customer purchases the suit for $1,431.00 after a 6% tax is added on to the price of the suit, what was the original price of the suit, in dollars?

Polynomial Operations and Functions

Operations on Polynomials

- Expressions with **like terms** have the same exact variables raised to the same powers.

  $3x^2$ and $2x^2$, abc and $5abc$, and $-9jk^3$ and $3jk^3$ are all examples of pairs of like terms.

  $2x^2$ and $4x^3$, $2abc$ and $-7ab^2c$, and $-9jk^2$ and $3j^2k$ are NOT examples of pairs of like terms.

- You can only add or subtract like terms.

$$3xy^2 + 9xy^2 = 12xy^2$$
$$6ab^2 + 7a^2b \text{ cannot be combined}$$

- To multiply terms, multiply coefficients, but add the exponents of like terms.

$$(3x^2y^6)(-6xy^{-1}) = -18x^3y^5$$

Distributive Property

- $3x(x - 5) = 3x(x) + 3x(-5) = 3x^2 - 15x$

FOILing

- When multiplying two binomials, remember the mnemonic device **FOIL**: **F**irst, **O**uter, **I**nner, **L**ast.
- To multiply $(3x - 4)(2x + 6)$, first multiply the first terms, then the outer terms, then the inner terms, then the last terms. Finally, simplify by combining like terms:

$$3x(2x) + 3x(6) + -4(2x) + -4(6) = 6x^2 + 10x - 24$$

Which of the following is equivalent to $(s - t)\left(\frac{s}{t}\right)$?

A) $\frac{s}{t} - s$

B) $\frac{s}{t} - st$

C) $\frac{s^2}{t} - s$

D) $\frac{s^2}{t} - \frac{s}{t^2}$

Let's start out by using our distributive property:

$$(s - t)\left(\frac{s}{t}\right) = \frac{s}{t}(s) - \frac{s}{t}(t) = \frac{s^2}{t} - \frac{st}{t} = \frac{s^2}{t} - s$$

Thus, our answer is **C.**

Functions

- A **function** is a relationship between a set of inputs and a set of outputs wherein each input is related to exactly one output.

  The image below contains a function on the left. Each input on the right goes to exactly one output on the left. The image below also contains a relation that is not a function on the right. The relation is not a function because an input of 4 leads to two outputs: 1 or 5.

- The inputs, or x-values of the function, are known as its **domain**. The outputs, or y-values of the function, are known as its **range**.

  In the image of the function below, the numbers on the left, 1, 2, –5, and 10, are the domain of the function, while the numbers on the right, 3, 6, and –2, are the range of the function.

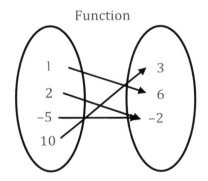 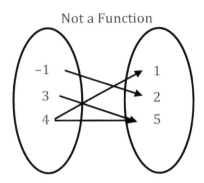

- In function notation, the input of the function is represented by x while the output of the function is represented as $f(x)$ or y. The ordered pair (x, y) is a solution to the function $f(x)$.

  $(2, 4)$ is a solution to the function $f(x) = 3x - 2$. Another way to write this is $f(2) = 4$.

  $$f(2) = 3(2) - 2 = 4$$

- Functions can be added, subtracted, multiplied or divided just like any other algebraic terms.

$$f(x) = 3x \qquad g(x) = 3 - x$$
$$f(x) + g(x) = 3x + 3 - x = 2x + 3$$
$$f(x) - g(x) = 3x - (3 - x) = 4x - 3$$
$$f(x) \times g(x) = 3x(3 - x) = 9x - 3x^2$$
$$f(x) \div g(x) = \frac{3x}{3 - x}$$

- Composition is the process by which one function becomes the input of another function.

$$f(x) = 3x \qquad g(x) = 3 - x$$
$$f(g(x)) = 3(3 - x) = 9 - 3x$$
$$g(f(x)) = 3 - (3x) = 3 - 3x$$

Note that $f(g(x))$ is not necessarily equivalent to $g(f(x))$.

If $f(x - 1) = 2x + 3$ for all values of x, what is the value of $f(-3)$?

A) –7

B) –5

C) –3

D) –1

In this question, we want to find the value of $f(-3)$, however, we're only given the function $f(x - 1)$ in terms of x. Therefore, we should set –3 equal to $x - 1$ and solve for x.

$$-3 = x - 1$$
$$-2 = x$$

Now we can plug -2 into our function and solve.

$$f(-2) = 2(-2) + 3 = -1$$

Thus, our answer is **D**.

1

If $f(2x) = 3x - 2$ for all values of x, what is the value of $f(7)$?

A) 8.5
B) 11.5
C) 17
D) 40

2

Which of the following is equivalent to $(s - t)(t + s)$?

A) $s^2 - t^2$
B) $s^2 - 2st - t^2$
C) $s^2 + 2st - t^2$
D) $t^2 - s^2$

3

If $f(x) = 3x^2$ and $g(x) = x - 3$, what is the value of $f(g(2)) - g(f(2))$?

A) -12
B) -9
C) -6
D) 0

4

If $f(x) = (x - 5)^{\frac{1}{2}}$, what is the value of $f(9) - f(6)$?

A) -3
B) -1
C) 1
D) 3

5

If $f(x) = \dfrac{2}{x} - x$ and $g(x) = 3 - x$, which of the following is equivalent to $g(f(x))$ for all values of $x \neq 0, 3$?

A) $\dfrac{2}{3-x} + x - 3$
B) $\dfrac{2}{3-x} + 3 - x$
C) $3 + x - \dfrac{2}{x}$
D) $3 + \dfrac{2}{x} - x$

6

If $f(x) = x^2 - 3x + 7$ and $g(x) = 3x^2 - 3x - 4$, which of the following is equivalent to $f(x) - g(x)$?

A) $2x^2 - 11$
B) $2x^2 - 6x + 3$
C) $-2x^2 + 11$
D) $-2x^2 + 6x - 3$

7

If $f(g(x)) = x^2 + 17x + 81$ and $f(x) = x^2 - x$, which of the following could be the value of $g(x)$?

A) $x - 9$
B) $x - 3$
C) $x + 3$
D) $x + 9$

8

If $f(2x - 4) = x^2$ for all values of x, what is the value of $f(6)$?

A) 16
B) 25
C) 36
D) 64

9

If $x \neq 0$, what is the value of $3(6x^2)(2x)^{-2}$?

10

If $x \neq 2$, what is the value of $\dfrac{-2(2-x)}{x-2}$?

Solving For A Term

Isolating and Identifying Terms

- Often times, the PSAT will ask you to solve for a quantity such as $x + 2$ or $3x$ instead of simply solving for x.

  We saw a question like this earlier:

  If $-\frac{9}{5} < -3t + 1 < -\frac{7}{4}$, what is one possible value of $9t - 3$?

- Many times, the easiest way to solve these is to simply solve for x, then plug your value of x into the indicated expression. Remember that the PSAT will usually include the value of x in the answer choices (if multiple choice) to try to trick you.

  Remember, that in this case, we can also solve the inequality for $9t - 3$ by multiplying each part of the inequality by –3:

  $$-3\left(-\frac{9}{5}\right) < -3(-3t + 1) < -3\left(-\frac{7}{4}\right)$$
  $$\frac{27}{5} > 9t - 3 > \frac{21}{4}$$

- Other times, it'll be impossible to solve for a single term or there will be multiple terms involved. In these cases, it'll be easier to adjust the initial expression in some way (add 2 to both sides, factor it out, multiply it by some number) to obtain the term that you're looking for.

  If $\frac{x+y}{x} = y$ and $x \neq 0$ or 1, what is the value of y in terms of x?

  To solve a problem like this, we should first get all of our y values on one side of the equation.

  $$\frac{x + y}{x} = y \rightarrow x + y = xy \rightarrow x = xy - y$$

  Now that all of our y values are on the right side of the equation, let's factor it out:

  $$x = xy - y \rightarrow x = y(x - 1)$$

  At this point, isolating y is easy: just divide both sides by $(x - 1)$.

$$x = y(x - 1) \rightarrow \frac{x}{x - 1} = y$$

- Only practice will allow you to figure out which way is best for a particular problem.

$$3(x + y) = y$$

If (x, y) is a solution to the equation above and $y \neq 0$, what is the ratio of $\frac{x}{y}$?

A) $-\frac{4}{3}$

B) $-\frac{2}{3}$

C) $\frac{1}{3}$

D) $\frac{2}{3}$

Since we're trying to solve for the term $\frac{x}{y}$, let's first simplify the initial equation as much as possible.

$$3(x + y) = y$$

$$3x + 3y = y$$

Next, we should put all of our y terms on one side and the x terms on the other.

$$3x + 3y - 3y = y - 3y$$

$$3x = -2y$$

To solve for $\frac{x}{y}$, let's do some dividing:

$$3x \div 3 = -2y \div 3$$

$$x = -\frac{2}{3}y$$

$$x \div y = -\frac{2}{3}y \div y$$

$$\frac{x}{y} = -\frac{2}{3}$$

Our answer must be **B**.

1

If $8 - 12x = 19$, what is the value of $3x - 2$?

A) $-\dfrac{19}{4}$

B) $-\dfrac{11}{12}$

C) $\dfrac{11}{12}$

D) $\dfrac{19}{4}$

2

If $4x - 9 = 13$, what is the value of $8x$?

A) $\dfrac{11}{2}$

B) 11

C) 22

D) 44

3

If $x + 2y = 12$ and $3x - y = 5$, what is the value of $4x + y$?

A) 17

B) $\dfrac{57}{7}$

C) 7

D) $\dfrac{22}{7}$

4

$$3x - 2y = 2x$$

If (x, y) is a solution to the equation above and $x \neq 0$, what is the ratio of $\dfrac{y}{x}$?

A) -2

B) $-\dfrac{1}{2}$

C) $\dfrac{1}{2}$

D) 2

5

$$4x^2 = 9y^2$$

If (x, y) is a solution to the equation above and $y \neq 0$, what is the ratio of $\frac{x}{y}$?

A) $\frac{9}{4}$

B) $\frac{3}{2}$

C) $\frac{2}{3}$

D) $\frac{4}{9}$

6

If $3x = 6 - 2y$ and $5 + 6y = 2x$, what is the value of $5x - 4y$?

A) -13

B) 6

C) 9

D) 11

7

If $\left(\frac{x}{3}\right)^{-2} = 12$, what is the value of x^2?

A) $\frac{1}{16}$

B) $\frac{3}{4}$

C) $\frac{4}{3}$

D) 16

8

$$3(xy - y^2) = 2y$$

If (x, y) is a solution to the equation above and $y \neq 0$, what is the value of $y - x$?

A) $-\frac{3}{2}$

B) $-\frac{2}{3}$

C) $\frac{2}{3}$

D) $\frac{3}{2}$

9

If $3x - 6 = -8$, what is the value of $-2x$?

10

If $-1 > 3x - 2y > -4$, what is one possible value of $4y - 6x$?

Quadratics

Solving Quadratic Expressions

- A quadratic expression of the form $ax^2 + bx + c = 0$ can be solved using the formula:

$$x = \frac{-b \pm \sqrt{b^2 - 4ac}}{2a}$$

$$3x^2 + 9x - 2 = 0$$

$$x = \frac{-9 \pm \sqrt{9^2 - 4(3)(-2)}}{2(3)}$$

$$x = \frac{-9 \pm \sqrt{81 + 24}}{6}$$

$$x = \frac{-9 \pm \sqrt{105}}{6}$$

- Some quadratic expressions can be solved by factoring, the opposite of FOILing, or by completing the square. Both of these methods are very situational and cannot be used on every problem. However, reviewing these methods will help you be successful when taking the PSAT. Every quadratic problem on the SAT can be solved with the quadratic formula above, however.

$$2x^2 + 7x - 15 = 0$$

If r and s are two solutions of the equation above and $r > s$, which of the following is the value of $r - s$?

A) $\frac{15}{2}$

B) $\frac{13}{2}$

C) $\frac{11}{2}$

D) $\frac{3}{2}$

Since we're looking for the two solutions to the equation, we can use the quadratic formula to find them.

$$x = \frac{-7 \pm \sqrt{7^2 - 4(2)(-15)}}{4}$$

$$x = \frac{-7 \pm \sqrt{169}}{4}$$

$$x = \frac{-7 \pm 13}{4}$$

$$x = \frac{3}{2}, -5$$

Since $r > s$, $r = \frac{3}{2}$ and $s = -5$. Thus $r - s = \frac{3}{2} - (-5) = \frac{13}{2}$. Our answer is **B**.

Let's also look at how we could solve this problem by factoring:

$$2x^2 + 7x - 15 = 0$$
$$(2x - 3)(x + 5) = 0$$
$$2x - 3 = 0 \quad x + 5 = 0$$
$$2x = 3 \quad x = -5$$
$$x = \frac{3}{2} \quad x = -5$$

From this point, the steps are identical and we get the same answer.

1

$$x^2 - 4x = 5$$

Which of the following is a solution to the equation above?

A) −5
B) −4
C) 1
D) 5

2

Which equation below has two solutions, $\frac{3}{4}$ and −2?

A) $4x^2 + 5x + 6 = 0$
B) $4x^2 + 5x - 6 = 0$
C) $4x^2 - 5x + 6 = 0$
D) $4x^2 - 5x - 6 = 0$

3

$$6x^2 + 3x - 3 = 0$$

If a and b are two solutions of the equation above and $a > b$, which of the following is the value of $b - a$?

A) $-\frac{3}{2}$
B) $-\frac{1}{2}$
C) $\frac{1}{2}$
D) $\frac{11}{2}$

4

$$0 = 3x^2 + bx - a$$

$x = -6$ and $x = 3$ are solutions to the equation above. Which of the following is a possible value of $a + b$?

A) 63
B) 54
C) 45
D) 36

$$f(x) = 2(x^2 + 4x + 8) - 4(x + j)$$

In the polynomial $f(x)$ defined above, j is a constant. If $f(x)$ is divisible by x, what is the value of j?

A) -4
B) -2
C) 2
D) 4

$$-6x^2 - 18x - 12$$

Which of the following is not a possible factorization of the polynomial above?

A) $-6(x + 2)(x + 1)$
B) $(-6x - 12)(x + 1)$
C) $(x + 2)(-6x - 6)$
D) $(-6x + 2)(x - 6)$

$$y = x - 3$$
$$y = x^2 - 4x - 9$$

Which of the following ordered pairs (x, y) is a solution to the system of equations above?

A) $(-1, 3)$
B) $(-1, -4)$
C) $(6, -3)$
D) $(6, 4)$

$$h = -4.9t^2 + 19.6t + 58.8$$

The height of a projectile, in meters, can be modeled by the equation above, where h is the projectile's height after it has been in the air for t seconds. After how many seconds will the projectile hit the ground?

A) 1.5
B) 2.4
C) 4.0
D) 6.0

9

If $x + 1$ is a factor of $x^2 + 2bx + b$, where b is a constant, what is the value of b?

10

If $x - a$ is a factor of $2x^2 + x - 6$ and $a > 0$, what is the value of a?

Graphs of Polynomials

Graphing Linear Equations

- The **slope**, m, of an equation represents the rate at which the y-values of the equation change as the x-values change.

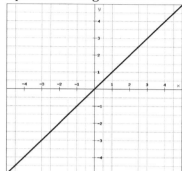   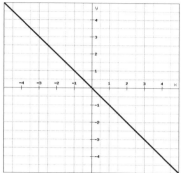

The line above has a slope of 1.   The line above has a slope of –1.

- Given two points, (x_1, y_1) and (x_2, y_2), of a linear equation, the slope, or change in rise divided by change in run, of the equation can be found by the equation $m = \frac{\text{rise}}{\text{run}} = \frac{y_2 - y_1}{x_2 - x_1}$.

The slope of the line that goes through the points (3, 4) and (7, –2) is $m = \frac{4 - -2}{3 - 7} = -\frac{3}{2}$

- The **y-intercept**, b, of an equation represents the initial point of the equation: the value of y when x equals 0.

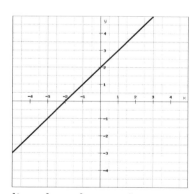

The line above has a y-intercept of 2.

- You can obtain the equation of a linear graph when you have either two of the points that lie on that line, one of the points that lies on the line and the line's slope, or one of the points and the line's y-intercept:

- Use the equation $y = mx + b$, where m is the slope of the linear equation and b is its y-intercept, when you are given both the slope and the y-intercept of the line.

The equation of the line that has a y-intercept of -2 and a slope of $-\frac{3}{5}$ is simply:

$$y = mx + b \rightarrow \mathbf{y = -\frac{3}{5}x - 2}$$

- Use the equation $y - y_1 = m(x - x_1)$ when you are given both the slope and a single point on the line or two points on the line (use the two points to calculate the slope).

The equation of the line that passes through the point $(-2, -4)$ and has a slope of 4 is:

$$y - y_1 = m(x - x_1) \rightarrow y - (-4) = 4(x - (-2)) \rightarrow y + 4 = 4x + 8 \rightarrow \mathbf{y = 4x + 4}$$

What is the slope of the line in the xy-plane that passes through the points $\left(-\frac{5}{2}, 1\right)$ and $\left(-\frac{1}{2}, 4\right)$?

A) -1

B) $-\frac{2}{3}$

C) 1

D) $\frac{3}{2}$

In this question, we're only asked to find the slope, so let's plug our two points into the slope formula:

$$m = \frac{\text{rise}}{\text{run}} = \frac{y_2 - y_1}{x_2 - x_1} = \frac{4 - 1}{-\frac{1}{2} - -\frac{5}{2}} = \frac{3}{2}$$

Our answer is **D**.

Graphing Linear Inequalities

- Graphing linear inequalities is similar to graphing linear equations, except you must shade all areas of the graph that satisfy the given inequality.
- When graphing inequalities with a < or > sign, use a dashed line instead of a solid line.
- When graphing inequalities with a ≤ or ≥ sign, use a solid line.
- The easiest way to check which part of the graph to shade involves picking a point that does not lie on the line of the inequality, then plugging that point into the inequality. If the point makes the inequality true, shade the portion of the graph that contains that point. If the point makes the inequality false, shade the other portion of the graph:

$$y < 3x - 2$$
Check point $(0, 0)$

$$0 < 3(0) - 2$$
$$0 < -2 \text{ false}$$

Shade the portion of the graph that does not contain $(0, 0)$

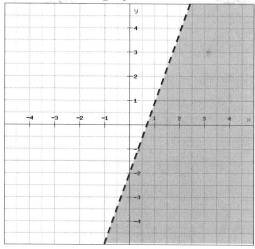

$$y < 3x - 2$$

Graphing Systems of Linear Equations or Inequalities

- To graph a system of linear equations, simply graph both lines. The point of intersection of the two graphs is the solution to the system of equations.

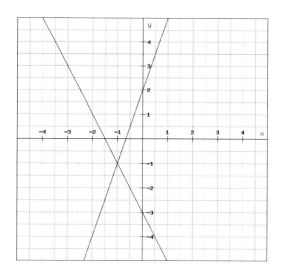

$$y = 3x + 2$$
$$y = -2x - 3$$

The solution to the system of equations above is $(-1, -1)$.

- To graph a system of linear inequalities, graph both inequalities as normal. The points that are shaded by both inequalities are all of the solutions to the system of linear inequalities.

Graphing Quadratic Equations

- The highest term of a quadratic equation is x^2. The graphs of these functions are symmetric – thus, they increase and then decrease, or decrease and then increase, as shown below:

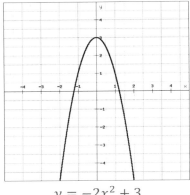

$$y = -2x^2 + 3$$

- The most common scenario modeled by a quadratic equation is projectile motion.

In the xy-plane, if the parabola with equation $y = ax^2 + bx + c$, where a, b, and c are constants, passes through the point $(-1, 1)$, which of the following must be true?

A) $a - b = 1$
B) $-b + c = 1$
C) $a + b + c = 1$
D) $a - b + c = 1$

Let's plug-in the values for x and y into our parabola's equation and simplify:

$$y = ax^2 + bx + c$$
$$1 = a(-1)^2 + b(-1) + c$$
$$\mathbf{1 = a - b + c}$$

So, our answer must be **D**.

Properties of the Graphs of Polynomials

- To match the sketch of a graph to a polynomial, remember these key points:
- Every zero of a polynomial is a place where its graph crosses the x-axis.

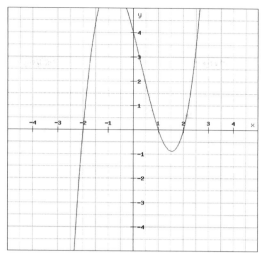

The above graph has three zeros: –2, 1, and 2

- The **degree** of a polynomial refers to the exponent of its highest-powered term.
- The **leading coefficient** of a polynomial refers to the coefficient in front of its highest-powered term.

$$y = 3x^4 + 2x^3 - 3$$

The degree of the above polynomial is 4, while its leading coefficient is 3.

- Polynomials of even degree with a positive leading coefficient have increasing end behavior on both ends, while those of even degree with a negative leading coefficient have decreasing end behavior on both ends.

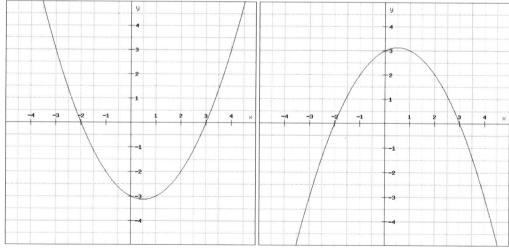

Polynomial of Even Degree and   Polynomial of Even Degree and
Positive Leading Coefficient   Negative Leading Coefficient

- Polynomials of odd degree and a positive leading coefficient have increasing end behavior as x increases (gets closer to ∞) and decreasing end behavior as x decreases (gets closer to $-\infty$).

- Polynomials of odd degree and a negative leading coefficient have decreasing end behavior as x increases (gets closer to ∞) and increasing end behavior as x decreases (gets closer to $-\infty$).

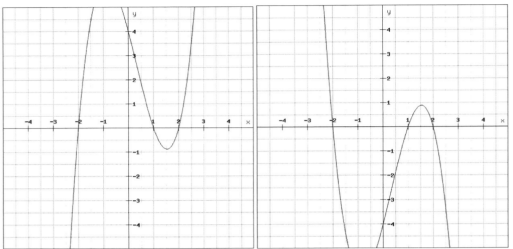

Polynomial of Odd Degree and
Positive Leading Coefficient

Polynomial of Odd Degree and
Negative Leading Coefficient

- The maximum (or minimum) of a polynomial's graph in a certain range is the highest (or lowest) y-value that is on that graph within that range.

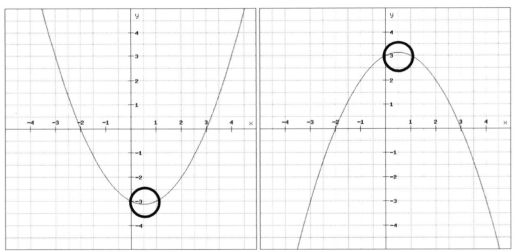

Minimum Value

Maximum Value

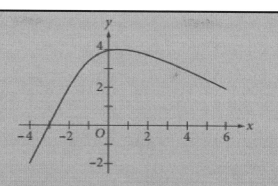

What is the minimum value of the function graphed on the xy-plane above, for $-4 \leq x \leq 6$?

A) $-\infty$

B) -4

C) -2

D) 1

Given the range above, the minimum, or lowest, point on the graph occurs when x is -4 and y is -2. Since only the y-value matters, our answer is **B**.

What is the equation of the line in the xy-plane that passes through the points $(3, 4)$ and $(9, 6)$?

A) $y = \frac{1}{3}x - 9$

B) $y = \frac{1}{3}x + 3$

C) $y = 3x - 9$

D) $y = 3x + 3$

What is the y-intercept of the line in the xy-plane that passes through the point $(-\frac{1}{2}, 2)$ and has a slope of -3?

A) $-\frac{3}{2}$

B) $-\frac{1}{2}$

C) $\frac{1}{2}$

D) $\frac{3}{2}$

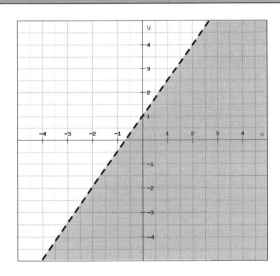

Which of the following best describes the solution set graphed above?

A) $y > \frac{3}{2}x + 1$

B) $y < \frac{3}{2}x + 1$

C) $y > -\frac{3}{2}x + 1$

D) $y > -\frac{3}{2}x + 1$

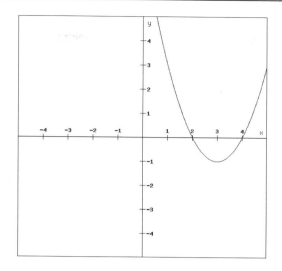

What is the minimum value of the function graphed on the xy-plane above, for $-5 \leq x \leq 5$?

A) $-\infty$
B) -1
C) 2
D) 3

In the xy-plane, if the parabola with equation $y = ax^2 + bx + c$, where a, b, and c are constants, passes through the point $(-1, -1)$, which of the following must be true?

A) $a + c = 1 - b$
B) $a + c = b - 1$
C) $a - c = 1 - b$
D) $a - c = b - 1$

In the xy-plane, the line with the equation $y = \frac{3}{5}x - 2$ is perpendicular to another line that passes through the origin. What is the equation of that line?

A) $y = \frac{5}{3}x$
B) $y = -\frac{5}{3}x$
C) $y = \frac{3}{5}x$
D) $y = -\frac{3}{5}x$

$$y \le x$$
$$y \le -2x + 2$$

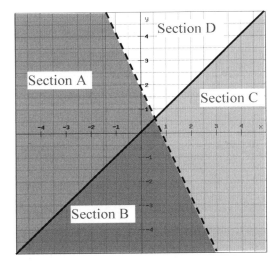

A system of inequalities and a graph are shown above. Which section or sections of the graph could represent all of the solutions to the system?

A) Section A
B) Section B
C) Sections A and D
D) Sections A, B, and C

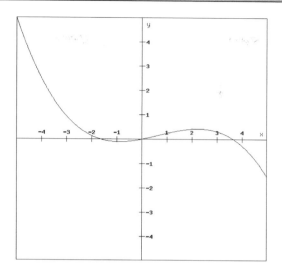

What is the maximum value of the function graphed on the xy-plane above, for $-5 \leq x \leq 5$?

A) $-\infty$
B) 0.75
C) 5
D) ∞

In the xy-plane, the line that passes through the points $(0, -3)$ and $(3, 6)$ intersects a line with a slope of -2 at the point $(a, 0)$. What is the y-coordinate of the y-intercept of the line with slope -2?

What is the length of the line segment AB with point A at the origin and point B at the midpoint of the line segment connecting the points $(3, 5)$ and $(7, 19)$?

Perimeter and Area

Perimeter

- The perimeter of a polygon is simply the sum of the length of all of its sides.

  What is the perimeter of a rectangle with length of 12 units and width of 4 units?

  $$P = 2l + 2w = 2(12) + 2(4) = \mathbf{32}$$

- The perimeter of a circle is known as its circumference. The circumference of a circle can be found by either of the two following equations:

  $C = 2\pi r$, where r is the radius of the circle
  $C = \pi d$, where d is the diameter of the circle

  A circle has a circumference of 20π inches. What is the length of its radius, in inches?

  $$C = 20\pi = 2\pi r \rightarrow r = \mathbf{10\ inches}$$

A rectangle has perimeter P, length l, and width w. Which of the following represents l in terms of P and w?

A) $l = P - w$
B) $l = \dfrac{2P - w}{2}$
C) $l = \dfrac{P - 2w}{2}$
D) $l = 2P - 2w$

Let's start by setting up our perimeter equation; then all we have to do is solve for l.

$$P = 2l + 2w$$
$$P - 2w = 2l$$
$$\frac{P - 2w}{2} = l$$

Our answer is **C**.

Area

- Typically, the PSAT will only ask us to find the area of polygons that are made up of triangles and/or rectangles.
- The area of a triangle can be found by the formula $A = \frac{1}{2}bh$. The base and height of a triangle must be perpendicular to each other.

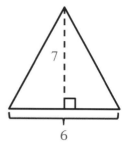 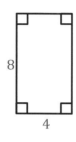 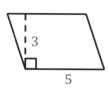

$$A = \frac{1}{2}bh = \frac{1}{2}(6)(7) = 21 \quad A = bh = (8)(4) = 32 \quad A = bh = (3)(5) = 15$$

- The area of a rectangle or parallelogram can be found by the formula $A = bh$. The base and height of a parallelogram must be perpendicular to each other.
- The area of a trapezoid can be found by the formula $A = \frac{1}{2}h(b_1 + b_2)$, where b_1 and b_2 are the lengths of the parallel bases of the trapezoid.

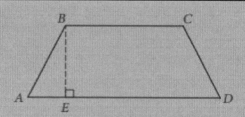

In the quadrilateral $ABCD$ above, $\overline{BC}$ is parallel to $\overline{AD}$, and $AB = CD$. If BC and AD were each doubled and BE was reduced by 50 percent, how would the area of $ABCD$ change?
A) The area of $ABCD$ would be decreased by 50 percent.
B) The area of $ABCD$ would be increased by 50 percent.
C) The area of $ABCD$ would not change.
D) The area of $ABCD$ would be multiplied by 2.

We know the area of the trapezoid above is $A = \frac{1}{2}h(b_1 + b_2)$. b_1 and b_2 are doubled, while h is reduced by 50%, or half of its original value. Let's insert these changes and compare.

$$A = \frac{1}{2}(\frac{1}{2}h)(2b_1 + 2b_2)$$

$$A = \frac{1}{4}h(2)(b_1 + b_2)$$

$$A = \frac{1}{2}h(b_1 + b_2)$$

In the end, the area does not change, so the answer must be **C**.

1

If the radius of Circle A is increased by 20%, the area of Circle A is increased by:

A) 10%
B) 20%
C) 40%
D) 44%

2

A circle has circumference C and diameter d. Which of the following represents d in terms of C?

A) $d = \pi C$
B) $d = \frac{\pi}{C}$
C) $d = \frac{C}{\pi}$
D) $d = \frac{C}{2\pi}$

3

A rectangle has a perimeter of 48 inches. What is the area of the rectangle?

A) 140 square inches
B) 144 square inches
C) 148 square inches
D) The area of the rectangle cannot be determined.

4

A rectangle has area A, length l, and width w. Which of the following represents w in terms of A and l?

A) $w = Al$
B) $w = \frac{l}{A}$
C) $w = \frac{A}{l}$
D) $w = \frac{A - 2l}{2}$

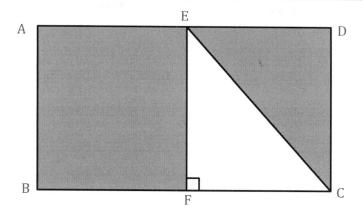

5

In the image above, Point F is the midpoint of BC. If the area of Rectangle $ABCD$ is 81, what is the area of right triangle EFC?

A) $\frac{81}{4}$

B) $\frac{81}{2}$

C) $81 - \frac{81}{4}$

D) It is unable to be determined from the information given.

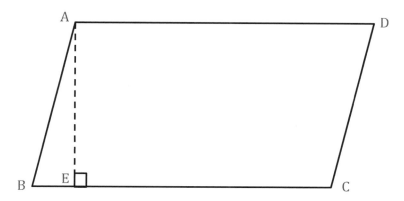

6

In parallelogram $ABCD$ above, AD and BC were each increased in length by 50% while the length of AE was decreased by 25%. How would the area of $ABCD$ change?

A) The area would be decreased by 25%.
B) The area would be decreased by 12.5%.
C) The area would be increased by 12.5%.
D) The area would be increased by 25%.

7

A circle is inscribed inside of a square with area 144. What is the length of the radius of the circle?

A) 3
B) 6
C) 9
D) 12

8

A square has a side length of 20. Which of the following changes would create the rectangle with the largest area?

A) Increase two parallel sides of the square by 15%
B) Increase each side of the square by 10%
C) Increase two parallel sides of the square by 20% and decrease the other two sides by 5%
D) Increase two parallel sides of the square by 30% and decrease the other two sides by 10%

9

A circle has an area of πx and a circumference of 24π. What is the value of x?

10

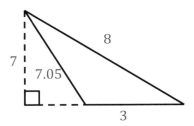

What is the area of the triangle above?

Triangles

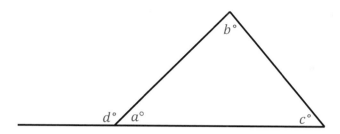

- The measures of the interior angles of a triangle sum to 180°

$$a + b + c = 180$$

- The measure of an exterior angle of a triangle is equal to the sum of the two interior angles of the triangle that are not adjacent to that exterior angle

$$d = b + c$$

- The longest side of a triangle is always opposite the largest interior angle of the triangle. Likewise, the shortest side of a triangle is always opposite the smallest interior angle of the triangle.

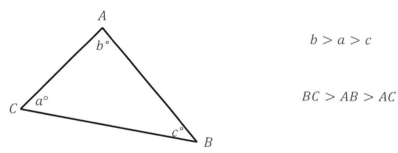

$$b > a > c$$

$$BC > AB > AC$$

- If two of the interior angles of a triangle have equal measures, then the sides opposite those two angles have equal lengths. These triangles are called **isosceles triangles**.

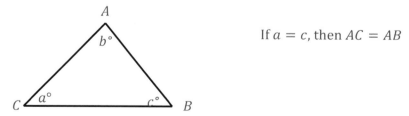

If $a = c$, then $AC = AB$

- A triangle with three equal sides and three equal angles is called an **equilateral triangle**.

- The lengths of any two sides of a triangle must add up to more than the third side of the triangle.

  The side lengths of a triangle can be 7, 8, and 9. However, they cannot be 3, 5, and 9, because $3 + 5 < 9$.

- If two triangles have at least two equal angles, then they are similar (their side lengths are proportional).

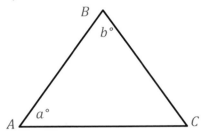
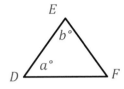

$$\frac{AB}{DE} = \frac{BC}{EF} = \frac{FD}{CA}$$

- Two triangles are congruent if they have exactly the same 3 side lengths and the same 3 angle measures. The following are enough to prove that two triangles are congruent:
    - SSS – Two triangles with all three side lengths equal
    - SAS – Two triangles with two side lengths and the angle between those side lengths equal
    - ASA – Two triangles with two angles and the side between those angles equal
    - AAS – Two triangles with two angles and a side adjacent to, but not between, those angles equal
    - HL – Two right triangles that have an equal pair of hypotenuses and an equal pair of legs

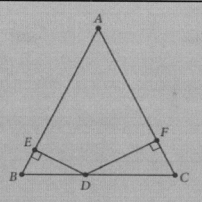

Note: Figure not drawn to scale.

Triangle ABC above is isosceles with $AB = AC$ and $BC = 48$. The ratio of DE to DF is $5 : 7$. What is the length of side length DC?

A) 12
B) 20
C) 24
D) 28

Since we know that the triangle is isosceles, the measures of angles B and C must be equal. Since triangles BED aand CFD both have two congruent angles (right angles are always congruent), they must be similar. The ratio of DE to DF is $5 : 7$, so the ratio of BD to DC must also be $5 : 7$.

$$BD + DC = 48$$
$$BD = 48 - DC$$
$$\frac{BD}{DC} = \frac{5}{7}$$
$$\frac{48 - DC}{DC} = \frac{5}{7}$$

Now we can cross multiply and solve for DC.

$$7(48 - DC) = 5DC$$
$$336 - 7DC = 5DC$$
$$336 = 12DC$$
$$\mathbf{28 = DC}$$

Our answer must be **D**.

A triangle has side lengths of 4 and 7. Which of the following is not a possible length of the third side of the triangle?

A) 3
B) 4
C) 7
D) 8

Use the following information for Questions 2 and 3.

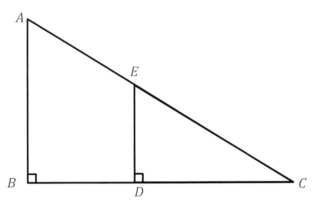

If the length of AB is 16, the length of ED is 8, and the perimeter of triangle ABC is 48, what is the perimeter of triangle EDC?

A) 12
B) 24
C) 36
D) It cannot be determined from the information provided.

If the length of BD is x, the length of ED is y, and the length of AB is $3y$, what is the length of DC in terms of x?

A) $\frac{1}{2}x$
B) x
C) $\frac{3}{2}x$
D) $2x$

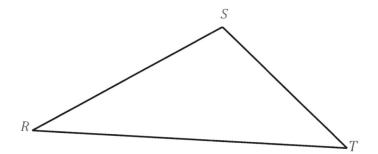

In the triangle above, $\angle S > \angle R > \angle T$. Which of the following statements is not true?

A) $RS < ST$
B) $RT < SR$
C) $ST < RT$
D) $RS < RT$

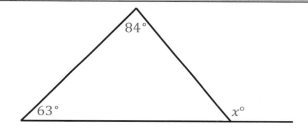

What is the value of x in the image above?

A) 21°
B) 33°
C) 147°
D) 159°

A triangle has side lengths of x, y, and z. Which of the following must be true about the triangle?

A) $x^2 + y^2 = z^2$
B) $x + y < z$
C) $x + y > z$
D) $x + y = z$

Questions 7 and 8 refer to the following information.

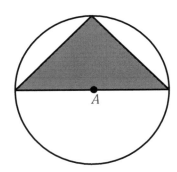

Circle A above has a radius of r.

What is the area of the shaded triangle inscribed in Circle A above in terms of r ?

A) $\frac{1}{2}r^2$
B) r^2
C) $\frac{3}{2}r^2$
D) $2r^2$

8

What is the area of the unshaded portion of the image above, in terms of r?

A) $2\pi r^2$
B) πr^2
C) $(\pi - 1)r^2$
D) $(\pi - 2)r^2$

9

A triangle has side lengths of y, 4, and 7. What is a possible value of y?

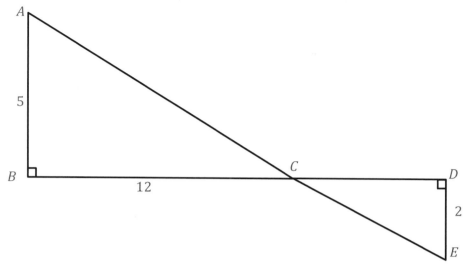

What is the length of *BD* above?

Trigonometry

Pythagorean Theorem

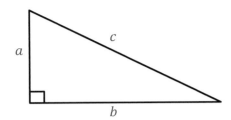

- For a right triangle with leg lengths a and b and hypotenuse of length c, the relation $a^2 + b^2 = c^2$ must hold true.

  A triangle has legs of length 7 and 12. What is the length of the hypotenuse of the triangle?

  $$7^2 + 12^2 = c^2$$
  $$49 + 144 = c^2$$
  $$193 = c^2$$
  $$\boldsymbol{\sqrt{193} = c}$$

- The most common right triangle lengths on the PSAT are in the ratio of $3:4:5$. The ratio $5:12:13$ is also common, as is the ratio $8:15:17$.

  A right triangle with a side length of 6 and a hypotenuse of 10 would have a second side length of 8. (multiply each term in the 3:4:5 ratio by 2).

Trigonometric Ratios

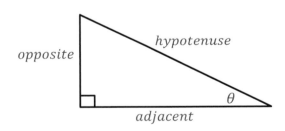

- Use trigonometric ratios to find missing side lengths or angle measurements of right triangles.
- **SOH CAH TOA**: $\sin \theta = \dfrac{opposite}{hypotenuse}$ $\cos \theta = \dfrac{adjacent}{hypotenuse}$ $\tan \theta = \dfrac{opposite}{adjacent}$

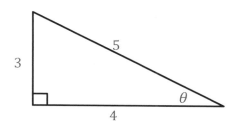

$$\sin \theta = \frac{3}{5}$$

$$\cos \theta = \frac{4}{5}$$

$$\tan \theta = \frac{3}{4}$$

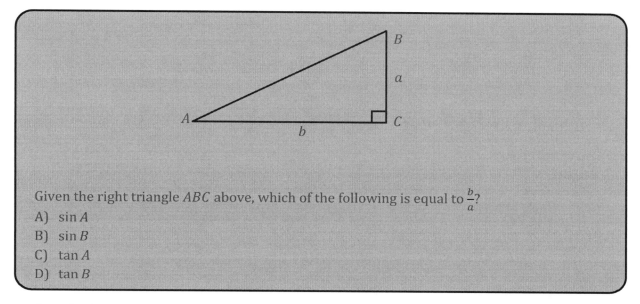

Given the right triangle ABC above, which of the following is equal to $\frac{b}{a}$?

A) $\sin A$

B) $\sin B$

C) $\tan A$

D) $\tan B$

Since both sides with given values, b and a, are legs, we know the relationship that connects them must be a tangent function. Since b is the numerator and a is the denominator, it must be **D**, $\tan B$.

Questions 1 and 2 use the following information.

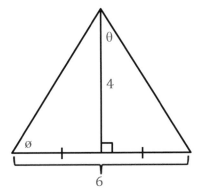

1

What is the value of tan ø?

A) $\frac{3}{5}$

B) $\frac{2}{3}$

C) $\frac{3}{4}$

D) $\frac{4}{3}$

2

What is the value of sin θ?

A) $\frac{3}{5}$

B) $\frac{2}{3}$

C) $\frac{3}{4}$

D) $\frac{4}{3}$

Use the information below for Questions 3 and 4.

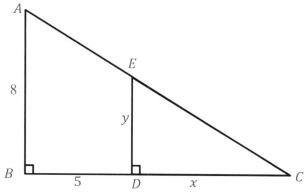

3

If the length of side AC is 17, what is the value of x?

A) 5
B) 7
C) 10
D) 12

4

If the length of side AC is 17, what is the value of y?

A) 8
B) $\frac{16}{3}$
C) 5
D) $\frac{8}{3}$

5

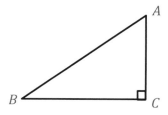

If $\sin A = \frac{1}{5}$ and $\cos B = \frac{1}{5}$, which of the following is true?

A) $AC = 4$
B) $AC = \sqrt{24}$
C) $\angle A = \angle B$
D) $m\angle A < m\angle B$

6

If $\sin(90 - x) = A$ and $0 < x < 90$, then $\cos x = ?$

A) $\frac{1}{A}$

B) A

C) $-A$

D) $-\frac{1}{A}$

7

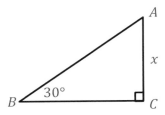

If the length of AB is 3, what is the value of x?

A) $\frac{3}{2}$

B) $\frac{3\sqrt{2}}{2}$

C) $3\sqrt{2}$

D) 6

8

An isosceles right triangle has a leg length of 12. What is the perimeter of the triangle?

A) 24

B) 36

C) $24 + 12\sqrt{2}$

D) $36 + 12\sqrt{2}$

Use the following information for Questions 9 and 10.

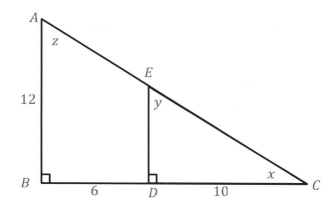

What is the value of tan x ?

What is the value of tan y ?

Measures of Center

- Usually, the mean of a dataset is the most commonly used measure of center. The **mean** of a dataset can be found by adding up each point in the data set, then dividing that sum by the number of points in the data set.

  The mean of the dataset {2, 4, 5, 7, 8} is $\frac{2+4+5+7+8}{5} = \frac{26}{5} = \mathbf{5.2}$

- However, the mean is an inappropriate measure of center when outliers (points that are very different from most other points in the data set) exist in the data set or when the data are heavily skewed in one direction.

  The mean of the dataset {2, 4, 5, 7, 100} is $\frac{2+4+5+7+100}{5} = \frac{118}{5} = \mathbf{23.6}$. Note how the mean is not representative of any piece of data in the dataset because 100 is so far away from the other points in the data set.

- The **median** of a data set is the point in the middle. To find the median, first make sure all the data points are in ascending (increasing) order.

  The median of the dataset {2, 4, 5, 7, 8} is **5.**

- If there are an even number of points in the data set, the median is the mean of the two middle points.

  The mean of the dataset {2, 4, 5, 7, 8, 10} is $\frac{5+7}{2} = \mathbf{6}$

- The median is the most appropriate measure of center when the data set is skewed or contains outliers.

  The median of the dataset {2, 4, 5, 7, 100} is **5**. This is a much better measure of the center of the dataset, as it is close to the majority of the numbers in the dataset.

- The **mode** of a data set is the most frequent data point. If two or more data points are the most frequent, all of them are considered to be the mode. Note that for a data point to be the mode, there must be more than one instance of that point in the data set. The mode is the most appropriate measure of center when you are looking for the most popular response.

  The mode of the dataset {2, 4, 4, 5, 7, 7, 8} is both **4 and 7.**

- The **range** of a data set is the difference between the largest and smallest data points.

  The range of the dataset {2, 4, 4, 5, 7, 7, 8} is $8 - 2 = \mathbf{6.}$

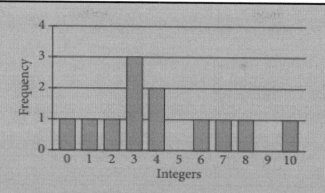

The graph above shows the frequency distribution of a list of randomly generated integers between 0 and 10. What is the mean of the list of numbers?

A) 3.0
B) 3.5
C) 4.25
D) 12.0

This is a pretty typical measure of center question, but the data is presented in an unusual way. Let's come up with a list of numbers in the dataset. The frequency of each number shows how many instances of that number there are:

{0, 1, 2, 3, 3, 3, 4, 4, 6, 7, 8, 10}

Now we can just add the numbers up and divide by the number of points in the dataset:

$$\frac{0 + 1 + 2 + 3 + 3 + 3 + 4 + 4 + 6 + 7 + 8 + 10}{12} = 4.25$$

The answer is **C**.

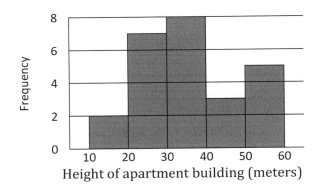

Height of apartment building (meters)

The histogram above shows the distribution of the heights, in meters, of 25 apartment buildings in Birmingham. Which of the following could be the median height of the 25 apartment buildings represented in the histogram?

A) 23 meters
B) 29 meters
C) 32 meters
D) 41 meters

Use the following information about the salaries of the employees of a company for Questions 2 and 3.

Number of Employees	Salary
18	$30,000
15	$40,000
25	$50,000
25	$60,000
10	$70,000
5	$80,000
2	$120,000

What is the mean salary of the 100 employees of the company shown above?

A) $52,300
B) $55,000
C) $59,800
D) $64,300

What is the median salary of the 100 employees of the company shown above?

A) $45,000
B) $50,000
C) $55,000
D) $60,000

$$\{3, 5, 7, 6, 9, 2, 1, 10, 9, 4\}$$

What is the positive difference between the range and the mode of the numbers above?

A) 0
B) 1
C) 9
D) 10

The heights of five students are as follows:

5 foot 6 inches   5 foot 4 inches   5 foot 8 inches   5 foot 11 inches   6 foot 0 inches

What is the approximate mean height of the students? (1 foot = 12 inches)

A) 5 foot 6 inches
B) 5 foot 7 inches
C) 5 foot 8 inches
D) 5 foot 9 inches

Questions 6 and 7 refer to the following information about the test scores of a class.

Test Score	Grade	Frequency
90-100	A	4
80-89	B	8
70-79	C	5
60-69	D	3

6

Which of the following could be the median test score of the class based on the above data?

A) 93
B) 91
C) 88
D) 78

7

The mean test grade of the students in the class is what grade?

A) A
B) B
C) C
D) It is impossible to be determined.

8

$$\{3, 3, 5, 6, 8, 8, 8, 9, 10, 12\}$$

The number 7.2 is added to the data set above. Which of the following measures of center and spread does this change?

A) Median
B) Mean
C) Range
D) The additional number does not change any of the above.

Questions 9 and 10 refer to the following information.

Inches of Precipitation for Santa Clara

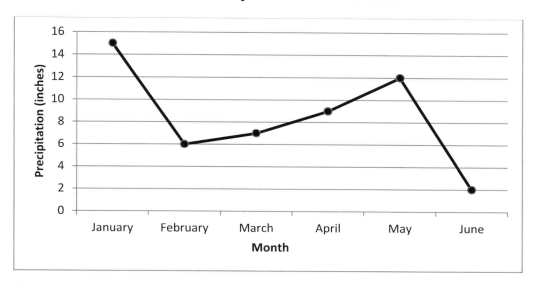

9

What is the range in monthly precipitation measurements, in inches, for the 6 months shown above?

10

What is the mean monthly precipitation for Santa Clara according to the information presented above, to the nearest tenth of an inch?

Graphs and Scatterplots

- A scatterplot shows the relationship between two sets of value. Look at the example below:

Length of Randomly Selected Pythons

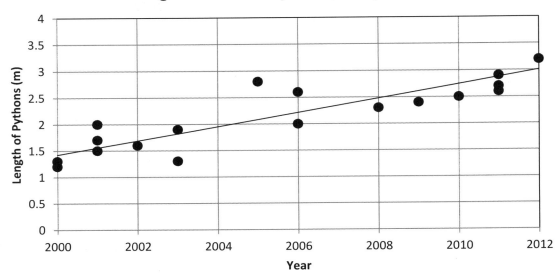

- Always check the title of each axis for the data that is being compared and the units of that data.

   The x-axis shows the year, while the y-axis shows the length of a randomly selected python in meters.

- The line of best fit shown above shows the general trend of how the length of a randomly selected python changes with respect to the year.

- Most of the lines of best fit on the PSAT will be linear, like the one shown above, though you will see the occasional quadratic or exponential line of best fit as well.

- Some scatterplot questions will give you the equation of the line of best fit of the data shown.

- To predict another data point that is not given, you should expand the line of best fit to points beyond those given. If the line of best fit is given, plug the point (x or y) into the equation to find the predicted data point.

In 1929, the astronomer Edwin Hubble published the data shown. The graph plots the velocity of galaxies relative to Earth against the distances of galaxies from Earth.

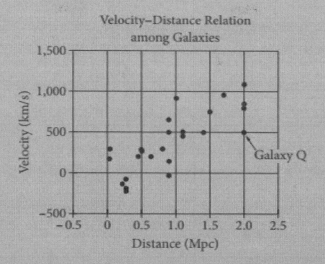

Hubble's data can be modeled by the equation $v = 500d$, where v is the velocity, in kilometers per second, at which the galaxy is moving away from Earth and d is the distance, in megaparsecs, of the galaxy from Earth. Assume that the relationship is valid for larger distances than are shown in the graph. (A megaparsec (Mpc) is 3.1×10^{19} kilometers.)

According to Hubble's data, how fast, in <u>meters</u> per second, is Galaxy Q moving away from Earth?

A) 2×10^6 m/s
B) 5×10^5 m/s
C) 5×10^2 m/s
D) 2.5×10^2 m/s

For this question, it is simple enough to find Galaxy Q in the data given. We can see that Galaxy Q has a Distance of 2.0 Mpc and a velocity of 500 km/s. Since we care about m/s, though, not km/s, we need to multiply the velocity by 1000.

500 km/s × 1000 m/km = 500,000, or **5.0 × 10⁵ m/s**. The answer is **B**.

There are four galaxies shown in the graph at approximately 0.9 Mpc from Earth. Which of the following is closest to the range of velocities of these four galaxies, in kilometers per second?

A) 100
B) 200
C) 450
D) 700

Let's start by examining the four galaxies referenced in the problem:

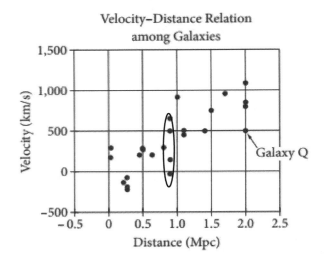

We've circled the four galaxies above. Since we're looking for the range of their velocities, we simply need to subtract the smallest of the four velocities from the largest of the four velocities.

650 km/s − −50 km/s = **700 km/s**. The answer is **D**.

Questions 1 and 2 refer to the following information.

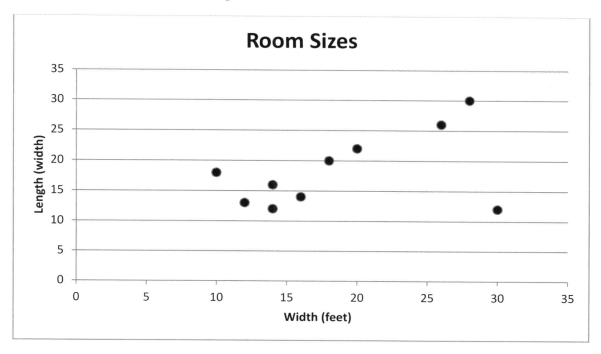

Room Sizes

1

The scatterplot above shows the lengths and widths of 10 different rooms in a resort. What is the length, in feet, of the room represented by the data point that is farthest from the line of best fit (not shown)?

A) 10
B) 12
C) 18
D) 30

2

The equation of the line of best fit to the data above is $l = 0.96w - 0.36$. Based on the model, what is the approximate width, in feet, of a room that is 24 feet long?

A) 20 feet
B) 22.5 feet
C) 24 feet
D) 25.5 feet

3

Which scatterplot shows a positive association that is not linear? (Note: A positive association between two variables is one in which higher values of one variable correspond to higher values of the other variable, and lower values of one variable correspond to lower values of the other variable.)

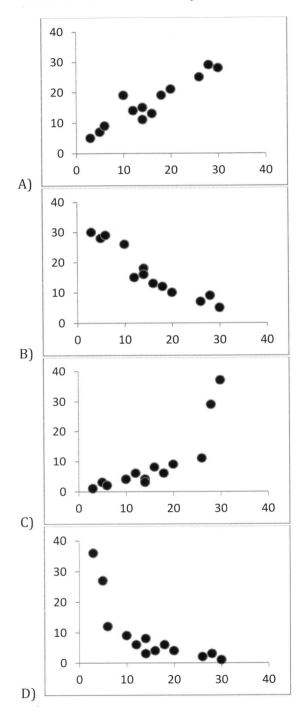

A)

B)

C)

D)

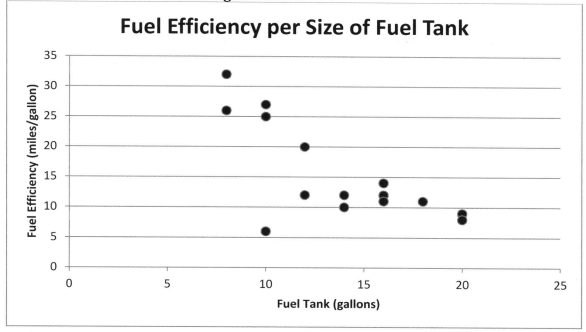

The data above can be modeled by the equation $y = -2.625t + 52.93$, where y is the fuel efficiency, in miles per gallon, and t is the fuel tank size, in gallons. Assume that the relationship is valid for larger and smaller fuel tank sizes than are shown in the graph.

4

There are three vehicles shown with a fuel tank size of 16 gallons. What is the range of fuel efficiencies of these three vehicles, in miles per gallon?

A) 1
B) 2
C) 3
D) 4

5

According to the data above, a vehicle with a fuel tank that holds 15 gallons should get what fuel efficiency?

A) 13.5 miles per gallon
B) 14.0 miles per gallon
C) 14.5 miles per gallon
D) 15.0 miles per gallon

Based on the model, a vehicle with a fuel efficiency of 40 miles per gallon would have a fuel tank that holds how many gallons?

A) 50
B) 15
C) 10
D) 5

A car company wants to increase its vehicle's fuel efficiency from 20 miles per gallon to 30 miles per gallon. Based on the model, by how much should the vehicle's fuel tank size, in gallons, decrease?

A) 2
B) 3
C) 4
D) 5

Questions 8 – 10 refer to the following information.

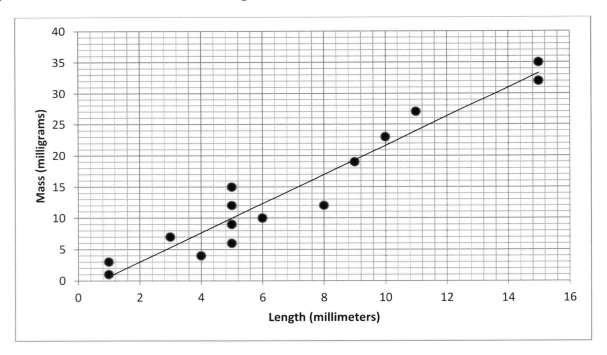

The above data models the length and mass of individual specimens of a newly discovered worm species. A line of best fit to the data is shown. Assume the relationship is valid for larger distances than are shown in the graph.

Based on the line of best fit to the data shown above, what is the approximate length, in cm, of a 40 mg specimen of the new worm species?

A) 2 cm
B) 4 cm
C) 20 cm
D) 40 cm

What is the range of masses, to the nearest mg, of the 4 worm specimens found that measure 5 mm in length?

Of the data points modeled above, how many have masses that are different from the mass projected by the line of best fit by more than 3 mg?

Two-Way Tables

- Two-way tables show data from one group that pertains to two distinct categories.
- Below is an example of a two-way table.

	VOTED YES	VOTED NO	DID NOT VOTE	TOTAL
18- to 39-year-olds	124	256	345	725
40- to 59-year-olds	223	298	136	657
People 60 years-old and over	89	76	23	188
Total	436	630	504	1,570

- Notice that each cell in the final row and final column is a total amount.
- The **relative frequency** of a value is the fraction or proportion of times the value occurs. So, the relative frequency of people 60 years-old and over in the survey above is $\frac{188}{1570}$.
- **Conditional frequency** is the ratio of a subtotal to the value of a total. In the two-way table above, the conditional frequency of 18- to 39-year olds who voted no is $\frac{256}{725}$. The conditional frequency of people who voted no who are 18 to 39 years-old, on the other hand, is $\frac{256}{630}$.

A survey of 170 randomly selected teenagers aged 14 through 17 in the United States was conducted to gather data on summer employment of teenagers. The data are shown in the table below.

	Have a summer job	Do not have a summer job	Total
Ages 14–15	20	69	89
Ages 16–17	39	42	81
Total	59	111	170

Which of the following is closest to the percent of those surveyed who had a summer job?

A) 22%

B) 35%

C) 47%

D) 53%

---

170 total people were surveyed, 59 of which had had a summer job. The percent surveyed who had a summer job is $\frac{59}{170} = $ **35**%, or **B**.

In 2012 the total population of individuals in the Unites States who were between 14 and 17 years old (inclusive) was about 17 million. If the survey results are used to estimate information about summer employment of teenagers across the country, which of the following is the best estimate of the total number of individuals between 16 and 17 years old in the United States who had a summer job in 2012?

A) 8,200,000
B) 3,900,000
C) 2,000,000
D) 390,000

Since the survey results can be used to estimate information about summer employment across the country, we know the proportions present in the table must be the same as the proportions for the population as a whole. There are 170 teenagers in the survey, and 39 of them have a summer job: 23%. Thus, 23% of the 17 million teenagers in the United States in 2012 also have a summer job. 23% of 17 million is **3.9 million**, or **B**.

Questions 1 through 3 refer to the following information.

A survey of 200 randomly selected college students aged 18 through 21 in the United States was conducted to gather data on employment while taking classes. The data are shown in the table below.

	Works while taking classes	Does not work while taking classes	Total
Ages 18-19	43	62	105
Ages 20-21	67	28	95
Total	110	90	200

1

Which of the following is closest to the percent of those surveyed who worked while taking classes?

A) 41%
B) 45%
C) 55%
D) 71%

2

In 2014, the estimated number of individuals in the United States between the ages of 18 and 21 who were attending college was about 10 million. If the survey results are used to estimate information about employment of college students in this age bracket around the country, which of the following is the best estimate of the total number of individuals between 20 and 21 years old in the United States who did not work in 2014?

A) 1.4 million
B) 1.5 million
C) 3.1 million
D) 3.2 million

3

Based on the data, how many times more likely is it for a 18-19 year old to work during college than it is for a 20-21 year old to work during college? (Round the answer to the nearest hundredth.)

A) 0.50
B) 0.58
C) 1.72
D) 2.00

Questions 4 through 7 refer to the following information.

A survey of 500 randomly selected voters in Oregon was conducted to gather data on support for Proposition 192a. The data are shown in the table below.

	Supports Proposition 192a	Does not support Proposition 192a	Total
Urban Voters	55	275	320
Rural Voters	136	44	180
Total	191	319	500

4

Which of the following percentages is greatest?

A) The percentage of urban voters who do not support Proposition 192a.
B) The percentage of rural voters who support Proposition 192a.
C) The percentage of Proposition 192a supporters who are urban.
D) The percentage of Proposition 192a supporters who are rural.

5

Based on the data, how much more likely is it for an urban voter to support the proposition than to not support it? (Round the answer to the nearest hundredth.)

A) 0.20 times as likely
B) 0.32 times as likely
C) 3.09 times as likely
D) 5.00 times as likely

6

The urban voters in the survey above were polled after the initial question to find out their opinions on Proposition 192b. Thirty percent of those surveyed supported Proposition 192b. What percentage of urban voters support both Propositions?

A) 5%
B) 24%
C) 47%
D) It is unable to be determined from the information provided.

7

Which of the following is closest to the percent of people who do not support Proposition 192a and are from rural areas of Oregon?

A) 8.8%
B) 13.8%
C) 24.4%
D) 91.2%

Questions 8 through 10 refer to the following information.

A survey of 300 randomly selected juniors and seniors at a local high school were polled about their future college plans. The data are shown in the table below.

	Plans on attending college	Does not plan to attend college	Total
Juniors	96	79	175
Seniors	83	42	125
Total	179	121	300

8

Based on the data, how many times more likely is it that a junior plans to attend college than a senior plans to attend college?

A) 0.74 times as likely
B) 0.83 times as likely
C) 1.21 times as likely
D) 1.34 times as likely

9

To the nearest tenth of a percent, what percent of the students surveyed plan on attending college?

10

To the nearest tenth of a percent, what percentage of the juniors surveyed plan on not attending college?

TEST PREP GENIUS

THIS PAGE IS LEFT INTENTIONALLY BLANK

Math Practice Answer Keys

Explanations can be found online at http://www.tpgenius.com/

Pre-Algebra Review	Algebra	%s, Rates, Unit Conversions	Polynomial Operations and Functions	Solving For A Term
1. C	1. B	1. A	1. A	1. A
2. C	2. B	2. A	2. A	2. D
3. D	3. A	3. B	3. C	3. A
4. C	4. C	4. C	4. C	4. C
5. A	5. B	5. C	5. C	5. B
6. A	6. C	6. B	6. C	6. D
7. C	7. D	7. B	7. D	7. B
8. C	8. D	8. D	8. B	8. B
9. C	9. 9	9. 75	9. 4.5	9. $\frac{4}{3}$
10. B	10. 7	10. 1500	10. 2	10. $2 < 4y - 6x < 8$

Quadratics	Graphs of Polynomials	Perimeter and Area	Triangles	Trigonometry
1. D	1. B	1. D	1. A	1. D
2. B	2. C	2. C	2. B	2. A
3. A	3. B	3. D	3. A	3. C
4. A	4. B	4. C	4. B	4. B
5. D	5. B	5. A	5. C	5. B
6. D	6. B	6. C	6. C	6. B
7. B	7. B	7. B	7. B	7. A
8. D	8. C	8. B	8. C	8. C
9. 1	9. 2	9. 144	9. $5 < y < 11$	9. $\frac{3}{4}$
10. 1.5	10. 13	10. 10.5	10. 16.8 or $\frac{84}{5}$	10. $\frac{4}{3}$

Measures of Center	Graphs and Scatterplots	Two-Way Tables
1. C	1. B	1. C
2. A	2. D	2. A
3. B	3. C	3. B
4. A	4. C	4. A
5. C	5. A	5. A
6. C	6. D	6. D
7. D	7. C	7. A
8. D	8. A	8. B
9. 13	9. 9	9. 59.7
10. 8.5	10. 4	10. 45.1

Explanations can be found online at http://www.tpgenius.com/

Section 5
Full-length Practice Tests

Reading Test

60 MINUTES, 47 QUESTIONS

Turn to Section 1 of your answer sheet to answer the questions in this section.

Questions 1-9 are based on the following passage.

This passage is excerpted from President Bill Clinton's First State of the Union Address, given on February 17, 1993.

When Presidents speak to the Congress and the nation from this podium, they typically comment on the full range of challenges and opportunities that face us. But these are not ordinary times. For all the many tasks that
5 require our attention, one calls on us to focus, unite, and act. Together, we must make our economy thrive once again.

We have always been a people of youthful energy and daring spirit. And at this historic moment, as
10 communism has fallen, as freedom is spreading around the world, as a global economy is taking shape before our eyes, Americans have called for change – and now it is up to those of us in this room to deliver.

Our nation needs a new direction. Tonight, I present
15 to you our comprehensive plan to set our nation on that new course.

The conditions which brought us to this point are well known. Two decades of low productivity and stagnant wages; persistent unemployment and underemployment;
20 years of huge government deficits and declining investment in our future; exploding health care costs, and lack of coverage; legions of poor children; educational and job training opportunities inadequate to the demands of a high wage, high growth economy.
25 I tell you this not to assign blame for this problem. There is plenty of blame to go around – in both branches of the government and both parties. The time for blame has come to an end. I came here to accept responsibility;

I want you to accept responsibility for the future of this
30 country, and if we do it right, I don't care who gets the credit for it.

Tonight, I want to talk about what government can do, because I believe our government must do more for the hard-working people who pay its way. But let me
35 say first: government cannot do this alone. The private sector is the engine of economic growth in America. And every one of us can be an engine of change in our own lives. We've got to give people more opportunity, but we must also demand more responsibility in return.
40 Our immediate priority is to create jobs, now. We will put people to work right now and create half a million jobs: jobs that will rebuild our highways and airports, renovate housing, bring new life to our rural towns, and spread hope and opportunity among our nation's youth
45 with almost 700,000 jobs for them this summer alone. And I invite America's business leaders to join us in this effort, so that together we can create a million summer jobs in cities and poor rural areas for our young people.

Second, our plan looks beyond today's business cycle,
50 because our aspirations extend into the next century. The heart of our plan deals with the long term. It has an investment program designed to increase public and private investment in areas critical to our economic future. And it has a deficit reduction program that will
55 increase savings available for private sector investment, lower interest rates, decrease the percentage of the federal budget claimed by interest payments, and decrease the risk of financial market disruptions that could adversely affect the economy.
60 Our plan invests in our roads, bridges, transit facilities; in high- speed railways and high-tech information systems; and in the most ambitious

environmental clean-up of our time.

But all of our efforts to strengthen the economy will
65 fail unless we take bold steps to reform our health care
system. America's businesses will never be strong;
America's families will never be secure; and America's
government will never be solvent until we tackle our
health care crisis.
70 The rising costs and the lack of care are endangering
both our economy and our lives. Reducing health care
costs will liberate hundreds of billions of dollars for
investment and growth and new jobs. Over the long run,
reforming health care is essential to reducing our deficit
75 and expanding investment.

Later this spring, I will deliver to Congress a
comprehensive plan for health care reform that will
finally get costs under control. We will provide security
to all our families, so that no one will be denied the
80 coverage they need. We will root out fraud and
outrageous charges, and make sure that paperwork no
longer chokes you or your doctor. And we will maintain
American standards – the highest quality medical care in
the world and the choices we demand and deserve. The
85 American people expect us to deal with health care. And
we must deal with it now.

If we work hard – and work together – if we
rededicate ourselves to strengthening families, creating
jobs, rewarding work, and reinventing government, we
90 can lift America's fortunes once again.

1

The central claim of the passage as a whole is that

A) the healthcare system must be reformed for the good
   of American families.
B) America's most pressing problem is a weak economy.
C) previous Presidents and leaders created the economic
   problems that Clinton must solve.
D) the economy cannot be addressed without reducing
   the budget deficit.

2

The speaker strongly suggests that he

A) believes the government is solely responsible for
   solving the nation's economic problems.
B) is interested in neither assigning blame for the current
   problem nor taking credit for solutions.
C) wishes to focus on short-term economic improvement
   before addressing long-term issues.
D) considers healthcare to be the most important issue
   facing Americans.

3

Which choice provides the best evidence for the answer
to the previous question?

A) Lines 27-31 ("The time...for it")
B) Lines 32-34 ("Tonight...its way")
C) Lines 49-51 ("Second...term")
D) Lines 82-86 ("And we...it now")

4

The author most likely used the phrase "youthful energy
and daring spirit" in order to

A) illustrate how young America is compared to other
   nations.
B) prove to his listeners that Americans are not too tired
   to address the current problems.
C) appeal to the listeners' sense of patriotic pride.
D) demonstrate that his primary audience is younger
   voters.

5

As it is used in line 17, "conditions" most nearly means

A) circumstances.
B) provisions.
C) preparations.
D) ailments.

6

As it is used in line 53, "critical" most nearly means

A) severe.
B) demanding.
C) precarious.
D) crucial.

7

Within the context of the passage as a whole, the ninth
paragraph (lines 64-69) serves to

A) demonstrate that Americans consider healthcare to
   be the most important issue of the day.
B) transition from a broad discussion about the
   economy to a discussion about healthcare.
C) illustrate how the economy impacts healthcare.
D) introduce the speaker's intentions to reform the
   healthcare system.

According to the passage, which of the following best describes the relationship between healthcare and the economy?

A) Bureaucracy and paperwork are costing too much money and harming the economy.
B) Without a strong economy, we cannot have a strong healthcare system.
C) A lack of healthcare results in early deaths, which shrinks the labor pool and hurts the economy.
D) Healthcare costs absorb funds that could otherwise be used to improve the economy.

Which of the following provides the best evidence for the answer to the previous question?

A) Lines 64-69 ("But all...crisis")
B) Lines 70-71 ("The rising...lives")
C) Lines 72-75 ("Reducing...investment")
D) Lines 80-82 ("We will...doctor")

The following passage is excerpted from Mary Shelley's *Frankenstein*.

"You must create a female for me, with whom I can live in the interchange of those sympathies necessary for my being. This you alone can do; and I demand it of you as a right which you must not
5 refuse."

"I do refuse it," I [Victor Frankenstein] replied. "Shall I create another like yourself, whose joint wickedness might desolate the world? Begone! You may torture me, but I will never consent."

10 "You are in the wrong," replied the fiend, "and, instead of threatening, I am content to reason with you. I am malicious because I am miserable; am I not shunned and hated by all mankind? You, my creator, would tear me to pieces, and triumph; remember that
15 and tell me why I should pity man more than he pities me? You would not call it murder, if you could precipitate me into one of those ice-rifts, and destroy the work of your own hands. Shall I respect man, when he contemns me? Let him live with me in the
20 interchange of kindness, and, instead of injury, I would bestow every benefit upon him with tears of gratitude at his acceptance. But that cannot be; the human senses are insurmountable barriers to our union. I will revenge my injuries: if I cannot inspire
25 love, I will cause fear; and chiefly towards you my arch-enemy, because my creator, do I swear inextinguishable hatred. Have a care: I will work at your destruction, nor finish until I desolate your heart, so that you curse the hour of your birth."

30 A fiendish rage animated him as he said this; his face was wrinkled into contortions too horrible for human eyes to behold; but presently he calmed himself, and proceeded—

"I intended to reason. This passion is detrimental
35 to me; for you do not reflect the cause of its excess. If any being felt emotions of benevolence towards me, I should return them an hundred and an hundred fold; for that one creature's sake, I would make peace with the whole kind! What I ask of you is reasonable and
40 moderate; I demand a creature of another sex, but as hideous as myself: the gratification is small, but it is all that I can receive, and it shall content me. It is true, we shall be monsters, cut off from all the world; but on that account we shall be more attached to one
45 another. Our lives will not be happy, but they will be harmless, and free from the misery I now feel. Oh!

my creator, make me happy; let me feel gratitude towards you for one benefit! Let me see that I excite the sympathy of some existing thing; do not deny me
50 my request!"

I was moved. I shuddered when I thought of the possible consequences of my consent; but I felt that there was some justice in his argument... He saw my change of feeling, and continued—

55 "If you consent, neither you nor any other human being shall ever see us again: I will go to the vast wilds of South America... Pitiless as you have been towards me, I now see compassion in your eyes; let me seize the favorable moment, and persuade you to
60 promise what I so ardently desire."

"You propose," replied I, "to fly from the habitations of man. How can you, who long for the love and sympathy of man, persevere in this exile? You will return, and again seek their kindness, and
65 you will meet with their detestation; your evil passions will be renewed, and you will then have a companion to aid you in the task of destruction. This may not be; cease to argue the point, for I cannot consent."

"How inconstant are your feelings! but a moment
70 ago you were moved by my representations, and why do you again harden yourself to my complaints? I swear to you, by the earth which I inhabit, and by you that made me, that with the companion you bestow, I will quit the neighborhood of man, and dwell, as it
75 may chance, in the most savage of places. My evil passions will have fled, for I shall meet with sympathy; my life will flow quietly away, and, in my dying moments, I shall not curse my maker."

His words had a strange effect upon me. I
80 compassionated him, and sometimes felt a wish to console him; but when I looked upon him, when I saw the filthy mass that moved and talked, my heart sickened, and my feelings were altered to those of horror and hatred. I tried to stifle these sensations; I
85 thought, that as I could not sympathize with him, I had no right to withhold from him the small portion of happiness which was yet in my power to bestow.

10

The passage is told from the point of view of

A) the scientist who created a monster.
B) the monster who was created by a scientist.
C) the mate who was ultimately created for the monster.
D) an omniscient third-person narrator.

11

It can be inferred from the passage that the narrator expects the monster to

A) become peaceful if his request is fulfilled.
B) offer rational arguments in support of his request.
C) react with violence when his request is refused.
D) continue on a path of violence regardless of whether his request is fulfilled.

12

Which of the following provides the best evidence for the answer to the previous question?

A) Lines 8-9 ("You...consent")
B) Lines 11-12 ("instead...you")
C) Lines 38-39 ("for that...kind")
D) Lines 51-52 ("I shuddered...consent")

13

As used in line 17, "precipitate" most nearly means

A) hasten
B) launch
C) fall
D) moisten

14

The monster explains his past violence by saying that

A) his violence has only been done in reaction to the hatred and violence committed upon him by others.
B) he has committed violence in response to his maker's hatred.
C) his maker has been and will continue to be the sole target of his violent actions.
D) he is only violent because he is so hideous.

15

Which of the following provides the best evidence for the answer to the previous question?

A) Lines 13-18 ("You...hands")
B) Lines 19-25 ("Let...fear")
C) Lines 25-29 ("chiefly...birth")
D) Lines 39-41 ("What...myself")

16

As it is used in line 44, "account" most nearly means

A) reason.
B) judgment.
C) deposit.
D) statement.

17

Which of the following best summarizes the monster's primary argument throughout the passage?

A) Without a female companion, the monster's race will die off and his maker's efforts will have been for nothing.
B) If he had a mate as ugly as himself, he would no longer be lonely and could stop seeking the company of man.
C) It is in his creator's best interest to make the monster a mate because that is the only way the monster will stop hunting him.
D) The monster cannot hope to avenge himself upon mankind without a companion to aid him.

18

The narrator does not believe that the monster will truly leave, even if his request is fulfilled, because

A) the monster will likely kill his new companion and become lonely again.
B) the monster loves his creator too much to part from him forever.
C) he believes that the monster is too naturally violent to accept a peaceful life in exile.
D) the monster longs for the acceptance of mankind and will therefore be unable to find happiness in exile.

19

The passage concludes by suggesting that

A) the narrator will refuse the monster's request because he so strongly hates the monster.
B) the narrator will consent to the monster's request out of fear.
C) the narrator will consent to the monster's request out of pity.
D) the monster will kill his creator.

Questions 20-29 are based on the following passages.

The following passages examine whether the Supreme Court has become too powerful. Ilya Somin, the author of Passage 1, is a professor at George Mason University of Law. Larry Kramer, the author of Passage 2, is a constitutional historian and a former dean of Stanford Law School. Both articles were written in 2015, following a series of contentious Supreme Court decisions.

Passage 1

Although the Supreme Court gets many things wrong, America would be a far worse society without it. If judicial review were curtailed, the executive and legislative branches of government would be free to
5 ignore the constitutional limits on their powers. This is a grave danger in a world in which government spends nearly 40 percent of our gross domestic product and regulates almost every aspect of human activity. The very reason that the framers of the Constitution
10 established an independent judiciary was to check the vast powers of federal and state governments, preventing them from censoring opposition speech, confiscating property, and otherwise persecuting those they disapprove of. Avoiding the potential tyranny of
15 a legislature run amuck is well-worth the price of dealing with a good many flawed judicial rulings.

Many point out that public opinion already imposes constraints on oppressive policies, but public opinion is not enough. Our government is large and complex,
20 leaving many of its abuses in the dark, particularly to a public that pays scant attention to policy. Moreover, a "tyranny of the majority" is certainly not conducive to a democratic society; mainstream public opinion would fail to protect those in the minority. Perhaps
25 most importantly, without judicial constraints, incumbents could easily insulate themselves against future electoral competition, rendering public opinion moot.

The court's historical record is mixed, but it has
30 long helped to protect the rights of racial minorities -- not only in iconic cases like Brown v. Board of Education, but in lesser-known decisions, like Buchanan v Warley, a 1917 ruling that struck down laws preventing blacks from moving into majority-
35 white neighborhoods. In addition, unpopular speech and religious worship have enjoyed far greater protection than would exist in the court's absence. The same is true of the rights of criminal defendants.

Historically, many of the court's worst decisions
40 were cases in which it chose not to strike down an oppressive unconstitutional policy -- cases like Plessy v. Ferguson, which permitted racial segregation, and Korematsu v. United States, which permitted Japanese internment camps during World War II. Such cases
45 are regrettable and undoubtedly caused pain and hardship, but they also merely upheld existing legislation. Imagine how many more such outrages would occur without the check of the Supreme Court.

Passage 2

In a nation populated by non-voters, one of the most
50 frequent arguments in favor of voting goes like this: "The next president will pick who sits on the Supreme Court!" That such a statement should even be made tells us that something is seriously flawed in our democracy. Certainly the Supreme Court has a role in
55 our government, but not the overblown one it has come to play.

Many on the left are currently pleased with the court because of a few big political wins this year. Although I happen to agree with these outcomes, I
60 don't understand why these same progressives are willing to overlook the fact that the court has systematically undermined liberal causes for the past four decades. The outcomes of 2015 could easily have gone the other way -- if Justice Kennedy had woken
65 up on the other side of the bed the day the court ruled, then same sex couples would have had fewer rights; if Chief Justice Roberts had been in a different mood, then the Affordable Care Act could easily have been overturned. These are major societal issues that rest on
70 the opinions of a small handful of non-elected individuals.

This is not a partisan issue. It's about how the meaning of our Constitution should be finally determined. Is it really the case that the fundamental
75 law of the land, made by "We, the People," depends on the ideologically driven whims of nine lawyers?

There is certainly a place for judicial review in a constitutional democracy, but not for judicial supremacy. The idea that the justices have final say
80 about the meaning of our Constitution ought to offend anyone who believes in democracy. It rests on the myth that the court needs this overweening power in order to protect minorities. The court has occasionally used its power to that end, but much more often it has
85 done the opposite. Time and time again, we have seen it undermine political movements and legislation intended to secure rights. Virtually no progress was

made on race until Congress enacted the Civil Rights
Acts of 1964 and 1965, laws the Supreme Court has
90 worked for years to weaken. That the people who
framed our Constitution wanted or expected the court
to have such power is wrong -- they emphatically did
not fight a revolution to replace a monarchy with an
oligarchy.

20

As it is used in line 10, "check" most nearly means

A) forcibly stop.
B) restrain.
C) verify.
D) inspect.

21

Which of the following best states the central claim of
Passage 1?

A) The Supreme Court is not too powerful because it is
   checked by public opinion.
B) The only time the Supreme Court makes truly
   terrible decisions is when it upholds poor legislative
   policy.
C) Despite some bad rulings, a strong judiciary is
   necessary in order to balance the powers of
   government.
D) The Supreme Court is necessary in order to protect
   the rights of racial minorities.

22

Which of the following best supports the answer to the
previous question?

A) Lines 14-16 ("Avoiding...rulings")
B) Lines 17-19 ("Many...enough")
C) Lines 29-30 ("The court's...minorities")
D) Lines 39-41 ("Historically...policy")

23

Which of the following best describes the primary
purpose of the second paragraph of Passage 1?

A) To strengthen the author's argument by refuting a
   possible counterclaim
B) To show the general corruption of the legislature in
   order to prove the necessity of the judiciary
C) To illustrate the importance of majority rule in a
   democratic society
D) To suggest that elected officials wish to dismantle
   the Supreme Court

24

The author of Passage 1 offers which of the following
types of evidence in support of his claims?

A) Quotes from the Constitution
B) Examples of Supreme Court cases
C) Public opinion polls showing the Court's popularity
D) A description of the history of the Supreme Court

25

How would the author of Passage 1 most likely respond
to the assertions made in the second paragraph of
Passage 2?

A) The decisions in question concern legislation that
   was passed by elected officials, not by non-elected
   justices, so the error lies with the legislature.
B) If the Supreme Court didn't exist, these decisions
   very likely would have gone the other way because
   the legislature would have decided the issue.
C) Whether people like it or not, the framers of the
   Constitution decided that the Supreme Court would
   make these kinds of important decisions.
D) Public opinion would have made worse decisions in
   these cases, so it is better that such decisions be left
   to the Supreme Court.

26

As it is used in line 72, "issue" most nearly means

A) distribution.
B) edition.
C) result.
D) question.

27

Which of the following best states the central claim of
Passage 2?

A) The Supreme Court is power-hungry and has
   awarded itself too much control over the
   government.
B) It is undemocratic for the justices, as unelected
   officials, to have ultimate power over interpretation
   of the Constitution.
C) The Supreme Court is too conservative to accurately
   reflect public opinion.
D) The Supreme Court has never shown an interest in
   protecting minorities.

28

Which of the following best supports the answer to the previous question?

A) Lines 52-56 ("That such...play")
B) Lines 59-63 ("Although...decades")
C) Lines 77-81 ("There is...democracy")
D) Lines 81-83 ("It rests...minorities")

29

Which of the following is one issue on which the authors of both Passage 1 and Passage 2 agree?

A) There have been numerous occasions in which the Supreme Court has failed to uphold the rights of minorities.
B) The bad decisions made by the Supreme Court are worth accepting in order to provide a check to worse decisions made by the legislature.
C) The Supreme Court should not have the ultimate power to determine the Constitutionality of laws passed by elected officials.
D) The framers of the Constitution clearly intended the Supreme Court justices to have the final say regarding interpretation of the Constitution.

Questions 30-39 are based on the following passage and supplementary material.

This passage is adapted from an article titled "Stop Blaming the Deer," published July 2015 by Quartz.

Each year, 300,000 US residents contract Lyme, estimates the US Centers for Disease Control (CDC). And given how inconsistently the condition is diagnosed and reported, it could be far more—as
5   many as 3 million cases a year, says Keith Clay, professor of biology at Indiana University. Worse yet, Lyme disease is spreading.

Two factors in particular seem to be making it easier for the tick that carries Lyme, the American
10 blacklegged tick (Ixodes scapularis), to spread the disease. One is an explosion in the populations of the creatures on whose blood it likes to feed. The other is global warming. Both, of course, are humanity's fault.

Ticks feed entirely on blood. They need a blood
15 meal to graduate from larva to nymph and from nymph to adult—the three stages of their life cycle. Females must take a third blood meal to lay eggs. All this usually happens in about the space of two years.

When they hatch in late spring, tick larvae seek a
20 suitable animal and grab hold. The tick latches into a nice patch of skin, inserts its straw-like mouth-tube, and starts sucking away on blood. Once it has gulped down this first blood meal, the tick drops to the ground, ready to molt into the next stage of its life
25 cycle: a nymph.

A larval tick isn't born carrying the Lyme spirochetes. It needs to pick up the bacteria from the host it feeds on. Only then, after reawakening as a hungry new nymph, can the tick pass Lyme on to the
30 next host it feeds on.

So what are those typical hosts? It is a common misconception that these ticks prefer deer. Although deer are a favorite blood source for adult female ticks, they are usually much too big for larvae and nymphs
35 to grab hold of -- which is why they're not the real culprit for the spread of Lyme.

"The resurgence of deer population is an overblown factor," says Richard Ostfeld, disease ecologist at the Cary Institute, one of the leading research centers
40 working on Lyme disease. "Our research suggests that white-footed mice are more important numerically."

White-footed mice infect 75%-95% of larval ticks that feed on them. Deer infect only about 1%. So while deer are key to helping the adult ticks get the
45 blood they need to reproduce, it's mice that are crucial in helping the disease-causing bacteria spread to infant ticks. And, thanks to our slicing and dicing of forests, these mice no longer have many natural predators, making the white-footed mouse one of the most
50 abundant small vertebrate in the woody areas of the northeast.

Adding to the spread of the white-footed mouse -- and the ticks that feed on them -- our changing climate seems to be making it easier for Lyme to spread by
55 altering the lifecycle of the blacklegged tick.

The Lyme transmission cycle goes like this. A nymph or adult tick that has already picked up Lyme disease bites an animal. It takes a few weeks for the bacteria to reproduce in the animal's bloodstream
60 enough for it to become infectious. Any larval ticks that then bite that critter will pick up the disease, passing it on after they in turn molt into nymphs.

Whether the Lyme bacteria keep spreading therefore depends a lot on when each generation of
65 larval ticks is feeding. If larvae happen to feed at the same time as newly emerged nymphs—what biologists call "synchronous feeding"—they're less likely to pick up the infection, since the bacteria won't have had enough time to reproduce inside the mammal
70 hosts. But if newly hatched larval ticks feed much later than the nymphs ("asynchronous feeding") they'll be more likely to pick it up—and to transmit it the next season as nymphs.

And what determines whether larval feeding is
75 synchronous or asynchronous? Biologists aren't sure, but the going theory, says Ostfeld, is that it depends on the weather. Chilly fall weather forces larvae into dormancy before they can molt, thus slowing the spread of Lyme disease. In the American northeast,
80 however, autumn temperatures are rising at nearly double the rate across the rest of the continental U.S., allowing a higher percentage of newborn larvae the opportunity to spend the winter as dormant nymphs. This allows the nymphs enough time to infect new
85 animal hosts in the spring before the next generation of larvae can hatch and feed.

Admittedly, climate is probably not the whole story. For instance, it doesn't explain why ticks feed synchronously in both frigid Minnesota and the much
90 more temperate UK. But if the theory is right, places where Lyme has been relatively muted up to now could be in for trouble.

Annual Cases of Lyme Disease in the US

■ Number of CDC-Reported Cases   ▣ CDC-Estimated Total Diagnosed Cases

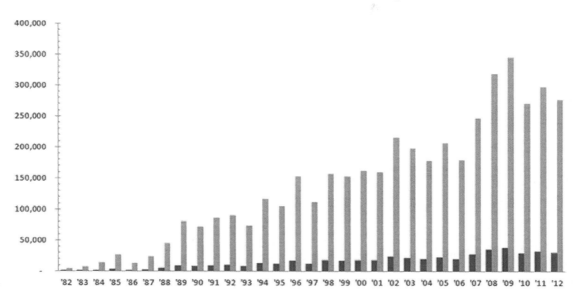

30

As it is used in line 1, "contract" most nearly means

A) condense.
B) agreement.
C) catch.
D) settle.

31

Which of the following best describes the purpose of the paragraphs in lines 14-30?

A) To suggest that we ought to eliminate ticks through any means necessary in order to halt the spread of Lyme disease
B) To persuade the reader that ticks are indeed the cause of the spread of Lyme disease
C) To establish the author's authority on the subject by showing that he knows about ticks
D) To illustrate the lifecycle of a tick and how it impacts Lyme disease transmission

32

It can best be inferred from the passage that

A) global warming has contributed to the increase in deer populations.
B) people who contract Lyme likely have an infestation of white-footed mice at home.
C) many blame deer for the spread of Lyme because deer populations have grown as Lyme has spread.
D) Lyme is unlikely to ever spread beyond the American northeast.

33

Which of the following best describes the relationship among Lyme disease, white-footed mice, and humans?

A) White-footed mice came into contact with human populations, which allowed the mice to pick up Lyme-carrying ticks.
B) Human activities contributed to the rise in mice populations, which helped spread Lyme-carrying ticks since they feed on the mice.
C) Humans caused climate change, which allowed the white-footed mouse population to grow, thereby spreading Lyme disease.
D) Lyme-carrying ticks feed on humans, who then transmit the ticks to mice by intruding on the forests in which the mice live.

Which of the following best supports the answer to the previous question?

A) Lines 40-41 ("Our...numerically")
B) Lines 45-51 ("it's...northeast")
C) Lines 52-55 ("Adding...tick")
D) Lines 56-62 ("The Lyme...nymphs")

As it is used in line 64, "generation" most nearly means

A) individuals born at the same time.
B) individuals with the same viewpoints.
C) interval of time between births.
D) creation of new energy.

According to the passage, how does climate change impact the spread of Lyme disease?

A) Rising temperatures change the lifecycle of the mice that carry ticks.
B) Rising temperatures hasten the spread of Lyme by altering the lifecycle and feeding of ticks.
C) As warmer temperatures spread beyond the northeast, so will the white-footed mice.
D) Climate change likely has no impact on the spread of Lyme disease.

Which of the following best supports the answer to the previous question?

A) Lines 52-55 ("Adding...tick")
B) Lines 74-77 ("And...weather")
C) Lines 79-83 ("In the...nymphs")
D) Lines 87-90 ("Admittedly...UK")

Which of the following best describes the evidence used throughout the passage?

A) Analogical reasoning
B) Results of a nationwide poll
C) Statistics from a scientific study
D) Expert testimony

The information in the graph best supports which of the following statements from the passage?

A) Lines 1-2 ("Each...CDC")
B) Lines 3-4 ("given...more")
C) Lines 4-6 ("as many...University")
D) Lines 8-11 ("Two...disease")

Questions 40-47 are based on the following passage.

This passage is adapted from "Insects May Feel After All" written by Carla Clark, PhD, a scientific consultant, writer, and researcher in the fields of psychology, neuropsychology, biotechnology, and molecular biology.

Almost any pet owner will insist that their animal companions are emotional creatures, sharing emotions with multiple species and not just their own, but it wasn't until 2012 that scientists finally agreed that
5　nonhuman animals are conscious beings. Meanwhile, in the laboratory, we have only just discovered that dogs display immensely complex, human-like emotions like jealousy, and we are only just deciphering how cows express positive emotions through the whites of their
10　eyes. But what about insects?

Emotions influence our perceptions and behaviors. If, for example, your house had been ransacked by burglars, you would likely feel shocked and angry. In fact, you might be so mad that despite your friends
15　doing everything possible to cheer you up, you become pessimistic and see the downside in everything. Even your favorite foods seem unappetizing.

This thoroughly emotional reaction to a traumatic event has actually been replicated with honeybees. A
20　group of bees were placed in a vortex (a machine used to vigorously mix chemicals) for one minute to simulate a badger attack on their hive.

Two groups of bees -- one that had been shaken and one that had not -- were then presented with different
25　solutions containing different proportions of two smelly chemicals: octanone, which both groups of bees had been trained to associate with a sugary treat, and hexanol, which they had been trained to associate with a bitter taste.
30　The bees that had been shaken became pessimistic. They were more likely to react to the nasty smelling mixtures and recoiled from the yummy smell. The unshaken bees remained optimistic, willing to approach even those mixtures containing the hexanol. Moreover,
35　there were emotionally relevant changes in neurotransmitter levels in the shaken bees, changing levels of serotonin and dopamine, for example.

Scientifically, the act of shaking the bees can be interpreted as having created an internal neurological
40　state that affected their subsequent behavior—all associated with changes in brain chemistry. This implies that agitated honeybees exhibit pessimistic cognitive biases.

A similar experiment was conducted with hungry
45　fruit flies. This time, the researchers tried to induce primal fear by casting a shadow over them to mimic the presence of an overhead predator. In a similar situation, a person would likely display behavioral and emotional changes until they feel safe again—and this is exactly
50　what seemed to happen with the fruit flies.

When the fake predator was introduced and then removed, potentially anxiety-ridden and hungry flies ignored their food until many minutes later. This suggests that an emotion-like state affected their
55　behavior even after the stimulus was gone. Other key building blocks of emotions like scalability were also demonstrated, i.e. repeating the predator's shadow simulation multiple times making the flies even more freaked out, taking them longer to calm down and dig
60　into their food.

Although researchers in both of these experiments agreed that the insects exhibited emotion-like states, in neither case were the researchers willing to say that the insects exhibited true emotions. After all, a key aspect
65　of emotion is allowing others to be aware of and respond to an individual's emotional state. In other words, emotions require a degree of empathy. Do insects lack empathy?

Another experiment, this time with woodlice, showed
70　that at least some insects have the capacity for empathy-like behavior. Researchers showed that calm woodlice reduced their more excited neighbors, causing them to also become calm.

Was this simply mimicking the behaviors of others?
75　If the same behaviors were exhibited by dogs or cats, we would probably term the behavior empathy. Why can we not imagine that the same might be true of bugs?

Hopefully, by mapping the neural circuitry that underlies the fear-like behavior in flies, anger-like
80　behavior in bees, or empathy-like behavior in woodlice, we may be one step closer to comparing insects' experiences of feelings with our own. With insect brains surprising even entomology experts in their extraordinary similarities with our own brains, we may
85　come to realize that the similarities are more profound than we would like to think.

While we cannot experience what it feels like for a bee to have a bee in its bonnet, a fly to feel like a bundle of nerves, or for a woodlouse to chill out with its
90　buddies, neither can we experience other humans' emotions. It is only because we can communicate (to a degree) that we know other humans have emotions too. Bear in mind that emotions are so subjective that we aren't especially accurate at understanding other

95 humans' emotions at the best of times—no less the
    emotions of another species!

40

Which of the following best describes the purpose of the
question in line 10?

A) To introduce the primary topic of the passage
B) To pose a question that has been definitively
   answered by recent research
C) To grab the reader's attention with a rhetorical
   question
D) To distract from the main idea of the paragraph

In the hypothetical situation presented in the second
paragraph (lines 11-17), "your house [being] ransacked"
is most analogous to

A) the bees being trained to associate certain smells
   with certain tastes.
B) the bees reacting pessimistically to different
   solutions.
C) the bees being presented with different solutions.
D) the bees being shaken in a vortex.

As used in lines 27 and 28, "associate" most nearly
means

A) relate.
B) colleague.
C) consort.
D) unite.

As it is used in line 40, "state" most nearly means

A) condition.
B) display.
C) declaration.
D) territory.

The passage suggests that scientists generally believe
that

A) humans and insects share the same thought
   processes.
B) other than humans, only dogs and cows experience
   true emotions.
C) only humans are capable of experiencing, displaying,
   and interpreting emotions.
D) insects may show emotion-like behaviors, but are
   likely incapable of true emotions.

Which of the following best supports the answer to the
previous question?

A) Lines 5-10 ("Meanwhile...eyes")
B) Lines 61-64 ("Although...emotions")
C) Lines 64-67 ("After...empathy")
D) Lines 82-86 ("With...think")

Based on information in the passage, we can assume
that the author most likely believes that

A) humans and insects share the same thought patterns
   and emotions.
B) humans have a certain prejudice against insects
   compared to mammals.
C) pets are likely less able to experience emotions than
   insects are.
D) insects likely mimic behaviors rather than
   experiencing true empathy.

Which of the following best supports the answer to the
previous question?

A) Lines 1-3 ("Almost...own")
B) Lines 69-73 ("Another...calm")
C) Lines 74-77 ("Was...bugs")
D) Lines 82-86 ("With...think")

Writing and Language Test
35 MINUTES, 44 QUESTIONS

Turn to Section 2 of your answer sheet to answer the questions in this section.

DIRECTIONS

Each passage below is accompanied by a number of questions. For some questions, you will consider how the passage might be revised to improve the expression of ideas. For other questions, you will consider how the passage might be edited to correct errors in sentence structure, usage, or punctuation. A passage or a question may be accompanied by one or more graphics (such as a table or graph) that you will consider as you make revising and editing decisions.

Some questions will direct you to an underlined portion of a passage. Other questions will direct you to a location in a passage or ask you to think about the passage as a whole.

After reading each passage, choose the answer to each question that most effectively improves the quality of writing in the passage or that makes the passage conform to the conventions of standard written English. Many questions include a "NO CHANGE" option. Choose that option if you think the best choice is to leave the relevant portion of the passage as it is.

Questions 1-11 are based on the following passage and

To Slash Costs of Homelessness, Give Homes Away

At night, Jack Jakups, Shannon McLaughlin, and **[1]** there dog, Cookie, burrowed beneath piles of blankets hoping to stay warm. It was the coldest winter on record for the state of Connecticut, so this was no easy feat. During the day, they sought warm food. If they were lucky, they might scrape together enough money to indulge in a day or two in a cheap motel, **[2]** allowing them time to wash every item of clothing they owned.

1
A) NO CHANGE
B) their
C) they're
D) its

2
Which of the following statements would least support the ideas presented in the initial paragraph?

A) NO CHANGE
B) providing a well-needed break from the elements.
C) providing solace from their emotional struggles.
D) letting them get the occasional bit of safe rest.

Theirs might easily have become just another bad luck story in the so-called land of opportunity, **3** but it's all behind them now. Jakups, McLaughlin, and Cookie now live in a one-bedroom apartment just two miles from where they once shivered under blankets. They were among the more than 400 people throughout Connecticut **4** that were housed through an innovative initiative called the 100-Day Challenge.

A joint public-private venture, the challenge included 140 agencies and providers and helped nearly 85% of the state's homeless population. Activists and advocates combined forces with government agencies and private business to use existing **5** resources to get people like Jakups and McLaughlin off the streets and into apartments.

It sounds so simple: **6**

[1] Those who live on the streets lack access to preventative medical care, so they often wind up in emergency departments suffering a medical crisis. [2] Many express concern about the costs of housing the homeless, but it actually costs more to keep people on the streets. [3] After all, the very state of homelessness lends itself to medical problems ranging from weather-related illnesses to nutritional deficiencies to physical assault. [4]As a result, the homeless spend significantly more time in hospitals than do those with homes. [5] In addition, the homeless are more likely both to become victims of crimes and to commit crimes, which means that they also spend more time in jails than do those with homes. [6]All of this costs public funds. **7**

3

A) NO CHANGE

B) so

C) and

D) however,

4

A) NO CHANGE

B) who were

C) that have been

D) who have been

5

All of the following words can be used here EXCEPT

A) NO CHANGE

B) capital

C) money

D) raw materials

6

To best transition from the first part of the essay to the second, which of the following should be inserted here?

A) Just as the solution to hunger is food, the solution to homelessness is homes.

B) But how can the government agencies trust the homeless to not take advantage of them?

C) I am glad to finally see the government doing something to combat this problem.

D) All Americans should do their part in helping the homeless find homes.

7

To make this paragraph most logical, sentence 1 should be placed

A) NO CHANGE

B) after sentence 2.

C) after sentence 3.

D) after sentence 4.

In fact, the cost to the government to help support the homeless is reduced by **8** <u>as much as 28%</u> when those people are placed into supportive housing instead of left on the street.

Traditionally, the response to homelessness is to place people in temporary shelters **9** <u>for the time being until permanent housing becomes available</u>, but access to permanent public housing is clogged by **10** <u>bureaucracy. People</u> often wait years for housing. Meanwhile, they are cycled and recycled through the shelter system, falling further and further into the abyss of homelessness and becoming less and less likely to be able to reestablish themselves.

11 <u>It's better</u> to house them. Not only does permanent housing cost less money, but it also helps to permanently solve the widespread issue of homelessness rather than simply putting a band-aid over the problem.

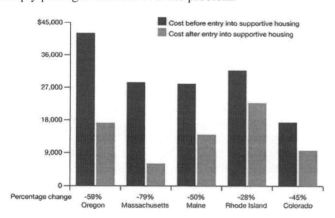

Source: Office of the Comptroller of the Currency, U.S. Department of the Treasury

---

8

A) NO CHANGE

B) at least 28%

C) no more than 28%

D) sometimes over 79%

9

A) NO CHANGE

B) until permanent housing becomes available for more than just the time being.

C) until permanent housing becomes available.

D) for now until permanent housing becomes available.

10

A) NO CHANGE

B) bureaucracy, but people

C) bureaucracy and people

D) bureaucracy: and people

11

A) NO CHANGE

B) Its better

C) Its best

D) The better things to do are

Questions 12-22 are based on the following passage.

Can the Sharing Economy Create Good Jobs?

Startups like Uber and Handy are transforming the way consumers access goods and services by matching those who need something with those willing to supply it. It's called the sharing economy, and roughly 7% of U.S. adults report working in this sector. Many more are likely to follow, attracted by flexible hours and the chance to be **12** his own boss.

13 Despite the growth of the sharing economy, these jobs have significant weaknesses. Today's sharing economy does not provide high-quality **14** jobs; instead, it compounds the increasingly precarious nature of 21st-century labor.

The sharing economy certainly has its benefits -- after all, its growth is fueled by a vast network of consumers who can now summon anything from a car to a housekeeper on demand. To a lesser degree, workers may also benefit. **15** The problem arises when people begin to rely on the sharing economy as their primary means of employment.

[1] The terms of service of this new sharing economy don't lend themselves to steady employment. [2] The jobs offered by these startups simply aren't traditional jobs. [3] By presenting themselves as software marketplaces, sharing companies consider themselves to be business platforms rather than employers. [4] They categorize their workers as independent contractors rather than permanent employees, allowing them to avoid providing benefits. **16**

12

A) NO CHANGE

B) his or her

C) their

D) they're

13

A) NO CHANGE

B) Because of

C) In addition to

D) From the time when

14

A) NO CHANGE

B) jobs, it

C) jobs, instead, it

D) jobs, instead; it

15

The author wants to add an example of a way in which workers may benefit. Which of the following best develops this idea?

A) NO CHANGE

B) Particularly for those hoping to earn extra money on the side, the gigs provided by the sharing economy are undoubtedly convenient.

C) Especially prominent in urban areas, many of the jobs provided by the sharing economy result in a higher tax rate for these employees.

D) In some areas of the country, these jobs and services have been outlawed for the effect they have on the local economy.

16

To improve the focus and flow of the paragraph, sentence 4 should be

A) left where it is now.

B) placed after sentence 1.

C) placed after sentence 2.

D) eliminated.

The result is that the sharing economy creates jobs that lack even the **17** miserable legal benefits of traditional employment. Sharing workers are burdened with all of the expectations of traditional employees, yet their jobs rarely provide health care, unemployment insurance, workers' compensation, and labor law protections.

In fact, the sharing economy is doing the opposite of generating good jobs; instead, it is **18** creating huge inequality between the owners of the platforms and the workers who sell their labor through **19** them. This new economy relies on venture-capital investment, which demands such huge returns that the creation of good jobs is simply impossible. The valuations of startups like Uber ($40 billion) and Airbnb ($20 billion) rest upon these companies treating workers as autonomous contractors without intrinsic economic rights. If these companies had the same obligations toward their employees as traditional enterprises, their radically profitable business model would be undermined and investors would have little incentive to pour billions into these startups. **20**

17

A) NO CHANGE
B) scornful
C) meager
D) derisive

18

A) NO CHANGE
B) generating big
C) widening the
D) helping create the

19

A) NO CHANGE
B) these owners.
C) these platforms.
D) themselves.

20

Which choice best establishes the main idea of the paragraph?

A) Many companies which benefit from the sharing economy would not survive if they gave their workers economic rights.

B) Venture capitalists are largely responsible for the success of many new businesses.

C) The sharing economy has led to many of the most successful new companies of the last 25 years.

D) The most important part of any economy is that its workers are treated justly and equitably.

The sharing economy doesn't work for labor. To create good jobs, it must provide workers with the minimal benefits that guarantee a decent standard of living, but such concessions would **21** <u>undermine</u> the profit margins of these startups and are thus anathema to its investors. **22**

21

A) NO CHANGE

B) empower

C) emasculate

D) demoralize

22

The author wants a concluding sentence that will highlight the hypocrisy of the phrase "sharing economy". Which choice best accomplishes this goal?

A) NO CHANGE

B) The sharing economy is actually more about being economical than it is about being kind.

C) In order to fix the sharing economy, less sharing needs to be done.

D) The sharing economy is actually a very selfish economy.

Questions 23-33 are based on the following passage.

Living Cells Armed with Lasers Fight Disease

The ability to direct tiny lasers on a fantastic voyage inside the body sounds like something out of a science fiction movie, but a Harvard team has actually made it happen. **23** They hope to use this development to enable a suite of medical applications, from delivering drugs to tackling tumor growth.

"We want to reinvent the laser for medical applications," says Seok-Hyun Yun of Harvard Medical School.

A typical laser excites atoms so that they emit light at a particular wavelength, then **24** bounce the light between a pair of mirrors to amplify the effect. One of the mirrors allows some light to escape in a narrow **25** beam—that's the laser. The key to building a laser inside a cell is creating an optical microresonator—a miniature version of this setup that **26** borders light so that it circulates inside a small sphere, where it's trapped by refraction at the sphere's surface.

Yun's team created both a soft version and a hard version of an optical microresonator. In each case, the entire cell was excited by a nanosecond pulse that produced **27** light; which then became trapped inside the sphere.

23
A) NO CHANGE
B) The team hopes to
C) The hope of the team is to
D) The team hopes that it may to

24
A) NO CHANGE
B) bounces
C) bounced
D) will be bouncing

25
A) NO CHANGE
B) beam, that's
C) beam. That's
D) beam, and that's

26
A) NO CHANGE
B) curbs
C) resigns
D) confines

27
A) NO CHANGE
B) light. Which
C) light, which
D) light what

"It's like when you're in an empty room and a certain voice frequency gets **28** resonated" Yun explains. "But if the room is squeezed, if the shape and size changes, the resonant frequency also gets altered. We do the same thing, **29** in principle, with the optical frequency scale. Certain light gets resonated and, as it circulates the cavity, it gets amplified and eventually turns into the laser output."

[1] The extreme precision of that output is one thing that makes the tiny lasers so promising. [2] The soft droplet versions shift shape ever so lightly when under stress, and that deformation makes a visible change in the laser's emission spectrum, so that even minute changes in the cell can be recorded in fine detail. [3] Similarly the team can produce lasers of slightly different wavelengths by changing the size of the hard beads—enabling them to uniquely color code an individual cell and potentially label thousands of different cells within a single tissue. **30**

28

A) NO CHANGE
B) resonated, Yun
C) resonated", Yun
D) resonated," Yun

29

A) NO CHANGE
B) in principal
C) while principled
D) with principals

30

Which sentence should be eliminated in order to improve the focus of the paragraph?

A) Sentence 1
B) Sentence 2
C) Sentence 3
D) None of the sentences should be eliminated.

[1] Living cells are the ideal delivery mechanism for getting these microlasers where they can do the most good. [2] Once in place, a finely tuned laser light could deliver highly detailed information about cell surfaces, hormones, and protein **31** production; tag individual cells to provide data about tumor growth; or track the movement of cells through the body. [3] For example, immune cells can be targeted to respond to specific problems, so they could deliver a laser to bind with a tumor or other disease location. **32**

33 Perhaps most promising of all is the potential to not only monitor aspects of human health but to actively improve them. Yun adds: "These laser-equipped cells could also potentially be loaded with light-activated drugs and delivered to a specific location, where they might be used to kill a tumor, for example."

31

A) NO CHANGE

B) production, tag

C) production or tag

D) production and tag

32

For the sake of the clarity of the paragraph, Sentence 2 should be placed where?

A) Where it is now.

B) Before Sentence 1

C) After Sentence 3.

D) It should be deleted from the paragraph.

33

Which of the following best establishes the main idea of the passage while maintaining the passage's style and tone?

A) NO CHANGE

B) Laser technology today has gone farther than some science-fiction authors could ever have imagined.

C) While many doctors and scientists remain skeptical of these laser-toting cells, Yun remains positive.

D) It is very possible that the function of these lasers may not endear them to the tumors they destroy.

How Nylon Stockings Changed the World

A pair of **34** ladies' stockings might seem out of place in the vaunted collections of the Smithsonian, but a pair of experimental stockings made in 1937 managed to impact nearly every facet of society.

The stockings were made to test the viability of the first manmade fiber developed entirely in a laboratory -- nylon. The new material was said to have the strength of steel and the sheerness of **35** cobwebs, promising a replacement for the delicate silk that was prone to snag and run. When nylon stockings were released for sale in 1940, demand was so high that four million pairs sold out in four days. **36** Nylon's impact on fashion was immediate, but the synthetics revolution sparked by the invention of nylon rapidly expanded beyond fashion, giving rise to a world of plastics that **37** have altered nearly every aspect of modern life.

34

A) NO CHANGE

B) ladies's

C) lady's

D) ladie's

35

A) NO CHANGE

B) cobwebs promising

C) cobwebs promised

D) cobwebs; promising

36

Should the author start a new paragraph with the sentence following question 36?

A) Yes, the author moves on from discussing nylon's effect on fashion to its effect on modern life.

B) Yes, because the author is discussing a completely different topic.

C) No, because the resulting paragraph will be only one sentence long.

D) No, because the following sentence is still discussing nylon.

37

A) NO CHANGE

B) has altered

C) have been altering

D) has been altered

38 Prior to the invention of nylon, a few other partly synthetic substances had been made by scientists in laboratories. Semi-synthetics such as Rayon and cellophane were derived from a chemical process that required wood pulp as a basic **39** element. Nylon, on the other hand, not only made great stockings, but was manufactured through human manipulation of nothing more than coal, air, and water.

Nylon's entirely synthetic nature seems undesirable in today's markets, but in 1940, on the heels of the Great Depression, the ability to control the elements through chemistry energized a people battered by forces beyond their control. **40**

38

Which of the following best establishes the main idea of the paragraph?

A) NO CHANGE

B) The discovery of the first completely synthetic substance completely overshadowed many of the scientific advancements made in the previous few years.

C) Unfortunately, the creation of synthetic materials like nylon is very toxic to the environment and should be stopped immediately.

D) Synthetic materials were not completely new, but until the breakthrough of nylon, no useful fibers had ever been synthesized entirely in the laboratory.

39

Which of the following choices is the least effective choice to complete the sentence?

A) NO CHANGE

B) molecule

C) component

D) constituent

40

The author is considering adding the following to the end of this paragraph:

Against this backdrop, industrial chemistry promised to lead mankind into a brighter future.

Should the author make this addition?

A) No, because it does not match the tone of the rest of the paragraph.

B) No, because this information is irrelevant.

C) Yes, because it provides a proper transition to the next paragraph.

D) Yes, because it provides an example that supports the ideas of the paragraph.

Just a few years after the release of nylon stockings, the outbreak of World War II provided a new demand for nylon. The new and improved stockings women had embraced were **41** wrenched unfairly away as nylon was diverted to the making of parachutes. Later, nylon was used to make tow ropes, aircraft fuel tanks, flak jackets, shoelaces, mosquito netting, and **42** hammocks earning it the moniker "the fiber that won the war."

[1] After the war, the re-introduction of nylon stockings unleashed consumer madness. [2] During the "nylon riots" of 1945 and '46, women stood in mile-long lines in hopes of snagging a single pair. [3] Nylon stockings remained the standard in women's hosiery for decades. [4] By the 1980s and 90s, stockings and pantyhose -- nylon or not -- simply fell out of favor. [5] In 2006, the New York Times referred to the hosiery industry as "An Industry that Lost its Footing."[6] Today, far fewer people use nylon stockings than they did just 20 years ago. **43**

No matter, they've made their point. Nylon has become an indispensable part of our lives found in everything from luggage and furniture to computers and engine parts. Chemistry and human ambition **44** is transforming the world in which we live.

41

A) NO CHANGE
B) wrenched away unfairly
C) wrenched from women like a baby from her mother
D) wrenched away

42

A) NO CHANGE
B) hammocks which earned
C) hammocks, earning
D) hammocks; earning

43

To make this paragraph less repetitive, which of the following sentences should be removed?

A) Sentence 1
B) Sentence 2
C) Sentence 3
D) Sentence 6

44

A) NO CHANGE
B) will transform
C) has transformed
D) have transformed

Math Test – No Calculator

25 MINUTES, 17 QUESTIONS

Turn to Section 3 of your answer sheet to answer the questions in this section.

DIRECTIONS

For questions **1-13**, solve each problem, choose the best answer from the choices provided, and fill in the corresponding circle on your answer sheet. **For questions 14-17**, solve the problem and enter your answer in the grid on the answer sheet. Please refer to the directions before question 14 on how to enter your answers in the grid. You may use any available space in your test booklet for scratch work.

NOTES

1. The use of a calculator **is not permitted**.
2. All variables and expressions used represent real numbers unless otherwise indicated.
3. Figures provided in the test are drawn to scale unless otherwise indicated.
4. All figures lie in a plane unless otherwise indicated.
5. Unless otherwise indicated, the domain of a given function f is the set of all real numbers x for which $f(x)$ is a real number.

REFERENCE

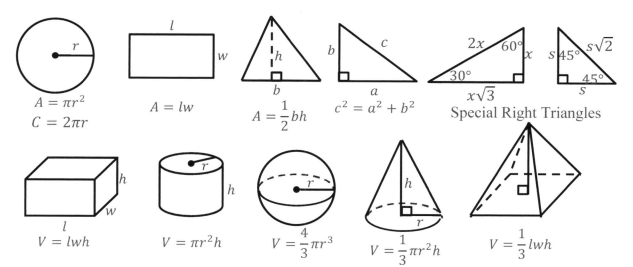

$A = \pi r^2$
$C = 2\pi r$

$A = lw$

$A = \frac{1}{2}bh$

$c^2 = a^2 + b^2$

Special Right Triangles

$V = lwh$

$V = \pi r^2 h$

$V = \frac{4}{3}\pi r^3$

$V = \frac{1}{3}\pi r^2 h$

$V = \frac{1}{3}lwh$

The number of degrees of arc in a circle is 360.

The number of radians of arc in a circle is 2π.

The sum of the measures in degrees of the angles of a triangle is 180.

1

$$3x - 6y = -3x$$

If (x, y) is a solution to the equation above, what is the value of $y - x$?

A) -1

B) 0

C) 1

D) It cannot be determined from the given information.

2

While playing a video game, Geoffrey earns 150 points for each target he shoots and an additional 75 points for each second he finishes the level in under 100 seconds. If Geoffrey finishes the level in 88 seconds, what expression could be used to determine how many points Geoffrey earned?

A) $150t + 88(75)$, where t is the number of targets Geoffrey shot

B) $150t + 12(75)$, where t is the number of targets Geoffrey shot

C) $75t + 88(150)$, where t is the number of targets Geoffrey shot

D) $75t + 12(150)$, where t is the number of targets Geoffrey shot

3

$$0.2a + 0.4b = 100$$

$$0.1a - 0.8b = 20$$

Which ordered pair (a, b) satisfies the system of equations above?

A) $(30, 440)$

B) $(50, 400)$

C) $(400, 50)$

D) $(440, 30)$

4

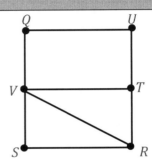

Note: Figure not drawn to scale.

Given rectangle $QURS$ above, segments QS and UR are bisected by segment VT. What is the ratio of the area of triangle RTV to the area of rectangle $QURS$?

A) $\frac{1}{4}$

B) $\frac{1}{3}$

C) $\frac{1}{2}$

D) $\frac{3}{4}$

5

A baker sells two types of dessert breads: banana and nut. Each nut bread requires 3 cups of flour, while each banana bread requires 2 cups of flour. If the baker uses 117 cups of flour to make 45 total dessert breads, how many nut breads did he make?

A) 9

B) 18

C) 27

D) 36

6

$$2x^2 + 7x - 15 = 0$$

If y and z are two solutions of the equation above, which of the following is the value of $y + z$?

A) $-\dfrac{7}{2}$

B) $-\dfrac{3}{2}$

C) $\dfrac{7}{2}$

D) 5

7

The temperature of an industrial cooler must be kept between –3°C and 5°C, inclusive. Which of the following inequalities gives the range of temperatures, T, at which the cooler can be kept?

A) $1 \leq |T - 4|$

B) $1 \geq |T - 4|$

C) $4 \leq |T - 1|$

D) $4 \geq |T - 1|$

8

If $f(3x) = 6x - 9$ for all values of x, what is the value of $f(-3)$?

A) -63

B) -27

C) -15

D) -3

9

A bus is traveling down the slope of a mountain. For every 100 meters the bus travels, the elevation of the mountain decreases by 5 meters. If the car starts at an elevation of 3,000 meters and is travelling at a rate of 20 meters per second, what is the elevation of the mountain, in meters, at the point where the bus passes t seconds after entering the road?

A) $3000 - t$

B) $3000 - 25t$

C) $3000 - 100t$

D) $3000 - 400t$

10

Which of the following is equivalent to $(f - g) \div fg$?

A) $\dfrac{1}{g} - \dfrac{1}{f}$

B) $\dfrac{1}{f} - \dfrac{1}{g}$

C) 1

D) 0

$$f = 263 - 1.5T$$

The equation above is used to model the relationship between the number of eggs, f, released by a fish at the current temperature, T, in degrees Fahrenheit. According to the model, what is the meaning of the 1.5 in the equation?

A) For every increase of 1.5°F, one more egg will be released.
B) For every decrease of 1.5°F, one more egg will be released.
C) For every increase of 1°F, one-and-a-half more eggs will be released.
D) For every decrease of 1°F, one-and-a-half more eggs will be released.

$$f(x) = -5(x^2 - 3x - 6) + 10(h - x)$$

In the polynomial $f(x)$ defined above, h is a constant. If $f(x)$ is divisible by x, what is the value of h?

A) -5
B) -3
C) 3
D) 5

13

In the xy-plane, if the parabola with equation $y = (x - a)(x - b)$, where a and b are non-zero constants, passes through the point $(1, 1)$, which of the following must be true?

A) $\frac{1}{a} + \frac{1}{b} = 1$

B) $\frac{1}{a} - \frac{1}{b} = 1$

C) $\frac{1}{b} - \frac{1}{a} = 1$

D) $\frac{1}{a} + \frac{1}{b} = -1$

For questions 14-17, solve the problem and enter your answer in the grid, as described below, on the answer sheet.

1. Although not required, it is suggested that you write your answer in the boxes at the top of the columns to help you fill in the circles accurately. You will receive credit only if the circles are filled in correctly.
2. Mark no more than one circle in any column.
3. No question has a negative answer.
4. Some problems may have more than one correct answer. In such cases, grid only one answer.
5. **Mixed numbers** such as $3\frac{1}{2}$ must be gridded as 3.5 or 7/2.

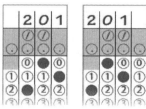

(If is entered into the grid, it will be interpreted as $\frac{31}{2}$, not $3\frac{1}{2}$.)
6. **Decimal answers:** If you obtain a decimal answer with more digits than the grid can accommodate, it may be either rounded or truncated, but it must fill the entire grid.

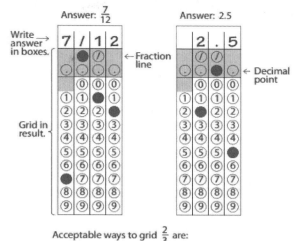

14

For what value of g is $-16 = 4 - \frac{g}{8}$?

15

What is the value of a if
$$\left(3a - \frac{1}{2}\right) - \left(\frac{3}{2}a - 2\right) = \frac{15}{4} \ ?$$

16

If x is not equal to zero, what is the value of
$16\frac{(1x)^{-1}}{(3x)^{-1}}?$

17

If $x + 3$ is a factor of $x^2 + 2ax + a^2$, where a is a constant, what is the value of a^2?

Math Test – Calculator

45 MINUTES, 31 QUESTIONS

Turn to Section 4 of your answer sheet to answer the questions in this section.

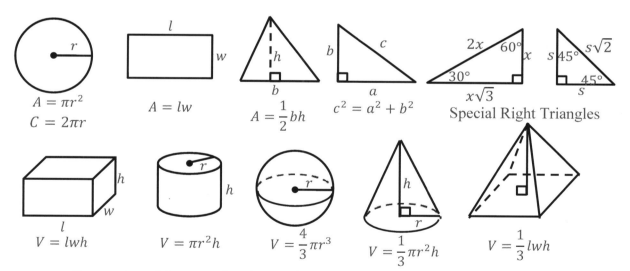

$A = \pi r^2$
$C = 2\pi r$

$A = lw$

$A = \frac{1}{2}bh$

$c^2 = a^2 + b^2$

Special Right Triangles

$V = lwh$

$V = \pi r^2 h$

$V = \frac{4}{3}\pi r^3$

$V = \frac{1}{3}\pi r^2 h$

$V = \frac{1}{3}lwh$

The number of degrees of arc in a circle is 360.

The number of radians of arc in a circle is 2π.

The sum of the measures in degrees of the angles of a triangle is 180.

1

Jonsi's water company charges a $12.50 monthly fee. Additionally, the company charges 25 cents per 100 gallons of water used monthly. Which of the following functions gives Jonsi's cost, $C(g)$, in dollars, for a month in which he uses g gallons of water?

A) $C(g) = 12.75t$

B) $C(g) = 12.50 + 0.25(g)$

C) $C(g) = 12.50 + 0.25(\frac{g}{100})$

D) $C(t) = 12.50 + 25.00(\frac{g}{100})$

A high school gym class is dividing its 82 students into groups of 3 and 4 students each. The class grouped some of its students into 6 groups of 3. Which equation shows the number of groups of 4 students, a, that were made that day?

A) $a = \frac{82-18}{3}$

B) $a = \frac{82-18}{4}$

C) $a = \frac{82}{4} - 18$

D) $a = \frac{82}{3} - 18$

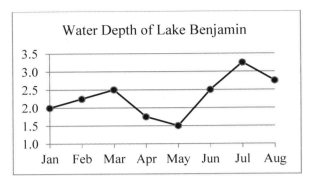

3

Water Depth of Lake Benjamin

The line graph above shows the monthly water depth, in feet, for Lake Benjamin last year from January to August. According to the graph, what was the greatest change (in absolute value) in the monthly rainfall between two consecutive months?

A) 12 inches

B) 9 inches

C) 6 inches

D) 1 inch

Which ordered pair (x, y) satisfies the system of equations shown below?

$$7x = 2y - 12$$
$$2y - 3x = 12$$

A) $(0, 6)$

B) $(0, -6)$

C) $(6, 0)$

D) $(-6, 0)$

5

A rectangle has side lengths of X and Y and area of A. Which of the following represents Y in terms of X and A?

A) $Y = XA$

B) $Y = X - A$

C) $Y = \frac{A}{X}$

D) $Y = \frac{X}{A}$

6

A peanut butter machine is filling jars of peanut butter from a tank that contains 500 pounds of peanuts. If 1.5 pounds of peanuts will make one 8-fluid ounce jar of peanut butter, approximately how many gallons of peanut butter will be produced by the machine? (1 gallon = 128 fluid ounces)

A) 20.83

B) 31.25

C) 46.86

D) 53.33

7

A snail traveled at an average speed of 10 feet per minute for 1.5 hours. Approximately how many miles did the snail travel in that time period? (1 mile = 5280 feet)

A) 0.08 miles

B) 0.11 miles

C) 0.17 miles

D) 0.23 miles

8

What is the length of the line in the xy-plane that passes through the points $(-2, 5)$ and $(-5, 9)$?

A) 4

B) 5

C) 7

D) 10.5

9

Length and Weight of Babies

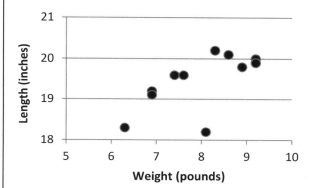

The scatterplot above shows the length, in inches, and weight, in pounds, of 11 different newborn babies. What is the weight, in pounds, of the baby represented by the data point that is farthest from the line of best fit (not shown)?

A) 8.2

B) 8.8

C) 18.2

D) 20.2

Fourty-four percent of the voters in a school election voted Mary for class president. Which of the following could be the total number of voters in the school?

A) 110

B) 220

C) 250

D) 440

$$85x + y = 1,700$$

A toy store is running a holiday event in which a number of free promos are given away each day. The equation above can be used to model the number of free promos, y, that remain to be given away x days after the promotion began. What does it mean that $(20, 0)$ is a solution to this equation?

A) It takes 20 days during the holiday event until none of the promos are remaining.
B) There are 20 promos available at the start of the holiday event.
C) During the holiday event, 20 promos are given away each day.
D) It takes 20 days during the holiday event to see 1,700 customers visit the toy store.

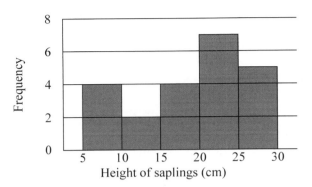

The histogram above shows the distribution of the heights, in centimeters, of 22 saplings in Talladega National Forest. Which of the following could be the median height of the 22 saplings in the histogram?

A) 15

B) 19

C) 24

D) 26

Which scatterplot shows a negative association that is not linear? (Note: A negative association between two variables is one in which higher values of one variable correspond to lower variables of the other variable, and vice versa.)

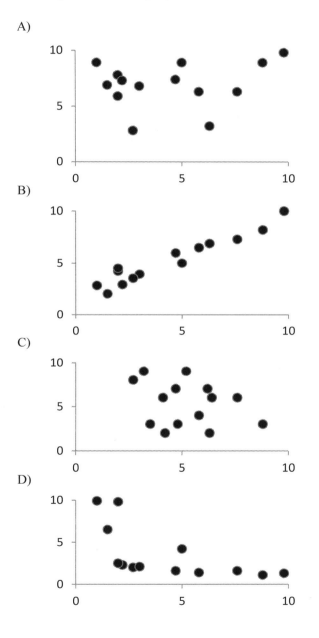

A)

B)

C)

D)

A survey of 170 randomly selected residents of a state was conducted to gather data on an upcoming election. The residents were broken up into whether they live in an urban or rural area. The data are shown in the table below.

	Voted for Candidate A	Voted for Candidate B	Total
Urban	20	76	96
Rural	62	12	74
Total	82	88	170

Which of the following is closest to the percent of rural residents who voted for Candidate B?

A) 16%

B) 21%

C) 54%

D) 84%

In 2015, the total population of the individuals in the state who were eligible to vote was about 8.5 million. If the survey results are used to estimate information about voting preferences of the state, and the ratio of rural to urban citizens is the same throughout the state as it is in the survey, which of the following is the best estimate of the total number of individuals who would vote for Candidate A?

A) 4.1 million

B) 4.2 million

C) 4.8 million

D) 4.9 million

Based on the data, how many times more likely is it for an urban resident of the state than a rural resident of the state to vote for Candidate B? (Round the answer to the nearest hundredth.)

A) 0.16 times as likely

B) 0.20 times as likely

C) 4.88 times as likely

D) 6.33 times as likely

Percent Carbohydrates in Five Energy Bars

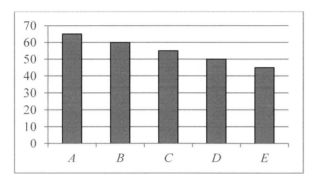

The graph above shows the amount of carbohydrates in five different brand energy bars, A, B, C, D, and E, as a percentage of their total weights. Each energy bar weighs the same amount. The cost of 1 energy bar of each brand A, B, C, D, and E is $1.69, $1.79, $1.85, $2.09, and $3.09, respectively. Which of the five energy bars supplies the least carbohydrates per dollar?

A) A

B) C

C) D

D) E

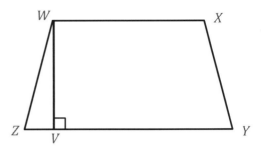

18

In quadrilateral $WXYZ$ above, WX is parallel to ZY and WV is perpendicular to ZY. If WV were reduced by 50%, how would the area of $WXYZ$ change?

A) The area of $WXYZ$ wold be increased by 50%

B) The area of $WXYZ$ would not change.

C) The area of $WXYZ$ would be reduced by 25%.

D) The area of $WXYZ$ would be reduced by 50%.

MultiComp computer company has two types of workers in its factory; 300 of the workers earn $10.50 an hour and 100 of the workers earn $12.50 per hour. Next year, MultiComp plans to hire 10% more of each type of worker, and pay each worker 10% more per hour. By what percentage does the total hourly cost to pay each of its employees for 1 hour of work increase for MultiComp from this year to next year?

A) 10 percent

B) 20 percent

C) 21 percent

D) 40 percent

Employee(s)	Salary
A	$30,000
B, C, D, E	$40,000
F, G	$45,000
H, I, J	$50,000
K, L, M, N	$60,000
O, P	$75,000
Q	$100,000

The graph above shows code letters for several different employees of a company and each employee's salary. Which of the following is closest to the approximate mean salary of the selected workers?

A) $40,000

B) $50,000

C) $55,000

D) $60,000

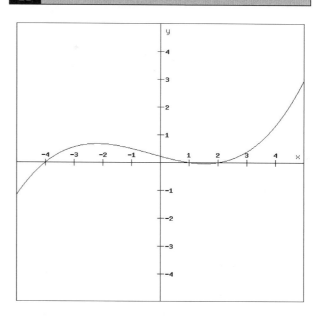

What is the maximum value of the function graphed above on the xy-plane above, for $-5 \leq x \leq 5$?

A) -2.5

B) 3

C) 5

D) ∞

Questions 22-24 refer to the following information.

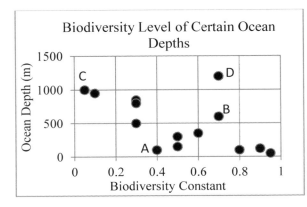

Biodiversity Level of Certain Ocean Depths

The data in the graph above can be modeled by the equation $950x + 0.9y = 950$, where y is the depth, in meters, in the ocean of several biological testing stations and x is a biodiversity constant that measures the number of different species present at that depth. The biodiversity constant is a number between 0 and 1, and the larger the number, the more species present.

22

According to the data above, what biodiversity constant would one expect to find at a depth of 200 meters?

A) 0.19

B) 0.75

C) 0.81

D) 0.95

Four of the testing stations are labeled in the data shown. It has been determined that the testing station with data farthest from that predicted by the line of best fit has been contaminated by impurities in its filters. Which testing station most likely has been contaminated?

A) A

B) B

C) C

D) D

24

Based on the model, if a biological testing station is moved 200 feet deeper, what change would be expected to happen to its biodiversity constant?

A)   Increase by approximately 0.2

B)   Increase by approximately 0.1

C)   Decrease by approximately 0.1

D)   Decrease by approximately 0.2

25

The area and circumference of a circle are both $x\pi$. What is the length of the diameter of the circle?

A) 1

B) 2

C) 4

D) 9

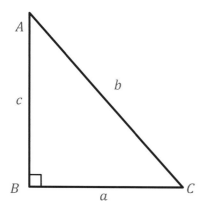

Given the right triangle ABC above, which of the following is equal to $\frac{a}{c}$?

A) $\sin A$

B) $\sin C$

C) $\tan A$

D) $\tan C$

$$y \geq 2 - 3x$$
$$y - 3 > -x + 2$$

A system of inequalities is shown above. Which point does not represent a solution to the system of inequalities above?

A) $(3, 3)$

B) $(0, 5)$

C) $(-1, 7)$

D) $(-2, 8)$

For questions 28-31, solve the problem and enter your answer in the grid, as described below, on the answer sheet.

1. Although not required, it is suggested that you write your answer in the boxes at the top of the columns to help you fill in the circles accurately. You will receive credit only if the circles are filled in correctly.
2. Mark no more than one circle in any column.
3. No question has a negative answer.
4. Some problems may have more than one correct answer. In such cases, grid only one answer.
5. **Mixed numbers** such as $3\frac{1}{2}$ must be gridded as 3.5 or 7/2.

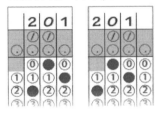

(If ⬚ is entered into the grid, it will be interpreted as $\frac{31}{2}$, not $3\frac{1}{2}$.)

6. **Decimal answers:** If you obtain a decimal answer with more digits than the grid can accommodate, it may be either rounded or truncated, but it must fill the entire grid.

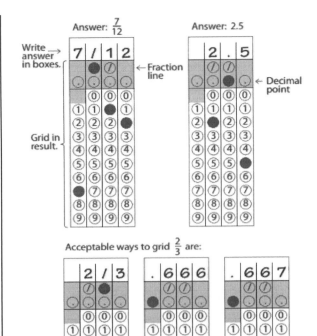

Acceptable ways to grid $\frac{2}{3}$ are:

Answer: 201 – either position is correct

NOTE: You may start your answers in any column, space permitting. Columns you don't need to use should be left blank.

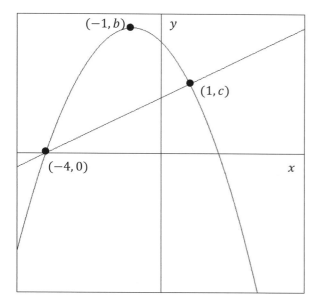

The xy-plane above shows both points of intersection of the graphs of a linear function $(y = \frac{1}{2}x + 2)$ and a quadratic function. The vertex of the quadratic function has coordinates (a, b). What is the value of $+b$?

A cellphone service provider charges $55.00 a month for service, plus an additional $2.50 per hour of talking time used. Another cellphone service provider charges $45.00 a month, plus an additional $3.125 per hour of talking time used. For how many hours of talking time used do the two providers charge the same monthly fee?

Questions 30 and 31 refer to the following information.

$$F_{Net} = ma$$
$$F_{Net} = \frac{mv^2}{R}$$
$$F_{Net} = \frac{4\pi^2 R}{T^2}$$

To the nearest tenth of a second, what is the period of the car?

The acceleration of an object moving in a circle with radius R can be determined by the equations above. T represents the period of the motion of the object, a represents its acceleration, v represents its velocity, and m represents its mass.

A 900-kg car moving at 10 m/s takes a turn around a circular-shaped track with a diameter of 50 meters.

30

What is the acceleration of the car, to the nearest tenth of a m/s^2?

TEST PREP GENIUS

THIS PAGE IS LEFT INTENTIONALLY BLANK

Practice Test 1 Answer Key

Explanations can be found online at http://www.tpgenius.com/

Section 1: Reading		Section 2: Writing		Section 3: Math – No Calc	Section 4: Math - Calc
1. B	25. A	1. B	23. B	1. B	1. C
2. B	26. D	2. C	24. B	2. B	2. B
3. A	27. B	3. A	25. A	3. D	3. A
4. C	28. C	4. B	26. D	4. A	4. A
5. A	29. A	5. D	27. C	5. C	5. C
6. D	30. C	6. A	28. D	6. A	6. A
7. B	31. D	7. B	29. A	7. D	7. C
8. D	32. C	8. B	30. D	8. C	8. B
9. C	33. B	9. C	31. A	9. A	9. C
10. A	34. B	10. A	32. C	10. A	10. A
11. C	35. A	11. A	33. A	11. D	11. A
12. D	36. B	12. C	34. C	12. B	12. C
13. B	37. B	13. A	35. A	13. A	13. D
14. A	38. D	14. A	36. A	14. 160	14. A
15. B	39. B	15. B	37. B	15. $\frac{3}{2}$ or 1.5	15. A
16. A	40. A	16. A	38. D	16. 48	16. C
17. B	41. D	17. C	39. B	17. 9	17. D
18. D	42. A	18. D	40. C		18. D
19. C	43. A	19. C	41. D		19. C
20. B	44. D	20. A	42. C		20. C
21. C	45. B	21. A	43. D		21. B
22. A	46. B	22. D	44. D		22. C
23. A	47. C				23. D
24. B					24. D
					25. B
					26. C
					27. B
					28. 7
					29. 16
					30. 4
					31. 0.5

Explanations can be found online at http://www.tpgenius.com/

Reading Test

60 MINUTES, 47 QUESTIONS

Turn to Section 1 of your answer sheet to answer the questions in this section.

DIRECTIONS

Each passage or pair of passages below is followed by a number of questions. After reading each passage or pair, choose the best answer to each question based on what is stated or implied in the passage or passages and in any accompanying graphics (such as a table or graph).

Questions 1-10 are based on the following passages.

Broad agricultural use of the herbicide glyphosphate, most commonly sold as Roundup, has resulted in the spread of resistant "super weeds." The following passages examine potential responses to these so-called "super weeds." Passage 1 is written by a farmer in Missouri. Passage 2 is written by a well-known food journalist.

Passage 1

We used to control weeds by cultivating. Three triangular shovels ran between each row of crops, rooting out weeds. We were left with weeds that had tap roots and tough stalks, which slid around the shovels.
5 Sort of a forerunner of herbicide-resistant weeds, when you think about it. We'd cut the escapes with a hoe, which was my summer job.

We used to control weeds the old-fashioned way — with hoes.

10 Then, we had an outbreak of shattercane, a grass closely related to grain sorghum, which seemed to thrive on the crop protection chemicals we had at the time. Shattercane seeded so profusely that the cultivator was ineffective, and would grow back from below the
15 ground after we cut it with a hoe. A plant that was hoe resistant.

Then, we had Roundup, which ended the threat from shattercane. For a time, we won the battle. But some of those wily weeds have evolved to defeat Roundup, and
20 the war between man and weed goes on, no different than it has since the beginning of time.

Many farmers are now plagued by Roundup-resistant weeds. The strongest tool in their arsenal has been

rendered ineffective because they came to rely on it so
25 strongly. By narrowing their response to weeds to focus almost entirely on herbicides like Roundup, many farmers have been the creators of their own enemy.

We haven't noticed a large problem with Roundup-resistant weeds on our farm because we only use
30 Roundup every other year, and we use crop protection chemicals with different modes of action to lessen the chance of resistant weeds. We will no doubt see an increase in resistant weeds, and we'll perhaps have to lengthen the time between applications of Roundup to
35 maintain its effectiveness.

None of this is surprising. Of course weeds evolve, and certainly some farmers have overused a wonderful tool. Being a technological optimist, I assume that weed scientists and crop geneticists are working overtime to
40 solve the problem. Surely the brilliant minds who developed tools like Roundup will soon create a new response to these resistant weeds; just as surely, the weeds will eventually find a way to survive whatever new tools we develop. Martial metaphors are disturbing
45 to those who imagine farming as a pastoral stroll with Gaia, but we're in an arms race with weeds, and thus has it always been.

Passage 2

What a surprise! Roundup-resistant weeds have shown up in fields that have been doused with Roundup!
50 Shocking!

Genetically modified Roundup Ready crops are not, as their creator, Monsanto, suggests, a shiny new paradigm.

What would have been truly surprising would be if
55 these weeds hadn't shown up -- the only real question

was the timing. The theory of natural selection predicts that resistance will appear whenever we attempt to eradicate a pest using such a heavy-handed approach. It is in the very nature of every creature -- plants included -- to survive. And if survival means evolving to resist an enemy, then that is what will happen.

In fact, the rise of these Roundup resistant weeds was predicted by food scientist Marion Nestle in her 2003 book *Safe Food* and by the Union of Concerned Scientists. At the time, Monsanto rejected such predictions as "hypothetical." Today, the hypothetical has become reality.

A few lessons may be drawn from this story.

First, we must recognize that any industrial approach to an agronomic problem -- from the widespread use of a pesticide or herbicide to the introduction of genetically modified crops -- is only temporary and destroys the conditions on which it depends. We've seen this with Roundup, which is no longer effective against the weeds it is intended to destroy, and, by extension, with genetically modified crops like Roundup Ready soy, which are no longer so attractive now that Roundup has lost its effectiveness. Lucky for Monsanto, the effectiveness of Roundup lasted almost exactly as long as its patent protection.

This brings us to our second lesson, which is that these genetically modified crops are not, as Monsanto suggests, a shiny new paradigm. They are simply a new iteration of the same pesticide treadmill, in which the farmer gets hooked on a chemical fix that then needs to be upgraded every few years as it loses its effectiveness. The only real beneficiaries of this treadmill are the companies that sell the products that must be reworked over and over again.

Finally, we ought to learn that monocultures are inherently precarious. Thanks in large part to Roundup and its cohort of Roundup Ready crops, farmers have taken to sowing acre upon acre with the same seed, dousing those acres with the same chemicals. This practice eliminates anything resembling natural diversity, allowing resistance to come quickly. Resilience and long-term sustainability come from diversifying fields, not planting them all to the same kind of seed.

1

According to Passage 1, the farmer and his family resorted to using Roundup because

A) they prefer to utilize the latest methods of weed and pest control.
B) controlling weeds by cultivating was difficult and inefficient.
C) Roundup was specifically designed to kill shattercane, a weed that plagued the farmer.
D) they experienced an infestation of a weed that could not be hoed and was not killed by their usual chemicals.

2

In line 20, the phrase "the war between man and weed" serves to

A) illustrate the author's severe hatred towards weed and weed control.
B) establish an angry and combative tone that is maintained throughout the rest of the passage.
C) introduce an extended metaphor comparing farming and warfare.
D) signal a shift in the discussion from acceptance of weeds to battling weeds.

3

As it is used in line 24, "rendered" most nearly means

A) made.
B) contributed.
C) displayed.
D) explained.

4

Based on information in Passage 1, currently, the best way to cope with resistant weeds is to

A) reduce reliance on Roundup.
B) increase applications of Roundup.
C) return to cultivating weeds.
D) wait for new chemicals to become available.

Which of the following provides the best support for the answer to the previous question?

A) Lines 8-9 ("We used...hoes")
B) Lines 25-27 ("By narrowing...enemy")
C) Lines 32-35 ("We will...effectiveness")
D) Lines 38-40 ("Being...problem")

Which of the following best describes the author of Passage 2's attitude toward herbicides like glyphosphate?

A) He finds it surprising that they failed.
B) He thought they might have a chance of success.
C) He believes they are doomed to failure.
D) He theorizes that they were intentionally designed to fail.

Which of the following provides the best support for the answer to the previous question?

A) Lines 48-50 ("What a...Shocking")
B) Lines 54-56 ("What...timing")
C) Lines 65-66 ("At the...hypothetical")
D) Lines 78-80 ("Lucky...protection")

As it is used in line 73, "conditions" most nearly means

A) illnesses.
B) restrictions.
C) social position.
D) circumstances.

Which of the following best describes the differing attitudes of the two authors towards organizations like Monsanto?

A) The author of Passage 1 considers them to be a help to farmers, while the author of Passage 2 considers them to be harmful to farmers.
B) Both authors believe them to be generally helpful to farmers.
C) Both authors believe them to be generally harmful to farmers.
D) The author of Passage 1 considers them to be harmful to farmers, while the author of Passage 2 considers them to be helpful to farmers.

10

Based on information in both passages, the issue of Roundup-resistant weeds is most analogous to

A) a puppy no longer listening when he is yelled at because he has been yelled at too often.
B) a child learning to resist going to bed by repeatedly requesting stories or drinks of water.
C) people using the wrong kind of pesticide to fight cockroaches.
D) the overuse of antibiotics leading to antibiotic-resistant bacteria.

Questions 11-19 are based on the following passage.

The following passage is excerpted from President John F. Kennedy's Inaugural Address, delivered on January 20, 1961.

The world is very different now. For man holds in his mortal hands the power to abolish all forms of human poverty and all forms of human life. And yet the same revolutionary beliefs for which our forebears

5 fought are still at issue around the globe-the belief that the rights of man come not from the generosity of the state, but from the hand of God…

Let every nation know, whether it wishes us well or ill, that we shall pay any price, bear any burden, meet

10 any hardship, support any friend, oppose any foe, in order to assure the survival and the success of liberty. This we pledge-and more.

To those old allies whose cultural and spiritual origins we share, we pledge the loyalty of faithful

15 friends. United, there is little we cannot do in a host of cooperative ventures. Divided, there is little we can do-for we dare not meet a powerful challenge at odds and split asunder.

To those new States whom we welcome to the ranks

20 of the free, we pledge our word that one form of colonial control shall not have passed away merely to be replaced by a far more iron tyranny. We shall not always expect to find them supporting our view. But we shall always hope to find them strongly supporting

25 their own freedom-and to remember that, in the past, those who foolishly sought power by riding the back of the tiger ended up inside.

To those peoples in the huts and villages across the globe struggling to break the bonds of mass misery,

30 we pledge our best efforts to help them help themselves, for whatever period is required-not because the Communists may be doing it, not because we seek their votes, but because it is right. If a free society cannot help the many who are poor, it cannot

35 save the few who are rich.

To our sister republics south of our border, we offer a special pledge-to convert our good words into good deeds-in a new alliance for progress-to assist free men and free governments in casting off the chains of

40 poverty. But this peaceful revolution of hope cannot become the prey of hostile powers. Let all our neighbors know that we shall join with them to oppose aggression or subversion anywhere in the Americas. And let every other power know that this Hemisphere

45 intends to remain the master of its own house.

To that world assembly of sovereign states, the United Nations, our last best hope in an age where the instruments of war have far outpaced the instruments of peace, we renew our pledge of support-to prevent it

50 from becoming merely a forum for invective-to strengthen its shield of the new and the weak-and to enlarge the area in which its writ may run.

Finally, to those nations who would make themselves our adversary, we offer not a pledge but a

55 request: that both sides begin anew the quest for peace, before the dark powers of destruction unleashed by science engulf all humanity in planned or accidental self-destruction.

We dare not tempt them with weakness. For only

60 when our arms are sufficient beyond doubt can we be certain beyond doubt that they will never be employed.

But neither can two great and powerful groups of nations take comfort from our present course-both

65 sides overburdened by the cost of modern weapons, both rightly alarmed by the steady spread of the deadly atom, yet both racing to alter that uncertain balance of terror that stays the hand of mankind's final war.

70 So let us being anew-remembering both sides that civility is not a sign of weakness, and sincerity is always subject to proof. Let us never negotiate out of fear. But let us never fear to negotiate.

Let both sides explore what problems unite us

75 instead of belaboring those problems which divide us.

Let both sides, for the first time, formulate serious and precise proposals for the inspection and control of arms-and bring the absolute power to destroy other nations under the absolute control of all nations.

80 Let both sides unite to heed in all corners of the earth and command of Isaiah-to "undo the heavy burdens…and to let the oppressed go free."

And if a beachhead of cooperation may push back the jungle of suspicion, let both sides join in creating a

85 new endeavor, not a new balance of power, but a new world of law, where the strong are just and the weak secure and the peace preserved.

11

As it is used in line 7, "state" most nearly means

A) dignity.
B) condition.
C) government.
D) declaration.

12

Which of the following best describes the effect of the speaker's choice of words in lines 8-11 ("Let...liberty")?

A) The strong diction creates a tone of warning to the nation's enemies.
B) The repeated sounds help to create an emotional appeal to patriotism.
C) The list of similar phrases clarifies the speaker's intentions.
D) The choice of words makes the speaker seem more impressive and dedicated to his purpose.

13

It can be inferred from the passage that the U.S. wishes to

A) gain the votes of "those peoples in huts and villages."
B) retain control in the entire Western hemisphere.
C) follow in the footsteps of old allies.
D) fight a war against the nation's adversaries.

14

Which of the following best supports the answer to the previous question?

A) Lines 13-15 ("To those...friends")
B) Lines 28-33 ("To those...right")
C) Lines 41-45 ("Let all...house")
D) Lines 53-58 ("Finally...self-destruction")

15

According to the speaker, one means of ensuring peace is to

A) help the poor in order to prevent the Communists from taking root in poor countries.
B) halt the spread of atomic weapons.
C) limit the strength and power of the United Nations.
D) create a strong arsenal to discourage enemies from attacking.

16

Which of the following best supports the answer to the previous question?

A) Lines 28-32 ("To those...doing it")
B) Lines 46-49 ("To that...support")
C) Lines 59-62 ("We dare...employed")
D) Lines 64-67 ("both...atom")

17

As it is used in line 68, "stays" most nearly means

A) waits.
B) supports.
C) visits.
D) halts.

18

Which of the following best describes the purpose of the final paragraphs of the passage, lines 70-87?

A) To surrender to the nation's adversaries
B) To warn the nation's adversaries
C) To appeal to the nation's adversaries for peace
D) To refuse to yield to the nation's adversaries

19

It can be inferred that the speaker's intended audience is

A) the United Nations.
B) the nation's allies.
C) only Americans.
D) people throughout the world.

The following passages was adapted from an article titled "Scientists Find a Natural Way to Clean Up Oil Spills," published in 2015 in *Smithsonian Magazine.*

Following an oil spill, the first priority is to find a way to contain and remove the oil. Anyone who has ever tried to skim oil off of soup or gravy has some small idea of how difficult it can be to separate oil
5 from water. After a spill, boat operators sometimes deploy physical booms to trap the oil so that it can be siphoned or burned off of the water's surface, but such methods are often highly ineffective. Instead, we often resort to other methods of containing oil by adding
10 manmade chemicals to the water.

Current techniques leave something to be desired. In a technique called dispersion, chemicals and wave action break the oil down into smaller particles, which then disperse and slowly biodegrade over a large area.
15 Another technique is known as chemical herding. To clean up an oil spill with a chemical herder, crews spray a chemical compound around the perimeter of the spill. The compound remains on the surface and eventually causes the oil to thicken. Once the oil
20 reaches the desired thickness, it can be burned off. Depending on the location of the spill and the prevailing weather conditions, chemical herding can be unreliable because it requires calm water; however, unlike mechanical removal or dispersion, chemical
25 herding gets all the oil. The technique has been around since the 1970s, but, until now, the chemicals used to herd the oil, called soap surfactants, didn't break down over time. As a result, even after the oil burned off, the chemicals remained in the surrounding ecosystem.
30 This problem may have finally been addressed. Researchers at the City College of New York, led by chemist George John and chemical engineer Charles Maldarelli, have developed a way to clean up oil using a chemical herder made of phytol, a molecule in
35 chlorophyll that makes algae green. It's the first non-toxic, natural way to remediate oil spills.

"We didn't want to add anything to the environment that would make it worse, so we decided to make molecules that came from natural products, so they
40 would automatically biodegrade," Maldarelli says. "We like the idea of using a molecule that's abundant in nature to arm against something humans have done to the environment."

The researchers settled on phytol, which they
45 harvest from algae. It is a natural molecule that

cleaves off as the chlorophyll breaks down, so they knew it would be stable in the environment. The phytol didn't quite do the job on its own, so they added a plant-based fat, called a lipid, which helped
50 align the molecules in a way that broke the water's surface tension.

In their Manhattan lab, the team tested the natural herder on fake oil spills to see if it could condense the oil as effectively as current chemical herders. Over
55 time, they fine tuned the balance of elements until it herded just as quickly as the chemical versions. Maldarelli says they closely examined both biodegradability and toxicity while also considering the feasibility of sourcing the new herder
60 commercially.

"The commercial ones, they're fairly non toxic—some are more than others," says Maldarelli. "But our claim is that if you start with natural products you're ahead of the game."

65 The researchers are currently testing the natural herder in wave tanks and monitoring how long it takes to break down. They're still unsure if the lipid they are currently using is truly the best option, so they are testing other options for binding agents. They hope to
70 scale up the manufacture of the new chemical herding in order to make it available for use in emergency situations.

The natural herder can be sprayed from a plane, so Maldarelli says its best use case will be in calm waters
75 where it's hard to navigate a boat. "The Arctic seas are usually calmer and have icebergs floating, so chemical herding works there," he says.

On July 22, 2015, President Obama approved two of Royal Dutch Shell's permits for drilling in the
80 Chukchi Sea, off the coast of northern Alaska. Shell had an accident the first time they tried to drill in the Arctic, in 2012. Other companies, including Exxon, have also had difficulties with oil in the Arctic. Given the history of Arctic drilling, a future oil spill certainly seems like a possibility. In that event, a safer, more environmentally-friendly means of addressing the problem would be useful.

20

As it is used in line 2, "contain" most nearly means

A) hold back.
B) stifle.
C) accommodate.
D) incorporate.

21

That author most likely included the sentence in lines 2-5 ("Anyone...water") in order to

A) provide an analogous situation to help the reader relate.
B) show how simple addressing oil spills ought to be.
C) illustrate the exact methods involved in addressing oil spills.
D) offer imagery that helps the reader picture what an oil spill looks like.

22

It can be inferred from the passage that an unexpected storm near an oil spill would likely

A) aid chemical herding efforts by emulsifying the oil with the water.
B) create rough waters that would make chemical herding impossible.
C) force oil to move to calmer water.
D) make mechanical removal or dispersion impossible.

23

Which of the following is the primary benefit of the newly developed chemical?

A) It can be used in rough waters, so it can be used in more locations.
B) It is easier to source than older chemical herders.
C) It biodegrades more quickly because it is made from natural materials.
D) It can be sprayed from a plane, unlike other chemicals.

24

Which of the following best supports the answer to the previous question?

A) Lines 21-23 ("Depending...water")
B) Lines 37-40 ("We...biodegrade")
C) Lines 59-60 ("the feasibility...commercially")
D) Lines 73-75 ("The natural...boat")

25

As it is used in line 53, "condense" most nearly means

A) compress.
B) summarize.
C) shorten.
D) thicken.

26

Which of the following is NOT a requirement the researchers had for their chemical?

A) Easily biodegraded
B) Non-toxic and environmentally friendly
C) Able to withstand rough waters
D) Effective in condensing oil

27

Which of the following best supports the answer to the previous question?

A) Lines 21-23 ("Depending...water")
B) Lines 24-25 ("unlike...oil")
C) Lines 55-58 ("they fine...toxicity")
D) Lines 65-67 ("The researchers...down")

28

It can be inferred from the passage that the new chemical is timely because

A) old chemical herders no longer work.
B) an Arctic oil spill seems to be a likely possibility.
C) governments now require non-toxic chemicals.
D) the Shell oil spill from 2012 has yet to be cleaned up.

The following passage is adapted from an article titled "Passage to America, 1750," published by Eyewitness History. It includes an excerpt from a diary entry by immigrant Gottelb Mittelberger, which was published in *Journey to Pennsylvania in 1750*.

Approximately 200,000 people lived in the British colonies in North America at the end of the seventeenth century. The population doubled about every 25 years after that in the following century. A
5 majority of these new immigrants were Scotch-Irish, Germans, or African slaves. From the start of the 1700s to the beginning of the American Revolution approximately 250,000 Africans, 210,000 Europeans, and 50,000 convicts had reached the colonial shores.
10 The journey to America was perilous. Many immigrants were far too poor to purchase passage to the colonies and therefore indentured themselves to wealthier colonialists. They would sell their services for a contracted period of time in return for the price
15 of passage. Even those who paid would have to endure the hardships of the voyage, crammed into small wooden spaces, rocking and rolling at the whims of the sea. Misery is the most accurate way to describe the journey that generally lasted seven weeks. One
20 immigrant described the journey as follows:
"During the voyage, there is much misery, stench, fumes, horror, vomiting, seasickness, fever, dysentery, headache, heat, constipation, boils, scurvy, cancer, mouth rot, and much more, all that came from terrible
25 food and very foul water, causing many to die miserably.
"All of those illnesses are paired with want for provisions, hunger, thirst, frost, heat, dampness, anxiety, afflictions, and emotions. The misery was so
30 high when a gale rages for several nights and days, making everyone believe that the ship will sink to the bottom of the sea killing all on board. During such visitations, people cry and pray most piteously.
"No one can envision the sufferings which the
35 women in confinement have to endure with their innocent children on board these ships. Few escape with their lives; many a mother is thrown into the ocean with her child as soon as she is dead. One day after a heavy gale, a woman on our ship, who was
40 about to give birth and could not due to the conditions, was pushed overboard through a porthole in the ship and dropped into the sea, because she was at the rear

of the ship and could not be brought forward.
"Young children under seven years rarely survived
45 the long journey; many times parents are forced to watch their children suffer miserably and die from hunger, thirst, and sickness, and then see them thrown away into the water. I witness such misery in no less than thirty-two children on our ship, all of whom were
50 tossed into the sea. The parents grieve to see their children find no resting place in the earth, but be devoured by sea monsters. It is notable that many children who have not yet had the measles or smallpox generally contract them on board and most of them
55 die.
"When the ships have pulled into port at Philadelphia, no one is allowed to leave the ships except those who have paid for their passage in full. The others, who cannot pay, must remain on board
60 until they are purchased and released from the ships by their purchasers. The healthy and strong are naturally preferred and purchased first, leaving the sick and weak on board. The sick and wretched must often stay on board in front of the city for several
65 weeks, and frequently die, where one who is healthy, purchased, or paid for passage would be able to leave the ship immediately, recover their health, and remain alive.
"The sale of human beings in the market on board
70 the ship is carried on as follows: Every day Englishmen, Dutchmen, and High German people come from Philadelphia and other cities, some from a great distance that could span from twenty to forty hours, and go on board the newly-arrived ships that
75 have brought and offer for sale passengers from Europe. They select from the groups the healthy persons that seem suitable for their business and bargain with them for how long they will serve for payment of their passage. When they have come to an
80 agreement, the adult persons bind themselves in writing to serve for three to six years for the amount due, according to their age and strength. However, very young people from the ages of ten to fifteen years must serve till they are twenty-one years old."

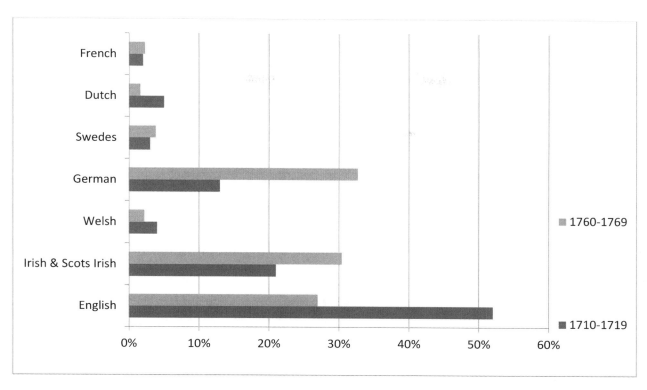

Populations of immigrants, comparison between 1710-1719 and 1760-1769

29

Which of the following can be inferred from the passage?

A) During the 1700s, it was not uncommon for convicts to be sent to America rather than imprisoned.
B) The majority of the population growth during the 1700s came from reproduction rather than immigration.
C) Almost all of the 210,000 Europeans who came to America during the 1700s were Scotch-Irish.
D) Almost all of the 210,000 Europeans who came to America during the 1700s were indentured servants.

As it is used in line 14, "contracted" most nearly means

A) condensed.
B) negotiated.
C) caught.
D) consumed.
.

Which of the following best describes the effect of the author's word choice in the paragraph in lines 21-26?

A) The phrasing in the paragraph places blame for many deaths on those who sailed the ships.
B) The simplistic list of single words shows that the author was not a well educated immigrant.
C) The list of words seems monotonous, reflecting the boredom inherent in such a long journey.
D) The list of descriptive words effectively paints a picture of misery.

As it is used in line 54, "contract" most nearly means

A) condense.
B) negotiate.
C) catch.
D) consume.

It can be inferred from the passage that

A) parents were usually thrown overboard with their children.
B) pregnant women were not allowed to give birth on the ship so they were thrown overboard.
C) any passenger that contracted smallpox was thrown overboard.
D) many communicable diseases spread among the passengers.

Which of the following best supports the answer to the previous question?

A) Lines 36-38 ("Few...dead")
B) Lines 38-43 ("One...forward")
C) Lines 48-50 ("I...sea")
D) Lines 52-55 ("It...die")

According to the passage, those who survived the voyage but arrived ill

A) were thrown overboard at the first chance.
B) were allowed to leave the ships.
C) were usually purchased quickly.
D) often perished while waiting to be purchased.

Which of the following best supports the answer to the previous question?

A) Lines 56-58 ("When...full")
B) Lines 59-61 ("The others...purchasers")
C) Lines 61-63 ("The healthy...board")
D) Lines 63-65 ("The sick...die")

37

According to the passage, which groups suffered the most aboard the ships?

A) Those who had already had measles and smallpox
B) Parents
C) Children and pregnant women
D) Indentured servants

According to the graph, which of the following groups of immigrants arrived in America in large numbers during the 1700s but were NOT identified in the first paragraph of the passage?

A) Germans and Scotch Irish
B) Irish and English
C) Dutch and Swedes
D) Irish and Scotch Irish

This passage is adapted from Leo Tolstoy's novel *Anna Karenina*.

The families of the Levins and the Shcherbatskys were old, noble Moscow families, and had always been on intimate and friendly terms. This intimacy had grown still closer during Levin's student days. He had both
5 prepared for the university with the young Prince Shcherbatsky, the brother of Kitty and Dolly, and had entered at the same time with him. In those days Levin used often to be in the Shcherbatskys' house, and he was in love with the Shcherbatsky household. Strange
10 as it may appear, it was with the household, the family, that Konstantin Levin was in love, especially with the feminine half of the household. Levin did not remember his own mother, and his only sister was older than he was, so that it was in the Shcherbatskys' house that he
15 saw for the first time that inner life of an old, noble, cultivated, and honorable family of which he had been deprived by the death of his father and mother. All the members of that family, especially the feminine half, were pictured by him, as it were, wrapped about with a
20 mysterious poetical veil, and he not only perceived no defects whatever in them, but under the poetical veil that shrouded them he assumed the existence of the loftiest sentiments and every possible perfection.

One would have thought that nothing could be
25 simpler than for him, a man of good family, rather rich than poor, and thirty-two years old, to make the young Princess Shcherbatsky an offer of marriage; in all likelihood he would at once have been looked upon as a good match. But Levin was in love, and so it seemed to
30 him that Kitty was so perfect in every respect that she was a creature far above everything earthly; and that he was a creature so low and so earthly that it could not even be conceived that other people and she herself could regard him as worthy of her.

35 After spending two months in Moscow in a state of enchantment, seeing Kitty almost every day in society, into which he went so as to meet her, he abruptly decided that it could not be, and went back to the country.

40 Levin's conviction that it could not be was founded on the idea that in the eyes of her family he was a disadvantageous and worthless match for the charming Kitty, and that Kitty herself could not love him. In her family's eyes he had no ordinary, definite career and
45 position in society, while his contemporaries by this time, when he was thirty-two, were already, one a colonel, and another a professor, another director of a bank and railways, or president of a board like Oblonsky. But he (he knew very well how he must
50 appear to others) was a country gentleman, occupied in breeding cattle, shooting game, and building barns; in other words, a fellow of no ability, who had not turned out well, and who was doing just what, according to the ideas of the world, is done by people fit for nothing else.

55 The mysterious, enchanting Kitty herself could not love such an ugly person as he conceived himself to be, and, above all, such an ordinary, in no way striking person. Moreover, his attitude to Kitty in the past—the attitude of a grown-up person to a child, arising from his
60 friendship with her brother—seemed to him yet another obstacle to love. An ugly, good-natured man, as he considered himself, might, he supposed, be liked as a friend; but to be loved with such a love as that with which he loved Kitty, one would need to be a handsome
65 and, still more, a distinguished man.

He had heard that women often did care for ugly and ordinary men, but he did not believe it, for he judged by himself, and he could not himself have loved any but beautiful, mysterious, and exceptional women.

70 But after spending two months alone in the country, he was convinced that this was not one of those passions of which he had had experience in his early youth; that this feeling gave him not an instant's rest; that he could not live without deciding the question, would she or
75 would she not be his wife, and that his despair had arisen only from his own imaginings, that he had no sort of proof that he would be rejected. And he had now come to Moscow with a firm determination to make an offer, and get married if he were accepted. Or ... he
80 could not conceive what would become of him if he were rejected.

39

The relationship between the Levin and Shcherbatsky households is most analogous to

A) an organization that has been around for decades and one that has just begun
B) two cousins separated by a vast family tree.
C) two illustrious businesses, one of which has recently suffered financial setbacks.
D) two politicians of equal stature and importance.

40

The passage suggests that Levin is in love with the Shcherbatsky household because

A) he is in love with Kitty.
B) he thought of the young Prince Shcherbatsky as a brother.
C) he lacked a strong family life in his early years and appreciates that of the Shcherbatskys.
D) he has longing dreams of joining the Moscow aristocracy.

41

Which of the following best supports the answer to the previous question?

A) Lines 4-8 ("He...with him")
B) Lines 12-17 ("Levin...mother.")
C) Lines 17-23 ("All... perfection.")
D) Lines 29-34 ("But...her.")

42

As used in line 23, "loftiest" most nearly means

A) most towering.
B) grandest.
C) worthiest.
D) most elevated.

43

As described in the passage, Levin's attitude towards Kitty is that of

A) a man suffering a hopeless obsession.
B) an older brother protective of his younger sister.
C) a social climber hoping to improve his position through an advantageous marriage.
D) a worshipper of an idealized object.

44

Which of the following is NOT an obstacle that Levin sees in his courtship of Kitty Shcherbatsky?

A) the difference in their ages.
B) another suitor.
C) his profession.
D) his low self-esteem.

45

The passage implies which of the following?

A) Levin rarely goes out into society for his own sake.
B) Kitty is too far above Levin for the marriage to work.
C) Levin's family disapproves of his profession and would prefer he be a banker or in the military.
D) Levin will be rejected by Kitty.

46

Which of the following best supports the answer to the previous question?

A) Lines 29-34 ("But... her.")
B) Lines 35-39 ("After... country.")
C) Lines 43-49 ("In... Oblonsky.")
D) Lines 79-81 ("Or... rejected.")

47

As it is used in line 37, "striking" most nearly means

A) attacking
B) distracting
C) impressive
D) startling

Writing and Language Test
35 MINUTES, 44 QUESTIONS

Turn to Section 2 of your answer sheet to answer the questions in this section.

DIRECTIONS

Each passage below is accompanied by a number of questions. For some questions, you will consider how the passage might be revised to improve the expression of ideas. For other questions, you will consider how the passage might be edited to correct errors in sentence structure, usage, or punctuation. A passage or a question may be accompanied by one or more graphics (such as a table or graph) that you will consider as you make revising and editing decisions.

Some questions will direct you to an underlined portion of a passage. Other questions will direct you to a location in a passage or ask you to think about the passage as a whole.

After reading each passage, choose the answer to each question that most effectively improves the quality of writing in the passage or that makes the passage conform to the conventions of standard written English. Many questions include a "NO CHANGE" option. Choose that option if you think the best choice is to leave the relevant portion of the passage as it is.

Questions 1-11 are based on the following passage.
The Changing Nature of Happiness

{1}

1 In 1938, one of the first scientific studies of happiness was conducted in the Lancashire town of Bolton in the United Kingdom. Mass Observation, a social research organization in the U.K., sent out questionnaires to **2** petition the feelings of average citizens. On March 28th, 1938, 226 Boltanians were sent a survey inviting them to 'give their opinion' on happiness. Ten 'qualities of life' were identified and participants were asked to rank them in order of importance.

1

The author is considering adding the following sentence as an introduction to the passage:

The contemporary obsession with happiness is not as recent as many experts would have us believe.

Should the author make this change?

A) Yes, the passage is incomprehensible without it.

B) Yes, it gives a reason for writing the passage.

C) No, it is irrelevant to the rest of the passage.

D) No, it does not fit with the tone of the rest of the passage.

2

A) NO CHANGE

B) appeal

C) lobby

D) request

{2}

In February 2014, a local newspaper offered readers an opportunity to participate in a re-run of this questionnaire. The original survey was updated to include modern topics, while preserving as much of the original meaning as possible. **3** Because of the original survey, heavy industry in Bolton has mostly been supplanted by the service and technology industries. Nowadays, Boltonians enjoy a standard of living that citizens in 1938 would **4** be astounded and astonished by. Better housing standards, a universal benefit system, national healthcare, and educational access from primary to university level are now accessible to average people. These advances bring other challenges, and thus, the debate regarding the core of happiness and the result of technological and economic change on well-being remains.

{3}

[1] How has the meaning of happiness changed in Bolton in the last 76 years? [2] In addition, weekends have become more **5** popular, the respondents reporting weekends as a happier time for them increased from **6** approximate 25 percent in 1938 to 41 percent in 2014. [3] Both surveys found that the majority of respondents reported that their happiness was the same at weekends or weekdays. [4] As to the role of luck, there was a 22 percent increase in those believing it influenced happiness. [5] Overall, the main differences between 1938 and 2014 were in the opinions on religion, leisure, and good humor. [6] Politics and leadership were rated lowest in significance in both periods. **7**

3

A) NO CHANGE
B) Since
C) Although
D) Despite

4

A) NO CHANGE
B) be astounded by.
C) find astounding.
D) find the most surprising.

5

A) NO CHANGE
B) popular; since the
C) popular; the
D) popular the

6

A) NO CHANGE
B) projectedly
C) estimated
D) approximately

7

The author plans to add the following sentence:

The majority of citizens in 1938 were most content in Bolton, but by 2014, 63 percent reported being happier away from the town.

This sentence would most logically be added

A) before sentence 1.
B) before sentence 2.
C) before sentence 3.
D) after sentence 6.

{4}

8 The Mass Observation happiness contests were conducted during some crucial world events. At this point in history, Hitler pushed into Vienna, and Franco gained the upper hand in Spain. Walt Disney released the first feature-length animated **9** movie and Preston North End won the FA Cup. But the degree to which external matters affect happiness is difficult to ascertain. The general impression from the survey in 1938 is that happiness was mostly entrenched in daily lives at home and in the community.

{5}

In the end, the Mass Observation team did not truly grasp the implications of its work. Happiness is more intricate than the Mass Observation team appreciated. Furthermore, **10** they ignore the significance of relationships, along with social and cultural factors. Nevertheless, this early inquiry was one of the first to examine the science of happiness and for that we are indebted. **11**

8

To best transition from the first part of the essay to the second, which of the following should be inserted here?

A) In reality, some very good and very bad things happened during this time.

B) Many of the world events during this time wee embarrassing to the entire world.

C) Could external factors have influenced the outcomes?

D) Who knows why any of this happened?

9

A) NO CHANGE

B) movie, and

C) movie; and

D) movie, but

10

A) NO CHANGE

B) it ignores

C) the team ignored

D) the team ignore

11

Which of the following paragraph orders would produce the most logical essay?

A) NO CHANGE

B) 1, 2, 4, 3, 5

C) 1, 3, 2, 4, 5

D) 1, 4, 2, 3, 5

Questions 12-22 are based on the following passage.

Cellular "Cheaters" Give Rise to Cancer

The story of how living protoplasm arose from lifeless matter could potentially **12** illuminate something darker: the origin of cancer. As primordial cells evolved, mercilessly vying for nutrients, some discovered a different **13** path cooperation. They began sharing resources and duties, giving rise to multicellular creatures—plants, animals and ultimately us.

14 Cells that work together are relatively rare in modern-day organisms. By yielding some of its autonomy, each cell thrives with the whole. But unsurprisingly, there are cheaters. In healthy organisms, a cell replicates only as often as necessary **15** to maintain the population and to allow for moderate growth. On the other hand, these cheaters begin replicating wildly, utilizing more than their share of resources and spewing toxins that reshape the environment to their advantage. **16** And so cancer begins.

12
A) NO CHANGE
B) eliminate
C) eradicate
D) irradiate

13
A) NO CHANGE
B) path; cooperation
C) path: cooperation
D) path. cooperation

14
Which choice best establishes the main idea of the paragraph?

A) NO CHANGE
B) How commonly do cells work with other cells?
C) An intricate web of biological concessions holds each of these cooperatives together.
D) Cells are the building blocks of living organisms.

15
A) NO CHANGE
B) to maintain and allow the population
C) to maintain the population and allow
D) to maintain the population and be allowing

16
Which concluding sentence would best transition to the next paragraph?

A) NO CHANGE
B) But cheaters never prosper.
C) These cheaters rarely get away with this selfishness.
D) But we have the technology to fight cancer.

Typically, a process called differentiation works to let normal cells specialize, becoming skin cells, muscle cells, bone **17** cells, and so forth and so on. This allows for an appropriate division of labor. However, cancer cells "dedifferentiate," deserting **18** there assigned roles for a course advantageous only to themselves. Under normal conditions, a cell that goes berserk is swiftly eradicated through a mechanism called programmed cell death, or cellular suicide. Cancer cells somehow manage to circumvent this safeguard by refusing to die.

[1] Interestingly enough, a recent review in a noted scientific journal describes cancer-like phenomena in almost every niche of the biosphere. [2] But not all biologists would agree that every occurrence described in the review should be classified as cancer-like. [3] What is clear from the wealth of examples is that multicellular existence is a constant struggle between competition and cooperation. [4] Tip the balance too far, and the outcome might be malignancy. **19**

In the long run, the trade-offs between cellular freedom and communalism have repeatedly paid off. Multicellularity, flawed as it has been, can be so beneficial that it has evolved independently several times throughout the history of the biosphere.

17

A) NO CHANGE

B) cells, and so forth.

C) cells, etc.

D) cells, and such other things.

18

A) NO CHANGE

B) their

C) its

D) they're

19

To improve the focus and flow of the paragraph, sentence 4 should be

A) Where it is now.

B) Before sentence 1.

C) Before sentence 2.

D) Before sentence 3.

Nevertheless, most of Earth's biomass **20** <u>are</u> still comprised of individual actors—bacteria and other single-celled organisms. Frequently, these microbes also yield some of their freedom, forming primitive collectives, like the invisible biofilms that coat surfaces of hospital equipment. These reciprocal support societies make the otherwise vulnerable individual practically invincible to antibiotics.

21 Yet here too, some research indicates, cooperation can give rise to cheaters. Taking advantage of the nourishment and shelter provided by the biofilm, some bacteria will waste resources and prosper at the expense of the others—a microscopic tragedy of the commons.

22 <u>Although,</u> once they have the upper hand, even cancer cells may join forces—to the advantage of the tumor and to the peril of its host. As the cancerous cells split and mutate, they diverge into distinct lineages, each with varying abilities. In a lethal symbiosis, one family of cells might manufacture a substance that aids the others, which in turn generates other chemicals the tumor needs to thrive in remote regions of the body.

In the end, there are no victors. The cancer annihilates its own ecosystem and perishes with its host.

20

A) NO CHANGE

B) is

C) was

D) were

21

The author of the passage is considering starting a new paragraph here. Should he do so?

A) Yes, because the author is shifting the topic of the paragraph.

B) Yes, because the author is shifting the tone of the paragraph.

C) No, because the author has not changed the topic of the paragraph.

D) No, because the paragraph is not too long to be split into two.

22

A) NO CHANGE

B) Before then

C) Nonetheless

D) Inasmuch as

Questions 23-33 are based on the following passage.

How Much Do We Really Know About Pocahontas?

As one of the most legendary figures in early America, Pocahontas is seen as the idealistic "princess" who rescues John Smith and the struggling Jamestown colony. **23** Later on, Jamestown becomes one of the most important towns in making the history of the burgeoning United States.

She was born Matoaka, in the mid-1590s, in what is now eastern Virginia. Her **24** father Chief Powhatan had dozens of children. But she drew special attention for her beauty and **25** vivacity, thus she gained the nickname Pocahontas, meaning "playful one." John Smith, an early leader in Jamestown, characterized her as attractive in "feature, countenance, and proportion" and full of "wit and spirit."

But unlike her portrayal in storybooks and films, Pocahontas was described by Smith as "A child of ten years old." There is no proof of a romance between her and Smith or that Pocahontas flung her own body over his to rescue the English captain from a death sentence. The sole source for this tale is Smith, who **26** decorated many of his exploits and failed to recount his rescue by Pocahontas until 17 years after the incident supposedly occurred.

23

Which of the following best establishes the main idea of the passage while maintaining the passage's style and tone?

A) NO CHANGE

B) Pocahontas went on to star as the central character in a film by Disney, as well as other pieces of fiction.

C) Oddly enough, many of the tales told about Pocahontas do not make much sense to modern day readers.

D) However, the true story of this young woman's short life is nothing like the fairy tales with which we are so familiar.

24

A) NO CHANGE

B) father Chief Powhatan, had

C) father, Chief Powhatan had

D) father, Chief Powhatan, had

25

A) NO CHANGE

B) vivacity,

C) vivacity so

D) vivacity; thus

26

A) NO CHANGE

B) adorned

C) embellished

D) festooned

[1] Nonetheless, she did protect Jamestown from famine and Native American attack. [2] She brought food to the colonists, served as a liaison, and **27** was cautioning the English about her father's ambush plans. [3] Smith praised Pocahontas for her assistance and even rewarded her with trinkets, but within a few years, she was abducted by the English, who planned to exchange her for a ransom of corn and captives held by Powhatan. [4] When Powhatan refused the deal, the now-teenager remained with the colonists. [5] Powhatan was the name of both the chief of the tribe and the tribe he ruled over.[6] Whether this was by choice is unclear, since all accounts of her came from the English. **28**

Eventually, one of the colonists, John Rolfe, became smitten by Pocahontas. In 1614, she was baptized Rebecca and married Rolfe, with both natives and colonists present. The marriage actually brought a **29** breakneck peace to Virginia. It also offered an opportunity for the **30** colonies stockholders to flaunt their accomplishments in planting a cash crop, tobacco, and "civilizing" heathen natives.

27

A) NO CHANGE

B) cautioned

C) cautions

D) were cautioning

28

Which sentence should be eliminated in order to improve the focus of the paragraph?

A) Sentence 2

B) Sentence 3

C) Sentence 5

D) Sentence 6

29

A) NO CHANGE

B) ethereal

C) fleeting

D) blistering

30

A) NO CHANGE

B) colonies'

C) colonys

D) colony's

Thus, in 1616, the Rolfes and their infant son set sail for London on a publicity tour funded by the Virginia Company. Pocahontas attended balls and plays, astounding the English with her etiquette and appearance, and sat for a painting adorned in courtly regalia. But like so many natives exposed to Europeans in this period, she and her young son became ill in England, likely from tuberculosis. Even though the Rolfes had set out for Virginia, Pocahontas' illness forced them back ashore to the Thames port of Gravesend. **31**

Rolfe, who "much lamented" her **32** passing upon returning to Virginia and eventually remarried. His son by Pocahontas, Thomas Rolfe, inherited his father's estate, married a colonist, and joined the militia, which crushed his mother's tribe during a rebellion. In later centuries, the **33** depressed history of Pocahontas would ultimately be exchanged by the romanticized version we know today.

31

The author is considering adding the following sentence at this point:

She perished there in March 1617, at the age of approximately 21.

Should the author make this addition?

A) No, because it does not meaningfully develop the ideas presented in the paragraph.

B) No, because the information it provides is repeated in the next paragraph.

C) Yes, because it provides a different point of view than the one presented in the next paragraph.

D) Yes, because it gives extra information about Pocahontas' death.

32

A) NO CHANGE

B) passing, returned to

C) passing and returning to

D) , passed and returned to

33

Which adjective, if placed here, best fits the tone of the passage?

A) NO CHANGE

B) tumultuous

C) unhappy

D) unbridled

Questions 34-44 are based on the following passage and graphic.

The Case for Vacation

The average American worker **34** ensues 18 vacation days and uses only 16. We leave hundreds of thousands of hours of paid time off **35** leftover each year. Contrast this with the average French worker, who typically takes twice as much vacation time. Based solely on these statistics, it might be reasonable to assume that the vacation-bereft American worker is the more productive of the two. **36**

[1] In 1999, an insurance company called New Century Global sought the help of the Cornell University Ergonomics Research Laboratory in order to improve worker efficiency. [2] Though the term "ergonomics" most commonly applies to furniture design and posture, in this context, it is the study of workplace efficiency. [3] The lab conducted a 10-week study at New Century Global, implementing a computer program that reminded some workers to take short breaks. [4] They found that workers who received the alerts were 13% more accurate in their work than those who were not reminded.

37

34

A) NO CHANGE

B) cultivates

C) increases

D) accrues

35

Which of the following idioms provides the best replacement for the underlined portion?

A) on the table

B) to wrap up

C) to make the best of

D) make headway with

36

Which of the following would best establish the main idea of the passage if inserted here?

A) The rest of the civilized world lags behind America in most economic measures.

B) European countries with more vacation days are simply too lazy to get much work done.

C) In fact, it may be the opposite: Europeans understand that breaks improve workplace efficiency.

D) The fact of the matter is that an increase in vacation days decreases the amount of work that can be done.

37

The author is considering removing sentence 2 from the paragraph. Should the author make this deletion?

A) Yes, because it adds irrelevant information.

B) Yes, because this information is redundant.

C) No, because it clarifies the meaning of an important idea.

D) No, because it provides an example that develops the ideas of the paragraph.

Today, we don't need software to remind us to take **38** breaks: we have the constant distraction of the Internet. Once study found that "Internet misuse" costs U.S. companies more than $178 billion annually in lost productivity. And yet, the National University of Singapore found that those who spent less than 20% of their time "misusing" the Internet -- whether by engaging on social media, reading a blog, or watching silly cat videos – **39** was 9 percent more productive than those who resisted going online.

The more we learn about human attention, the more limited it seems. Study after **40** study indicate that short bursts of attention punctuated with equally deliberate breaks are the surest way to harness our full capacity to be productive. For example, a study published in the journal *Cognition* found that short breaks allow people to maintain **41** there focus on a task without the loss of quality that normally occurs over time.

[1] Just as small breaks improve concentration, long breaks replenish job performance.[2] But what about vacations? [3] "The impact that taking a vacation has on one's mental health is profound," said Francine Lederer, a clinical psychologist in Los Angeles specializing in workplace health. [4] Vacation deprivation increases mistakes and resentment at co-workers, Businessweek reported in 2007.[5] "Most people have better life perspective and are more motivated to achieve their goals after a vacation, even if it is a 24-hour time-out." **42**

38
A) NO CHANGE
B) breaks, we
C) breaks we
D) breaks, because we

39
A) NO CHANGE
B) are
C) were
D) is

40
A) NO CHANGE
B) studies indicate
C) study indicates
D) studies indicates

41
A) NO CHANGE
B) they're
C) its
D) their

42
To improve the focus and flow of the paragraph, sentence 2 should be placed where?
A) Where it is now.
B) Before sentence 1.
C) Before sentence 4.
D) Before sentence 5.

43 <u>Overtime is tearing the United States' economy apart.</u> Where you get your break -- from an hour on blogs, a day in the park, or a week golfing at Martha's Vineyard -- doesn't matter so much as that you get it. The United States should take a lesson from other European countries and drastically increase the number of legally required paid days off. **44** <u>A five-day increase would put it even with the countries with the least number of required days off.</u>

Source: Center for Economic and Policy Research

43

Which of the following provides the best transition between the previous paragraph and this paragraph?

A) NO CHANGE

B) Many liberals want to drastically increase the number of breaks given to workers – and they couldn't be more wrong.

C) Breaks should even be extended to school children, as they benefit education greatly as well.

D) The bottom line is that breaks are better for our brains than overtime

44

A) NO CHANGE

B) A twenty-five-day increase would put it even with the countries with the least number of required days off.

C) A thirty-five-day increase would put it even with the countries with the least number of required days off.

D) A ten-day increase would put it even with the countries with the least number of required days off.

Math Test – No Calculator
25 MINUTES, 17 QUESTIONS

Turn to Section 3 of your answer sheet to answer the questions in this section.

DIRECTIONS

For questions **1-13**, solve each problem, choose the best answer from the choices provided, and fill in the corresponding circle on your answer sheet. **For questions 14-17**, solve the problem and enter your answer in the grid on the answer sheet. Please refer to the directions before question 14 on how to enter your answers in the grid. You may use any available space in your test booklet for scratch work.

NOTES

1. The use of a calculator **is not permitted**.
2. All variables and expressions used represent real numbers unless otherwise indicated.
3. Figures provided in the test are drawn to scale unless otherwise indicated.
4. All figures lie in a plane unless otherwise indicated.
5. Unless otherwise indicated, the domain of a given function f is the set of all real numbers x for which $f(x)$ is a real number.

REFERENCE

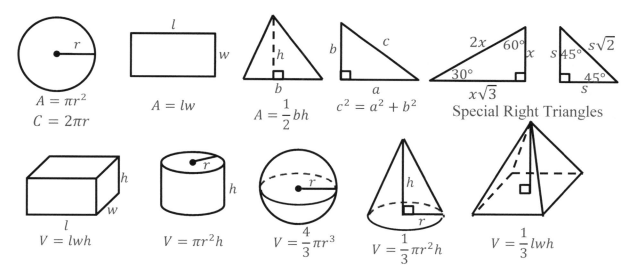

$A = \pi r^2$
$C = 2\pi r$

$A = lw$

$A = \frac{1}{2}bh$

$c^2 = a^2 + b^2$

Special Right Triangles

$V = lwh$

$V = \pi r^2 h$

$V = \frac{4}{3}\pi r^3$

$V = \frac{1}{3}\pi r^2 h$

$V = \frac{1}{3}lwh$

The number of degrees of arc in a circle is 360.
The number of radians of arc in a circle is 2π.
The sum of the measures in degrees of the angles of a triangle is 180.

$$6xy - 2x = -1(12 + 2x)$$

If (x, y) is a solution to the equation above, what is the value of yx?

A) -2

B) 0

C) 2

D) 12

2

While selling vacuum cleaners door to door, Kenji earns \$12.50 for each vacuum he sells and an additional \$65.00 bonus each time he sells 20 vacuums. If Kenji sells vacuums only in multiples of 20, what expression could be used to determine how many money Kenji earned?

A) $65v + \frac{v(12.50)}{20}$, where v is the number of vacuums Kenji sold

B) $65v + 20(12.50v)$, where v is the number of vacuums Kenji sold

C) $12.50v + v(65)$, where v is the number of vacuums Kenji sold

D) $12.50v + \frac{v(65)}{20}$, where v is the number of vacuums Kenji sold

$$3 - 2y = 4x$$

$$3x - 4y = 17$$

At which of the following points, (x, y), do the above equations intersect?

A) $\left(1, \frac{7}{2}\right)$

B) $\left(1, -\frac{7}{2}\right)$

C) $\left(-1, \frac{7}{2}\right)$

D) $\left(-1, -\frac{7}{2}\right)$

The area of the ground floor of a new rectangular-shaped office building must be at least 300 square meters, but no more than 400 square meters. If the width of the office building is 15 square meters, which of the following inequalities gives all of the possible lengths, l, of the office building?

A) $300 \leq 15l < 400$

B) $300 < 15l \leq 400$

C) $300 < 15l < 400$

D) $300 \leq 15l \leq 400$

Alexa and Ali are competing in a gameshow. Each question a contest gets right is worth x points, while each obstacle course a contestant completes is worth y points. Alexa answers 8 questions correctly and finishes 3 obstacle courses for 53 points. Ali answers 7 questions correctly and finishes 4 obstacle points for 56 points. How many points is completing 2 obstacle courses worth?

A) 4

B) 7

C) 8

D) 14

$$Ax^2 + Bx - 16 = 0$$

If 2 and –4 are two solutions of the equation above, which of the following is the value of $A + B$?

A) 2

B) 4

C) 6

D) 8

A cylinder has a height of 20 meters and a volume of 80π cubic meters. What is the length of the diameter of the cylinder?

A) 2

B) 4

C) 8

D) 16

If $f(2x - 1) = \frac{1}{2}x^2 + x$ for all values of x, what is the value of $f(7)$?

A) 4

B) 12

C) 31.5

D) 97.5

A motorcycle is traveling up the slope of a mountain. For every 60 meters the motorcycle travels, the elevation of the mountain increases by 6 meters. If the car starts at an elevation of 800 meters and is travelling at a rate of 30 meters per second, what is the elevation of the mountain, in meters, at the point where the motorcycle passes t seconds after entering the road?

A) $800 + 3t$

B) $800 + 6t$

C) $800 + 30t$

D) $800 + 60t$

10

Which of the following is equivalent to $(q - r) \times (\frac{q}{r-q})$?

A) q

B) $-q$

C) $\frac{q(q-r)}{r+q}$

D) 0

$$m = 53 - 0.2T$$

The equation above is used to model the relationship between the number of male alligators, m, hatched from a group of alligator eggs at the current temperature, T, in degrees Fahrenheit. According to the model, what is the meaning of the 53 in the equation?

A) For every increase of 0.2°F, 53 more males will be hatched
B) For every decrease of 0.2 °F, 53 more males will be hatched
C) Initially, 53 eggs are in the group, and as the temperature increases, the number of males who hatch increases.
D) Initially, 53 eggs are in the group, and as the temperature decreases, the number of males who hatch increases.

$$f(x) = x^2 + 6x + 12 + h$$

In the polynomial $f(x)$ defined above, h is a constant. If $f(x)$ is divisible by $x + 2$, what is a possible value of h?

A) -8
B) -4
C) 4
D) 8

13

In the xy-plane, if the parabola with equation $y = (x + a)(x - b)$, where a and b are non-zero constants, passes through the point $(0, ab)$, which of the following must be true?

A) $a = 0$
B) $b = 0$
C) $ab = 0$
D) $ab = -1$

For questions 14-17, solve the problem and enter your answer in the grid, as described below, on the answer sheet.

1. Although not required, it is suggested that you write your answer in the boxes at the top of the columns to help you fill in the circles accurately. You will receive credit only if the circles are filled in correctly.
2. Mark no more than one circle in any column.
3. No question has a negative answer.
4. Some problems may have more than one correct answer. In such cases, grid only one answer.
5. **Mixed numbers** such as $3\frac{1}{2}$ must be gridded as 3.5 or 7/2.

    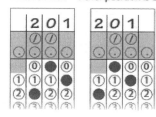

    (If [ ] is entered into the grid, it will be interpreted as $\frac{31}{2}$, not $3\frac{1}{2}$.)
6. **Decimal answers:** If you obtain a decimal answer with more digits than the grid can accommodate, it may be either rounded or truncated, but it must fill the entire grid.

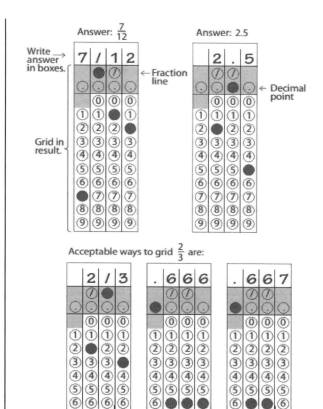

Acceptable ways to grid $\frac{2}{3}$ are:

Answer: 201 – either position is correct

NOTE: You may start your answers in any column, space permitting. Columns you don't need to use should be left blank.

14

For what value of g is $-\frac{3}{5} = 2 - \frac{1}{g}$?

15

What is the value of a if
$2a + \frac{5}{6} = 3(a - \frac{1}{6})$?

16

If x is not equal to zero, what is the value of $\frac{5x^4}{(-5x^2)^2}$

17

If $2x - 3$ is a factor of $4x^2 - a$, where a is a constant, what is the value of $2a$?

Math Test – Calculator
45 MINUTES, 31 QUESTIONS

Turn to Section 4 of your answer sheet to answer the questions in this section.

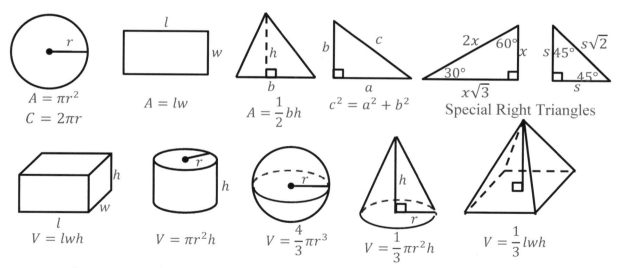

1

Ana's cable company charges a $16.75 monthly fee for the first 5 channels she subscribes to. Additionally, the company charges $3.95 per additional channel purchased beyond the fifth. Which of the following functions gives Ana's cost, $C(x)$, in dollars, for a month in which she purchases total x channels?

A) $C(g) = 16.75 + 3.95x$

B) $C(g) = 16.75 + 3.95(x - 5)$

C) $C(g) = 16.75 + 3.95(5 - x)$

D) $C(t) = (16.75 + 3.95)(x - 5)$

2

An organic foods store is selling granola bars both individually and in cases of 12. If the store sold 1076 granola bars yesterday, and 8 of the bars were sold individually, which of the following equations provides the number of cases of granola bars sold, c?

A) $c = \dfrac{1076 - 12}{8}$

B) $c = \dfrac{1076 - 8}{12}$

C) $c = \dfrac{1076}{8} - 12$

D) $c = \dfrac{1076}{12} - 8$

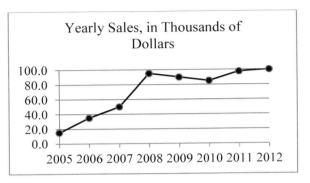

The line graph above shows the yearly sales, in thousands of dollars, for a national company from 2005 to 2012. According to the graph, what was the greatest increase in yearly sales between two consecutive years?

A) $45.00

B) $15,000.00

C) $20,000.00

D) $45,000.00

Which ordered pair (x, y) satisfies the system of equations shown below?

$$\frac{3}{2}x = 3 - y$$
$$5y - 2x + 4 = 0$$

A) $(0, 2)$

B) $(0, -2)$

C) $(2, 0)$

D) $(-2, 0)$

A circle has circumference C and area A. Which of the following represents A in terms of C?

A) $A = \frac{C^2}{4\pi}$

B) $A = \frac{C^2}{4\pi^2}$

C) $A = \frac{C^2}{2\pi}$

D) $A = \frac{C^2}{2\pi^2}$

A secretary is writing reports that must be exactly 700 words each. If the secretary can write at a rate of 75 words per minute, how many full reports can the secretary finish in an 8-hour work day?

A) 49

B) 50

C) 51

D) 52

Matisse's car uses fuel at a rate of 35 miles per gallon when driving 70 miles per hour on the interstate. If Matisse drives at 70 miles per hour on the interstate for 8 hours immediately after filling up his 20-gallon fuel tank, how many gallons of fuel does he have remaining after the trip?

A) 4 gallons

B) 8 gallons

C) 12 gallons

D) 16 gallons

What is the slope of the line in the xy-plane that passes through the points $(-3, 7.5)$ and $(-6, 7.5)$?

A) -3

B) 0

C) 3

D) The slope of the line is undefined.

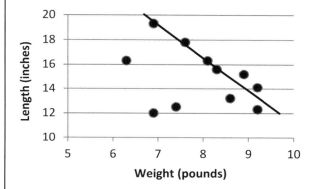

Length and Weight of Smallmouth Bass

The scatterplot above shows the length, in inches, and weight, in pounds, of 11 different smallmouth bass. Based on the line of best fit to the data shown above, how many of the smallmouth bass were at least 2 inches longer than predicted by their weight?

A) 0

B) 1

C) 2

D) 3

The ratio of boys to girls in a calculus class is 6 to 7. Which of the following is not a possible number of students in the class?

A) 26

B) 39

C) 42

D) 52

$$y + 104x = 1{,}248$$

A Korean restaurant is participating in a food festival in which a number of free samples are given away each hour. The equation above can be used to model the number of free samples, x, that remain to be given away y hours after the promotion began. What does it mean that $(12, 0)$ is a solution to this equation?

A) There are 12 free samples at the beginning of the festival.

B) During the food festival, 12 free samples are given out each sample until they run out.

C) After 12 hours of the festival, all of the free samples are gone.

D) It takes 12 hours for the restaurant to make 1,248 free samples.

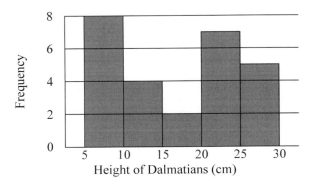

The histogram above shows the distribution of the heights, in centimeters, of 26 Dalmatian puppies at a pet store. Which of the following could be the median height of the 26 Dalmatians in the histogram?

A) 8

B) 12

C) 17

D) 21

Which scatterplot shown below features the most linear line of best fit to the data?

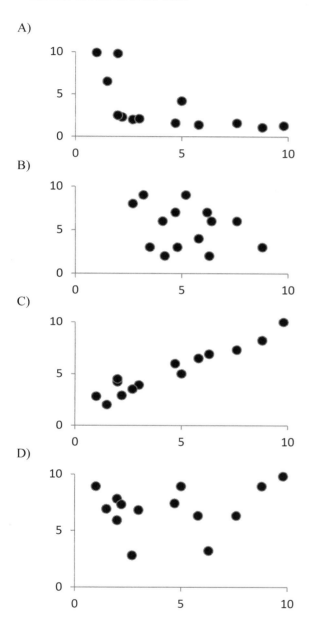

A)

B)

C)

D)

A survey of 200 randomly students was conducted to gather data on hereditary traits. The residents were divided based on whether they had attached or detached earlobes and whether or not they could roll their tongues. The data are shown in the table below.

	Can Roll Tongue	Cannot Roll Tongue	Total
Attached Earlobes	26	49	75
Detached Earlobes	57	68	125
Total	83	117	200

14

Which of the following is closest to the percent of people who have both attached earlobes and who can roll their tongues?

A) 13%

B) 25%

C) 31%

D) 34%

15

The entire school has 2,400 students, and the all of the proportions shown in the two-way table are consistent throughout all of the school's students. Approximately how many students in the entire school cannot roll their tongues?

A) 588

B) 816

C) 996

D) 1,404

16

Based on the data, which of the following situations is most likely?

A) A student with attached earlobes cannot roll his or her tongue
B) A student who cannot roll his or her tongue has attached earlobes
C) A student with detached earlobes cannot roll his or her tongue
D) A student who can roll his or her tongue has detached earlobes

Percent Protein in Four Protein Shakes

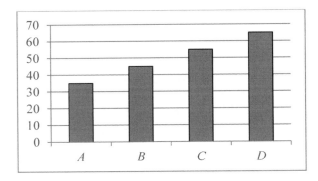

The graph above shows the amount of protein in four different brand protein shakes, A, B, C, and D, as a percentage of their total weights. Each protein shake weighs the same amount. The cost of 1 protein shake of each brand A, B, C, and D are $3.49, $4.09, $4.79, and $5.99, respectively. Which of the four protein shakes supplies the most protein per dollar?

A) A

B) B

C) C

D) D

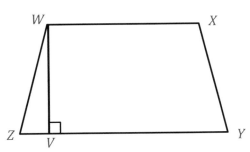

18

In quadrilateral $WXYZ$ above, WX is parallel to ZY and WV is perpendicular to ZY. If WV was increased by 50%, how would the area of $WXYZ$ change?

A) The area of $WXYZ$ would be multiplied by 2.
B) The area of $WXYZ$ wold be increased by 50%
C) The area of $WXYZ$ would not change.
D) The area of $WXYZ$ would be reduced by 50%.

Jasmine sells two colors of sweatpants: black and gray. Last month, she sold 250 pairs of black sweatpants for $10.00 each and 200 pairs of gray sweatpants for $9.00 each. This month, she plans to increase the price of black sweatpants for 10% more and gray sweatpants for 10% less. If she ends up selling 10% fewer black sweat pants and 10% more gray sweat pants, by what percentage will the money she take in increase or decrease when compared to last month?

A) 10 percent decrease

B) 1 percent decrease

C) 1 percent increase

D) 10 percent increase

Number of Students	Age
3	9
5	10
6	11
8	12
2	13
3	14
1	15

The graph above shows the ages of the students at an after-school tutoring center. What is the mode of the student ages?

A) 10

B) 11

C) 12

D) 13

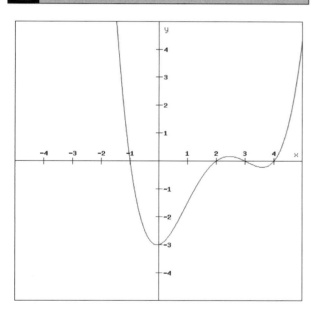

21

What is the minimum value of the function graphed above on the *xy*-plane above, for $-5 \leq x \leq 5$?

A) $-\infty$

B) -5

C) -3

D) 0

Questions 22-24 refer to the following information.

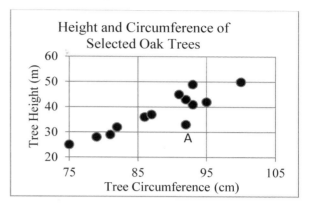

The data can be modeled by the equation $y = 0.95x - 45.5$, where y is the height, in meters, of an oak tree and x is the circumference, in cm, of the same tree. Assume that the relationship is valid for larger heights and circumferences than are shown in the graph.

According to the data above, an oak tree with a height of 63 m would be expected to have approximately what circumference, in m?

A) 0.114

B) 1.14

C) 11.4

D) 114

Based on the data shown, the tree labeled A in the data is how many meters shorter than its expected height?

A) 0.8

B) 1.5

C) 10

D) 18

Based on the model, a tree that is 50 meters tall would be expected to have what radius, assuming that the tree trunk is approximately circular?

A) 8 cm

B) 16 cm

C) 32 cm

D) 100 cm

What is the value of i^{100}? (Note: $i = \sqrt{-1}$).

A) -1

B) $-i$

C) i

D) 1

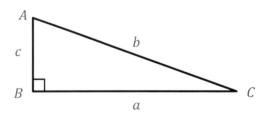

Given the right triangle ABC above, which of the following is always equal to $\cos A$?

A) $\sin A$

B) $\sin C$

C) $\cos A$

D) $\tan C$

$$2x > 3y - 5$$
$$3x - 2 < 2y$$

A system of inequalities is shown above. Which point represents a solution to the system of inequalities above?

A) $(-1, -1)$

B) $(0, -1)$

C) $(1, 3)$

D) $(2, 1)$

DIRECTIONS

For questions 28-31, solve the problem and enter your answer in the grid, as described below, on the answer sheet.

1. Although not required, it is suggested that you write your answer in the boxes at the top of the columns to help you fill in the circles accurately. You will receive credit only if the circles are filled in correctly.
2. Mark no more than one circle in any column.
3. No question has a negative answer.
4. Some problems may have more than one correct answer. In such cases, grid only one answer.
5. **Mixed numbers** such as $3\frac{1}{2}$ must be gridded as 3.5 or 7/2.

   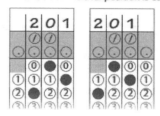

   (If is entered into the grid, it will be interpreted as $\frac{31}{2}$, not $3\frac{1}{2}$.)
6. **Decimal answers:** If you obtain a decimal answer with more digits than the grid can accommodate, it may be either rounded or truncated, but it must fill the entire grid.

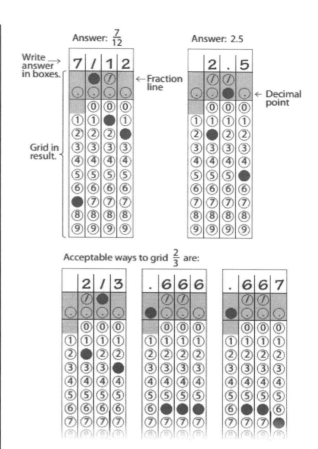

Answer: $\frac{7}{12}$

Answer: 2.5

Acceptable ways to grid $\frac{2}{3}$ are:

Answer: 201 – either position is correct

NOTE: You may start your answers in any column, space permitting. Columns you don't need to use should be left blank.

$$y = 2x^2 - 3$$
$$y = 12 - x$$

The two equations above are graphed on the xy-plane. If (x, y) is a solution to the system of equations above, and $x > 0$, what is the value of x?

$$y = \sqrt{\frac{(abc)^3}{a^2 b^4 c^1}}$$

In the equation above, $a = 9, b = 1$, and $c = 25$. What is the value of y?

Questions 30 and 31 refer to the following information.

$$\rho = \frac{m}{V}$$

The density of a substance, ρ, can be found by dividing its mass, m, in grams, by its volume in cubic cm.

An empty cylinder has negligible mass and volume, a radius of 3 cm, and a height of 9 cm.

30

The cylinder referenced above is filled with a liquid and now has a mass of 269 g. What is the density of the water used to fill the cylinder, in grams per cubic cm, to the nearest tenth?

31

The container is emptied of liquid, then filled with a new liquid with density 2.43. What is the mass of the liquid in the cylinder, to the nearest tenth of a kg?

Practice Test 2 Answer Key

Explanations can be found online at http://www.tpgenius.com/

Section 1: Reading		Section 2: Writing		Section 3: Math – No Calc	Section 4: Math - Calc
1. D	25. D	1. B	23. D	1. A	1. B
2. C	26. C	2. A	24. D	2. D	2. B
3. A	27. C	3. B	25. D	3. B	3. D
4. A	28. B	4. C	26. C	4. D	4. C
5. C	29. A	5. C	27. B	5. D	5. A
6. C	30. B	6. D	28. C	6. C	6. C
7. B	31. D	7. B	29. C	7. B	7. A
8. D	32. C	8. C	30. D	8. B	8. B
9. A	33. D	9. B	31. D	9. A	9. A
10. D	34. D	10. C	32. B	10. B	10. C
11. C	35. D	11. A	33. C	11. D	11. C
12. B	36. A	12. A	34. D	12. B	12. C
13. B	37. C	13. C	35. A	13. C	13. C
14. A	38. B	14. C	36. C	14. $\frac{5}{13}$	14. A
15. D	39. D	15. C	37. C	15. $\frac{4}{3}$ or 1.33	15. D
16. C	40. C	16. A	38. A		16. D
17. D	41. B	17. B	39. C	16. $\frac{1}{5}$ or 0.2	17. C
18. C	42. B	18. B	40. C	17. 18	18. B
19. D	43. D	19. A	41. D		19. B
20. A	44. B	20. B	42. B		20. C
21. A	45. A	21. A	43. D		21. C
22. B	46. B	22. C	44. D		22. B
23. C	47. C				23. C
24. B					24. B
					25. D
					26. B
					27. A
					28. 2.5 or $\frac{5}{2}$
					29. 75
					30. 1.1
					31. 06

Explanations can be found online at http://www.tpgenius.com/

How to Calculate Your Scores

Once you have completed an assessment, use the following steps to calculate your scores. The score(s) you calculate will be *general estimates* of your official scores for a number of reasons:

- Because standardized test score calculations are based on normative scaling and statistical analysis, your scores will differ depending your official test date – the final score calculations are impacted by the number of students, per-question performance by all students on each test date, and other numerical factors.
- College Board determines the final curve for official tests. Therefore, the scores you calculate for yourself on Test Prep Genius tests are within a general range of scores.

Calculate Your Raw Scores

Evidence-based Reading and Writing Section Raw Score

1) Count the number of correct answers you got on Section 1 (Reading Test). There is no penalty for wrong answers. The number of correct answers is your raw score.
2) Go to the Raw Score Conversion Table on the next page. Look in the "Raw Score" column for your raw score and match it to the number in the "Reading Test Score" column.
3) Do the same with Section 2 (Writing Test) to determine your Writing and Language Test Score. Make sure to use the "Writing Test Score" column.
4) Add your Reading Test Score and your Writing and Language Test Score.
5) Multiply that number by 10. This is your final Evidence-based Reading and Writing Section Score.

Math Section Score

1) Count the number of correct answers you got on Section 3 (Math Test – No Calculator) and Section 4 (Math Test – Calculator). There is no penalty for wrong answers.
2) Add the two numbers together.
3) Use the Raw Score Conversion Table on the next page to your final Math Section Score.

Use the following Raw Score Conversion Table to determine your test scores

Raw Score Conversion Table							
Raw Score (# of correct answers)	Math Section Score	Reading Test Score	Writing Test Score	Raw Score (# of correct answers)	Math Section Score	Reading Test Score	Writing Test Score
0	160	8	8	25	560	26	25
1	190	9	9	26	570	26	26
2	210	10	10	27	580	27	27
3	240	11	11	28	580	27	27
4	270	12	12	29	590	28	28
5	290	14	13	30	600	28	28
6	320	15	14	31	610	29	29
7	340	16	14	32	620	29	29
8	360	16	15	33	630	30	30
9	370	17	15	34	640	30	30
10	390	18	16	35	650	31	31
11	400	18	16	36	670	31	32
12	420	19	17	37	680	32	32
13	430	19	18	38	690	32	33
14	440	20	18	39	710	33	34
15	460	20	19	40	720	34	35
16	470	21	20	41	730	34	36
17	480	21	20	42	730	35	37
18	490	22	21	43	740	36	37
19	500	22	21	44	740	37	38
20	510	23	22	45	750	37	
21	520	23	23	46	750	38	
22	530	24	24	47	760	38	
23	540	24	24	48	760		
24	550	25	25				

For Evidenced-based Reading and Writing and Language Test Scores, add them together and multiply by 10 for your final Section Score for Reading and Writing and Language.

Add your two Section Scores together to get your final Score on a 320-1520 scale

Calculating Subscores

The Redesigned, New SAT will offer more detailed information in specific areas within math, reading, and writing. These subscores are reported on a scale of 1-15.

Math: Heart of Algebra

The Heart of Algebra subscore is calculated based on questions from the two Math Tests that focus on linear equations and inequalities.

1) Each practice test's Heart of Algebra questions are specified below. Add up your total correct answers from the specified set of questions for each test to get your raw scores for each test.
   Practice Test 1:

          Math Test – No Calculator: Questions 1-3; 5; 7; 9; 11; 14; 15

          Math Test – Calculator: Questions 1-2; 4; 11; 23-24; 29

   Practice Test 2:

          Math Test – No Calculator: Questions 1-5; 9; 11; 14-15

          Math Test – Calculator: Questions 1-2; 4; 8; 11; 30-31

2) Use the Subscore Conversion Table on Page 313 to calculate your Heart of Algebra Subscore.

Math: Problem Solving and Data Analysis

The Problem Solving and Data Analysis subscore is calculated based on questions from the two Math Tests that focus on quantitative reasoning, interpretation and synthesis of data, and solving problems with rich and varied contexts.

1) Each practice test's Problem Solving and Data Analysis questions are specified below. Add up your total correct answers from the specified set of questions for each test to get your raw scores for each test.
   Practice Test 1:

          Math Test – No Calculator: No Questions

          Math Test – Calculator: Questions 3; 6-7; 9-10; 12-17; 19-20; 26; 30-31

   Practice Test 2:

          Math Test – No Calculator: No Questions

          Math Test – Calculator: Questions 3; 6-7; 9-10; 12-20; 22-23

2) Use the Subscore Conversion Table on Page 313 to calculate your Problem Solving and Data Analysis Subscore.

Math: Passport to Advanced Math

The Passport to Advanced Math subscore is calculated based on questions from the two Math Tests that focus on topics critical to the ability of students to handle more advanced math topics, such as expressions, complex equations, and analysis of functions.

1) Each practice test's Passport to Advanced Math questions are specified below. Add up your total correct answers from the specified set of questions for each test to get your raw scores for each test.
   Practice Test 1:

          Math Test – No Calculator: Questions 6-8; 10; 12-13; 16-17

          Math Test – Calculator: Questions 5; 8; 21; 28; 30-31

   Practice Test 2:

          Math Test – No Calculator: Questions 6; 8; 10; 12-14; 17

          Math Test – Calculator: Questions 5; 18; 24-26; 30-31

2) Use the Subscore Conversion Table on Page 313 to calculate your Passport to Advanced Math Subscore.

Writing and Language: Expression of Ideas

The Expression of Ideas subscore is calculated based on questions from the Writing and Language Test that focus on topic development, organization, and rhetorical, effective use of language.

1) Each practice test's Expression of Ideas questions are specified below. Your total number of correct answers in the specified set below is your raw score.

    Practice Test 1: Questions 2; 6-7; 13; 15-16; 17-18; 20-22; 23; 26; 30; 32-33; 36; 38-40; 43

    Practice Test 2: Questions 1; 3-4; 6-8; 11; 12; 14; 16; 19; 21-22; 23; 26; 28-29; 31; 33; 34-37; 42-43

2) Use the Subscore Conversion Table on Page 313 to calculate your Expression of Ideas Subscore

Writing and Language: Standard English Conventions

The Standard English Conventions subscore is calculated based on questions from the Writing and Language Test that focus on sentence structure, usage, and punctuation (basic grammar).

1) Each practice test's Standard English Conventions questions are specified below. Your total number of correct answers in the specified set below is your raw score.

    Practice Test 1: Questions 1; 3-4; 9-11; 12; 14; 19; 24-25; 27-29; 31; 34-35; 37; 41-42; 44

    Practice Test 2: Questions 2; 5; 9-10; 13; 15; 17-18; 20; 24-25; 27; 30; 32; 38-41; 44

2) Use the Subscore Conversion Table on Page 313 to calculate your Standard English Conventions Subscore

Writing and Language + Reading: Words in Context

The Words in Context subscore is based on questions from both Reading and Writing Tests that focus on the meaning of words in context and rhetorical word choice.

1) Each practice test's Words in Context questions are specified below. Your total number of correct answers in the specified set below is your raw score.

    Practice Test 1:

    Reading Test: Questions 5-6; 13; 16; 20; 26; 30; 35; 42-43

    Writing Test: Questions 5; 8; 17-18; 26; 30; 39; 41

    Practice Test 2:

    Reading Test: Questions 3; 8; 11; 17; 20; 25; 30; 32; 42; 47

    Writing Test: Questions 3; 6; 12; 26; 29; 33; 34-35

2) Use the Subscore Conversion Table on Page 313 to calculate your Words in Context Subscore

Writing and Language + Reading: Command of Evidence

The Command of Evidence subscore is based on questions from both the Reading and Writing Tests that focus on the student's ability to interpret and use evidence found in passages and informational graphics such as tables, graphs, and charts.

1) Each practice test's Command of Evidence questions are specified below. Your total number of correct answers in the specified set below is your raw score.

    Practice Test 1:

    Reading Test: Questions 3; 9; 12; 15; 22; 28; 34; 39; 45; 47

    Writing Test: Questions 2; 6; 15; 20; 30; 33; 36; 43

    Practice Test 2:

    Reading Test: Questions 5; 7; 14; 16; 24; 27; 34; 36; 41; 46

    Writing Test: Questions 1; 7; 14; 16; 23; 31; 37; 43

2) Use the Subscore Conversion Table on Page 313 to calculate your Command of Evidence Subscore